D0918498

HAITI'S INFLUENCE
ON
ANTEBELLUM
AMERICA

HAITI'S INFLUENCE
ON
ANTEBELLUM
AMERICA

*Slumbering Volcano
in the Caribbean*

ALFRED N. HUNT

LOUISIANA STATE UNIVERSITY PRESS
BATON ROUGE AND LONDON

Designer: Sylvia Malik Loftin
Typeface: Trump Medieval
Typesetter: G&S Typesetters, Inc.
Printer: Thomson-Shore, Inc.
Binder: John H. Dekker & Sons, Inc.

10 9 8 7 6 5 4 3 2 1

Library of Congress Cataloging-in-Publication Data
Hunt, Alfred N., 1941–
Haiti's influence on antebellum America.

Includes index.
1. Haitians—United States—History—19th century.
2. Haiti—History—Revolution, 1791–1804—Influence.
3. Haiti—Foreign public opinion, American—History—
19th century.   4. Public opinion—United States—
History—19th century.   5. Immigrants—United States—
History—19th century.   I. Title.
E184.H27H86   1987   973'.049697294   87-12488
ISBN 0-8071-1370-0

TO MY CHILDREN
Meta-Margret and Brian

Might not the *San Dominick*, like a slumbering volcano,
suddenly let loose energies now held?
—Herman Melville, "Benito Cereno"

CONTENTS

ILLUSTRATIONS

ACKNOWLEDGMENTS

Scholars leave a trail of debts to many people who often give valuable help or support without realizing it; I have left such a trail over the years. My mentor, William H. Goetzmann of the University of Texas, is the most stimulating teacher I have ever seen. Robert Crunden and William Stott of Texas, Claude Nolen of St. Edward's University, and Edwin Redkey of SUNY, Purchase, were most helpful as colleagues and critics. The late Bell Wiley of Emory and Jack Greene of Johns Hopkins patiently endured my single-minded dedication to Haitian influences on American culture, in their respective National Endowment for the Humanities Summer Seminars. Special thanks go to three close friends with whom I have shared so much and who have given me so much: Brian Dippie of the University of Victoria, British Columbia, Raymund Paredes of UCLA, and Michael Hammond of SUNY, Purchase. Anyone involved in research knows what librarians do for them. I was fortunate enough to have three of the best to give me assistance: Jo Ann Hawkins of Texas, Connie Griffith of Tulane, and Paula Hane of SUNY, Purchase. I also want to thank the staffs of the following libraries and archives: Alderman Library, University of Virginia, Charlottesville; Boston Public Library; Charleston Historical Society; Haitian Bureau d'Ethnologie; Historic New Orleans Society; Howard-Tilton Memorial Library, Tulane University, New Orleans; Ilah Dunlap Little Memorial Library, University of Georgia, Athens; James P. Magill Library, Haverford College, Haverford, Pa.; Maryland Historical Society, Baltimore; Troy H. Middleton Library, Louisiana State University, Baton Rouge; National Archives, Washington, D.C.; New Orleans Public Library; Pennsylvania Historical Society, Philadelphia; William R. Perkins Library, Duke University, Durham; Schomburg Center for Research in Black Culture, the New York Public Library; Earl G. Severn Library, College of William and Mary, Williamsburg; South Carolina Archives, Charleston; South Caroliniana Library, University of South Carolina, Columbia; Southern Historical Collection, University of North Carolina, Chapel Hill; Virginia Historical Society, Richmond; and Robert R. Woodruff Library, Emory University, Atlanta. A Ford Foundation Grant, two NEH Summer Seminars, and a SUNY Research Grant greatly aided me in the costly business of archival research. I am grateful for the efforts of the staff at LSU Press, particularly Barbara O'Neil Phillips, whose insistence on accuracy and clarity was profound. Any errors of fact or interpretation of the material are the responsibility of the author. My assistant, Selma Aronson of SUNY, Purchase, graciously helped with typing earlier versions and took care of many details in my office while I finished the manuscript. Margaret and Bob Callahan provided parental nurture even before I started this project some years ago.

HAITI'S INFLUENCE
ON
ANTEBELLUM
AMERICA

INTRODUCTION

"Negro entered into white man as profoundly as white man entered into Negro—subtly influencing every gesture, every word,
every emotion and idea, every attitude." These incisive words of
southerner Wilbur J. Cash, written in the 1940s, foreshadowed the
interest in black history and the recognition of its importance to
the American experience. In pre–World War II America, the primary perspective from which whites viewed blacks was that of
the master, atop his horse, overseeing his slaves toiling below.
Slavery bequeathed a state of mind about the color line that precluded white Americans, and especially southerners, from per-
ceiving the validity of Cash's observation. Happily, this distorted
image is changing—due in part to the recognition that Cash was
correct. Whites' and blacks' destinies have been intertwined, and
black history is an intrinsic part of American history.

The influence of the Caribbean, particularly of Haiti, on the
United States remains a neglected area of historical scholarship
despite this new awareness of blacks' role in American history.
Interest in Haiti becomes evident only when spectacular events,
such as the American occupation during the early twentieth century or the Haitian refugees' desperate flight from poverty and
oppression in the early 1980s, cause Americans to pause momen-
tarily to consider the black republic. For the most part, however,
Americans are not aware of Haiti's historical significance and its
influence on American life. Haiti provides a useful tool to get behind whites' fears and blacks' aspirations in the early nineteenth
century. Further, the history of that republic suggests that in
many ways the lower South, particularly the South of literary and
political imagery, was the northern extremity of Caribbean culture. To view the South as an aberrant version of traditional
American society (as is the opinion in the Northeast) is to misun-
derstand its history and to diminish the role that the Caribbean
played in the development of the South up to the Civil War.

During the first half of the nineteenth century, many Americans, poets as well as politicians, used images of natural catastro-

phe—particularly hurricanes, volcanoes, and violent storms—to characterize the times. No single event more suited these images than did the Haitian Revolution, which began in 1791 as a slave revolt in the French colony on the island of St. Domingue, and was unique as a servile insurrection because of the nature of the conflict, its duration, and its outcome. For thirteen years, the black population struggled against intransigent masters and foreign invaders to establish, in 1804, an independent black republic symbolically recaptured by rejecting its colonial name, "St. Domingue," in favor of its aboriginal name, "Haiti." This revolution had a significant impact upon both America and France, and provided the focal point for American attitudes toward the French Revolution, black freedom, and slavery.

Although many Americans expressed a lively interest in the insurrection in St. Domingue, slaveholding southerners were most concerned with the ominous events that led to the establishment of the first black republic in the New World. Indeed, that successful revolt may well have been the most important event causing slave owners to become increasingly recalcitrant about the abolition of slavery in the United States during the early nineteenth century. Vivid reports of the massacres in St. Domingue convinced southerners that the only thing they could expect from freed slaves was vicious retaliation. A Virginia newspaper stated that "between five and six hundred white persons fell under the bloody hatchet of the Haitians, and the warm stream of blood which ran from them, quenched the thirst of their murderers, who went to their knees to receive it."[1] Thus three generations of white southerners believed that race war would be the only result of the universal emancipation of slaves. Furthermore, southerners used the example of St. Domingue in support of their conviction that blacks were incapable of civilization on their own. To those looking for failure in the emancipation of the former French colony, Haiti represented an affront to the laws of nature and the republic was therefore doomed to fail. These lessons of the Haitian Revolution helped forge an ideology that differed significantly from the humanistic traditions of Western civilization, one that denies the ultimate humanity of blacks. This proslavery inter-

1. Richmond *Enquirer*, June 9, 1804. There were hundreds of such newspaper accounts between 1791 and 1804.

pretation was based not on a sense of paranoia but rather on southerners' erroneous interpretation of events in the French West Indies.

While slaves' successfully overthrowing a white government made an indelible impression upon southern whites, the Haitian example was not lost on American blacks, free or slave. To evaluate an intangible such as pride is difficult, but American blacks constantly cited the Haitian republic as an indication of the potentialities of black people. Haiti became a primary symbol for those blacks who were striving to counter the argument that free blacks were incapable of sustaining civilization outside the confines of slavery. Obviously, the founding of a black republic in the New World also contributed to the development of a sense of black nationalism. In this way, Haiti was related to later black militancy and Pan-Africanism.

A particular source of pride for America's oppressed black population was the well-known Haitian leader, Pierre Dominique Toussaint Louverture.[2] This remarkable black man was respected by his contemporaries and was revered by blacks who were ridiculed as unfit for authority or freedom. Free blacks and slaves alike named their children and some of their groups after the liberator of Haiti. Some went to the West Indies to start a new life: Haiti was the primary symbol of black regeneration in the New World. If Thomas Jefferson and Thomas Hart Benton inspired whites with their visions of American destiny, the Republic of Haiti gave blacks assurances that they too could participate in these New World dreams and aspirations. Some intrepid American blacks even migrated to Haiti, but most chose to stay in the United States and endeavored to broaden their role in American society by often using Haiti as an example of their aptitude for citizenship.

As blacks pointed with pride to the revolution's accomplishments, and proslavery whites agonized over the horrors of St. Domingue, white antislavery leaders, particularly the more militant abolitionists, chose to see the violence in St. Domingue as a portent. If slave owners in the United States did not repent the sin of slavery, Armageddon might come at the hands of vengeful

2. The black leader wrote his name as Louverture, not L'Ouverture. I have used his spelling throughout.

slaves. The message was clear: abolish slavery or suffer the consequences. And the consequences were all too clear, as witness the unfortunate victims of the carnage in St. Domingue. These antislavery advocates also used Haiti to counter the notion that blacks were incapable of being trained in the craft of citizenship.

While these different constituencies in the United States were pondering the lessons of St. Domingue, a significant number of refugees fleeing the upheaval in the French West Indies arrived in southern ports. Many of these French Creoles, free people of color, and slaves were soon dispersed all along the North American coast; a smaller number of whites returned to France. Because of its Gallic flavor and its location, New Orleans became the site of the largest concentration of émigrés, earning the title Creole Capital of North America. Here the survivors of St. Domingue made their most enduring contributions to American culture, influencing agriculture, architecture, language, politics, medicine, religion, and the arts, and giving life in New Orleans and the Gulf region a distinctiveness that was predominantly Caribbean and Creole. Those responsible for introducing both the French opera and voodoo to the United States came to New Orleans and the seaport towns of the South in the same refugee boats.

Given this history, it is not surprising that throughout the antebellum period many Americans on both sides of the Mason-Dixon Line and the slavery controversy portrayed the South as somehow Caribbean. The presence of a large black population and the institution of slavery caused many observers to associate the South with the slaveholding tropics. For instance, in 1791 the governor of South Carolina, Charles Pinckney, wrote to the besieged colonial assembly in St. Domingue, offering his sympathy and support to the planters there because of the implications that the events in St. Domingue had for the South. Like most slaveholders, Pinckney could easily imagine the situation reversed, with South Carolinians embroiled in an insurrection that would require their asking for outside help. Indeed, southerners often used events in St. Domingue as an omen of what could happen in the southern states. This consistent identification of the mutual interests of the two slave societies was further evidence of their common heritage. No less an observer than Thomas Jefferson remarked, "Nature has connected the United States and these islands by the strong link of mutual necessity." References to the "Africanization" of the lower South also conjured up images of the Caribbean. For instance, James G. Birney, a moderate southerner with anti-slavery convictions, wrote to a friend that "by . . . South, I mean Alabama, Mississippi, Louisiana. In twenty years they must be overrun by the blacks. . . . Indeed I am by no means certain but that Lower Mississippi and the country bordering on the gulf of Mexico will ultimately be peopled almost entirely by blacks." Birney's opinions were shared by those who looked upon the South, particularly the lower South, as a sinister area. Typically, the Richmond *Enquirer* warned its readers of the "dark and growing evil at our doors," referring to the increase in the black population in the Deep South.[3]

Those proslavery advocates who said that whites were unable to work under the hot southern sun furthered the identification of the South with the tropics. As one apologist noted: "The Saxon race cannot labor in a tropical country; they must have slaves, or leave it; it seems the great law of nature for the protection of the tropical races of men." The same author dismissed the Haitian Revolution: "Haiti has shown the white man that he cannot colonize a tropical country; it must revert to those races of whom nature has bestowed a constitution adapted to labor under the tropical sun."[4] Southerners further acknowledged the common cultural bond in their desire to create an empire in the Caribbean. There was a need to extend slavery into areas where it would thrive, since, as was apparent to many slave owners, the American West was closed, politically and environmentally, to plantation culture. Southern imperialism thus echoed the national cry of "Manifest Destiny." Many southerners looked to the Caribbean for the solution to the race problem as well. The West Indies, espe-

3. Charles Pinckney to the assembly, September, 1791, in San Domingo file, South Carolina Archives, Charleston; Paul L. Ford (ed.), *The Writings of Thomas Jefferson* (10 vols.; New York, 1892), VI, 349; Dwight Dumond (ed.), *Letters of James G. Birney* (2 vols.; New York, 1938), I, 40; Richmond *Enquirer* reprinted in *Niles' Weekly Register*, XLI (January, 1832), 369.

4. Joseph Campbell, *Negro-Mania, Being an Examination of the Falsely Assumed Equality of the Various Races of Men* (Philadelphia, 1851), 280–81. Also see Samuel Cartwright, "Diseases and Peculiarities of the Negro Race," *De Bow's Review*, XI (1851), 64–69; Philadelphia *Inquirer*, March 4, 1861; *Congressional Globe*, 37th Cong., 2nd Sess., Appendix, 97; Benjamin Hunt, *Remarks on Hayti as a Place of Settlement for Afric-Americans . . .* (Philadelphia, 1860); and Howard C. Perkins (ed.), *Northern Editorials on Secession* (2 vols.; New York, 1942), I, 508–10, 519.

cially Haiti, became a logical place for potentially dangerous individual slaves. George Washington instructed that his unmanageable slaves be sent there, and Thomas Jefferson supported colonization because he thought that the West Indies would be the permanent home of the black race. Northern proslavery or antiblack opinion supported that view: Haiti "lies in the tropic zone, the proper residence of the negro."[5]

Antislavery spokesmen also drew upon tropical images in depicting the South, but they stressed the moral rather than the climatic aspects. They portrayed southerners as the English had characterized Spaniards in the *leyenda negra* (black legend), according to which Spaniards were cruel, immoral tyrants. Abolitionist tracts and slave narratives were replete with stories about brutal and sadistic masters, and abolitionist newspapers regularly published atrocity stories on their front pages. The *Anti-Slavery Record* angrily charged that "the Slave States are Sodoms and almost every village family is a brothel [*sic*]." The abolitionist Wendell Phillips also saw the South as "one great Brothel, where half a million of women are flogged to prostitution, or worse still, are degraded to believe it honorable." Northern clergymen condemned slavery as a barbaric institution that not only was "blind to the wickedness of breaking sacred ties, of separating man and wife, of beating women till they dropped down dead, or organizing licentiousness and sin into commercial systems" but also fostered ignorance, indolence, and political intimidation. Another charged that "planters are 'prodigal sons,' who spend their substance with harlots and in riotous living."[6]

Nor were the literary images of the South less hyperbolic. Harriet Beecher Stowe's powerful novel *Uncle Tom's Cabin* epitomized the tendency to characterize the lower South as the most dreadful area of the slaveholding states. Being "sold down the

5. John C. Fitzpatrick (ed.), *The Writings of George Washington* (39 vols.; Washington, D.C., 1931–41), II, 211–12; Ford (ed.), *Jefferson*, IV, 420–21; Philadelphia *Inquirer*, March 11, 1861. Also see U.S. Department of State, Consular Despatches . . . Aux Cayes, September 21, 1838.

6. Raymund Paredes, "The Image of the Mexican in American Literature" (Ph.D. dissertation, University of Texas at Austin, 1973); *Anti-Slavery Record*, December, 1836, p. 155; Wendell Phillips, *The Philosophy of the Abolitionist Movement*, Anti-Slavery Tract no. 8 (New York, 1860), 11; Chester F. Dunham, *The Attitude of the Northern Clergy Toward the South, 1860–65* (Philadelphia, 1974), 98–99; Ronald Walters, "The Erotic South: Civilization and Sexuality in American Abolitionism," *American Quarterly*, XXII (May, 1973), 177–201.

river" meant leaving American society for the cruel world of the tropics. One abolitionist journal claimed that "in Louisiana, the treatment of slaves in almost all respects, is doubtless worse than in any other part of the United States." This image resulted from Louisiana's being identified with the tropics, its association with the arduous production of sugar, and its French and Catholic flavor. One traveler stated that "the French planters were looked upon generally by the Americans of the North as very severe and even cruel masters in the treatment of their slaves, much more so than the planters of Louisiana of English ancestry."[7]

These twin heresies to antislavery Protestants—slavery and Catholicism—were at the heart of Louisiana's negative image. A New England schoolteacher in Louisiana wrote home: "I have such a hearty aversion to slavery and Catholicism. . . . One who has never been in a stable state can form no just idea of the blighting influence of the system upon the whole face of society." A Philadelphia merchant, Thomas P. Cope, commented on the impiety of the Catholic religion, suggesting that when the Americans took possession of Spanish New Orleans, "they could not after diligent search find a Bible in the place to swear their officers into power." He concluded that Roman Catholics like those in control of New Orleans wanted to keep the common people ignorant of true religion.[8]

This theme, that the South was not wholly American but was largely African, was also employed by two prominent American literary figures who wrote a century apart. Both Herman Melville and William Faulkner dealt with the influence of St. Domingue and Haiti on the American South, albeit somewhat obliquely. The specter of slave insurrection looms large in Melville's *Mardi*, where Nulli (modeled after militant proslavery advocate John C. Calhoun) warns the voyagers against any attempt to instigate an insurrection among his slaves: "Incendiaries! . . . Come ye, fire-brands, to light the flame of revolt? Know ye not that here are

7. *Niles' Weekly Register*, I (December, 1835), 136; James T. Edwards (ed.), *Some Interesting Papers of John McDonough: Chiefly Concerning the Louisiana Purchase and the Liberian Colonization* (McDonough, Md., 1898), 63. Also see Thomas Hamilton, *Men and Manners in America* (New York, 1833), 320.

8. Sarah Furber to Thomas Furber, May 7, 1844, in Sarah Furber Papers, Troy H. Middleton Library, Louisiana State University, Baton Rouge. Thomas P. Cope Diary, V (1812–14), November 25, 1813 (MS in Quaker Collection, James P. Magill Library, Haverford College, Haverford, Pa.).

many serfs who, incited to obtain their liberty, might wreak some dreadful vengeance?"[9] Nulli, incidentally, is from the extreme south of Vivenza, Melville's mythical United States. The most obvious reference to the events of St. Domingue is found in Melville's short story "Benito Cereno," which centers on a slave revolt aboard the *San Dominick*. The slave ship represents the decadence of slavery in the New World, and the three principal characters represent the key elements of antebellum society—the northern philanthropist, the southern slave owner, and the slave who is at once docile and fierce. The northerner is killed for naïvely trusting the slave, the slave is put to death for his bold mutiny, and the southerner dies with the self-knowledge that he has sinned immeasurably against humanity.

The same sense of intertwined destiny, black and white, permeates the fiction of William Faulkner. In his epic novel *Absalom, Absalom!*, Thomas Sutpen, white émigré from Haiti, attempts to build a dynasty with the help of Haitian slaves and a French architect. Ironically, it is Sutpen's own rejected son, a Haitian named Charles Bon, who finally kills his father's dream by threatening an incestuous miscegenation with his half sister. The history of slavery in all its ramifications haunts the white man who rejects and denies it. At least one theme of these works by Melville and most of Faulkner's fiction was aptly summed up by Benito Cereno after he was saved. His rescuer asked, "What has cast such a Shadow upon you?" Cereno replied (as Shakespeare's Prospero might have as well), "The Negro."

9. Herman Melville, *Mardi and A Voyage Thither* (1849; rpr. Chicago, 1970), 532.

ONE

ST. DOMINGUE AND THE CARIBBEAN

After Columbus landed near Môle St. Nicolas in 1492, the Spanish government hoped that the island he named Hispaniola would be the center of a vast, opulent empire in the West. But the colony's potential as a source of surface wealth proved disappointing and Spanish attention shifted to more exciting conquests on the American mainland. Spanish colonial administrators moved to Santo Domingo in the eastern part of the island, and the western part remained virtually uninhabited except for French freebooters and buccaneers who roamed the area during the seventeenth century. Spain officially acknowledged this casual French presence by ceding the western part of the island to France in 1697 under the terms of the Treaty of Ryswick. Santo Domingo continued to be an underdeveloped colony in the vast Spanish empire, but St. Domingue flourished as the most important of the French colonies in the West Indies.[1]

By the time of the French Revolution (1789), St. Domingue had assumed a position of importance unsurpassed in the history of European colonialism. In about eighty years the western portion of the island had been transformed into the busiest colony in the Western Hemisphere. The steady importation of black slaves from Africa helped establish a plantation system that in turn stimulated a trade estimated at over 200,000 tons annually, worth some $130 million. In 1788 alone, ninety-eight vessels carried 29,506 black slaves from Africa to work in the sugar, coffee, cotton, and indigo fields of the French colonists in St. Domingue. One contemporary historian of the prerevolutionary French West Indies estimated the population to more than one-half million—40,000 whites, 28,000 *affranchis* (free blacks), and 452,000 slaves. They worked chiefly in the production of plantation staples for export,

---

1. For a full account of the French buccaneers' role in settling St. Domingue, see James Burney, *History of the Buccaneers of America* (London, 1816); and Nellis Crouse, *The French Struggle for the West Indies, 1665–1715* (New York, 1966). Americans in the eighteenth and nineteenth centuries made no distinction between the two parts of the island, constantly referring to "Saint Domingue" as "St. Domingo," probably because the older Spanish version was easier to pronounce and spell.

9

primarily to France. Over five hundred vessels traded with that country, and another seven hundred foreign carriers combined to import large amounts of flour, wine, butter, salt, pork, soap, oil, dry goods, and slaves in exchange for large quantities of sugar and coffee and lesser amounts of cotton and indigo. In 1788, the livestock on the island numbered roughly 245,000, and none of the animals was indigenous.[2]

St. Domingue was not only a prosperous island that offered planters the opportunity to make their fortune in the Caribbean and return to France as parvenus, it was also a strategically important colony and port for France. Fifty miles across the Windward Passage from Môle St. Nicolas was Cuba, the center of Spain's Caribbean empire. Spain and France, fearing the ubiquitous British presence in the Caribbean, allied themselves in a mutual defense pact to counter any British attempt to control this important passage between the British colonies of Jamaica and the Bahamas. St. Domingue was also a thorn in the British side because British trade suffered from the French colony's sugar production and its well-known illicit trade with Britain's American colonies.

St. Domingue is the most mountainous area in the Antilles, and its 10,000-square-mile area is mostly untillable except for several highly productive belts scattered through the western portion of the colony. Understandably, French colonial administrative departments and the major commercial activity were located in these agricultural areas. The northern plain, verdant because of favorable winds and the absence of mountain obstructions, was the center of St. Domingue's staple-crop production at the time of the revolution, and was dominated by the entrepôt of Le Cap François (Cap Haitien). In the west, Port-au-Prince and St. Marc domi-

2. Philadelphia *Gazette of the United States and Daily Advertiser,* May 21, 1795; Ludwell L. Montague, *Haiti and the United States* (Durham, N.C., 1940), 5. For contemporary sources, see Bryan Edwards, *An Historical Survey of the French Colony in the Island of St. Domingo; Comprehending an Account of the Revolt of the Negroes in the Year 1791* . . . (3 vols.; London, 1819), III, 218–20; M. L. E. Moreau de Saint-Méry, *Description Topographique, Physique, Civile, Politique et Historique de la Partie Française de l'Isle Saint-Domingue* (3 vols.; Philadelphia, 1797), I, 28–29; Francis A. Stanislaus, Baron de Wimpffen, *A Voyage to St. Domingo in the Years 1788, 1789 and 1790* (London, 1817), 251–54. For modern sources, consult Thomas Ott, *The Haitian Revolution, 1789–1804* (Knoxville, 1793); and C. L. R. James, *The Black Jacobins: Toussaint Louverture and the San Domingo Revolt* (New York, 1938).

nated the green belt along the Artibonite River basin and the nearby cul-de-sac of central St. Domingue. To the south, on the western peninsulas, were smaller regions of agricultural activity contiguous to the ports of Jacmel, Les Cayes, and Jérémie. In contrast to the north, irrigation was necessary in both the central and southern areas of St. Domingue.[3]

Two government functionaries under the minister of marine administered St. Domingue for France. The governor, usually a nobleman, was the king's representative, and he had military responsibility for the colony. There were only two or three thousand regular troops in 1789; the fifty-one parishes were required to furnish an additional six thousand men-at-arms for the National Guard.[4] The governorship usually served as a stepping-stone to prominence in France—several former governors later became minister of marine, the most lucrative and important post in the French colonial system. The governor's counterpart was the intendant, who dealt with legal, financial, and commercial matters. The hallmark of this divided jurisdiction was inconsistent and arbitrary administration, and many times the two officials were openly antagonistic toward each other.

Furthermore, a rigid caste system existed in eighteenth-century St. Domingue that divided society into four well-defined groups, the *grands blancs* and their rivals, the *petits blancs*, the *gens de couleur (affranchis)*, and the slaves. There was internal tension and external conflict, and eventually these groups participated in the social and political upheaval that led to the destruction of the existing order in St. Domingue.

European-born Frenchmen enjoyed the highest status in the French West Indies. They occupied most of the important positions in the colonial administration and seemed to lord it over the proud but insecure Frenchmen born in the West Indies. Saint-Méry, a contemporary author and observer of colonial culture, reported that the European French were appalled at the tendency of Creoles at "take on the character of opulence." A Creole was a white Frenchman born in the Western Hemisphere (the term did not have the connotation of miscegenation that characterized the North American usage in the nineteenth century). The Creole

3. T. Lothrop Stoddard, *The French Revolution in San Domingo* (Boston, 1914), 6–8.
4. Edwards, *Historical Survey*, III, 7.

was nevertheless regarded as slightly inferior to the native-born Frenchman. This attitude can in part be traced to the influential writings of eighteenth-century French scholars such as the Abbé Raynal and the Comte de Buffon, who theorized that animals and plants in the New World had degenerated in comparison with their Old World counterparts.[5] These proponents of European superiority implied that the same fate awaited those who spent much time in the tropics. The competition between native-born and island-born Frenchmen permeated white society to such an extent that colonists' wives jealously sought the dubious distinction of having the most beautiful slaves at their command. Dubious indeed, since every white woman on the island feared that the accessible black woman would, wittingly or not, "sully" her conjugal bed.[6] Regardless of whites' views on the importance of one's birthplace, the rebellious blacks made no such distinctions.

From the seventeenth century onward, Spain, France, Great Britain, and Holland viewed their Caribbean colonies as conflicted societies that were "beyond the line" of civilization. This attitude was in part due to the unstable societies in the islands. The first immigrants were predominantly male, without families, looking for quick wealth, and unhindered by traditional laws or customs. The presence of black slavery further reinforced the sense of aristocratic leisure. It was assumed that any man willing to venture into this unsalubrious environment would make his fortune and return swiftly to Europe to live. The Caribbean was a place to make fortunes, not spend them. St. Domingue on the eve of the French Revolution had a reputation for opulence and hedonistic indulgence. In the European view, Creoles were the product of a sybaritic environment that reflected their machismo, their penchant for gambling, and their fondness for women. The situation worried slave owners and antislavery advocates alike, as both groups thought that much of this behavior was caused by the presence of blacks. Some even thought that the "insidious" practice of allowing Negro women to suckle white children was the beginning of this corruption. These black surrogate mothers, theorized

5. Saint-Méry, *Description,* I, 33–34; Abbé Raynal, *A Philosophical and Political History of the Settlement and Trade of the Europeans in the East and West Indies,* trans. J. O. Justamond (6 vols.; London, 1777), IV, 446–53. Also see Henry S. Commager and Elmo Giordanetti, *Was America a Mistake?* (New York, 1967).

6. Wimpffen, *Voyage,* 65, 109; Saint-Méry, *Description,* I, 34.

one racist observer, "seldom reach the period of weaning without communicating to the infant they nourish, the venom of a corrupted milk, and the vices of a temperament to . . . a lascivious and fiery nature."[7]

The climate also played a role in the popular image of the Creole and his exotic culture. One traveler to St. Domingue explained that the apparent languor of Creole society was the result of the relaxation caused by excessive heat that beats "on the organs of the body, and is equally extended over the faculties of the mind. There is an indolence of thought, as well as action." The French were familiar with justifying slavery by the African's peculiar adaptability to the heat and thus chaining the slave to the production of tropical staple crops. And yet, Creoles were also considered brave, amiable, and hospitable.[8] All these traits were later applied to Creoles in the lower South region during the nineteenth century, thus reinforcing the notion that many of the attitudes toward the lower South had their origins in West Indian culture.

The decided class division was a further complication. Notable officials and planters, the *grands blancs* were arbiters of high culture on the island and, as such, were contemptuous of the lower classes. This attitude caused resentment among the *petits blancs*, artisans, overseers, and those engaged in more prosaic vocations. After the outbreak of the revolution, this undercurrent of class antagonism played a significant role in creating a schism within white society that even the threat of black dominance could not mend. As was the case in France, the *grands blancs* supported the royalists at one point and British intervention at another, and the *petits blancs* thought that their interests could best be served by the radicals, the Jacobins.[9]

Black proscription was the only issue that united the divergent factions within white society. Free blacks, the *affranchis* in St. Domingue, constituted a class that applied constant pressure against white discrimination based on color instead of legal and economic status. Anomalies in any black slave society, free blacks

7. Wimpffen, *Voyage*, 286.
8. *Ibid.*, 39, 51; Pierre de Vaissière, *Saint-Domingue: La Société et la Vie Créole sous l'Ancien Régime* (Paris, 1909), 303–305; Saint-Méry, *Description*, I, 34–38; Jean-Bernard Bossu, *Travels in North America, 1751–1752*, trans. and ed. Seymour Feiler (Norman, Okla., 1962), 18–19.
9. Vaissière, *Saint-Domingue*, 229; Stoddard, *French Revolution*, 25–26.

(usually but not exclusively mulattoes) were marginal people who identified emotionally with the dominant white culture, yet had visibly different physical characteristics. After the Code Noir of 1685, which gave equal rights to free blacks, their legal and social privileges slowly eroded under the unsympathetic tutelage of French colonists and officials. By the late 1760s, the *affranchis* were subject to discriminatory laws that not only kept them out of the elite positions and professions but also excluded them from being considered French citizens by white society. Although most of the *affranchis* were mulattoes blanched by miscegenation, interracial marriages were very rare. Many free blacks were wealthy planters, some fortunate enough to have been educated in Paris, yet a nonstatutory caste system developed around the institution of concubinage that prevented their being accepted as Frenchmen. Considered bastards by white society, the *affranchis* nonetheless regarded themselves as superior to and distinct from the black slaves.[10]

Whatever the expectations and tribulations of the French, the Creoles, and the *affranchis* in St. Domingue, there was nothing ambiguous about the status of the slaves, the largest group on the island. Inexorably tied to the large-scale cultivation of staple crops, the slaves were totally subservient to the whims of their masters, French, Creole, or *affranchi*. Although there is some evidence that the French colonial administration at least attempted to enforce the mild humanitarian aims of the Code Noir of 1685, the effort was largely unsuccessful. The Roman Catholic church in some Spanish colonies was an effective institution for influencing the character of Creole society, but in St. Domingue and the other French colonies the church played a lesser role.[11] Witnesses noted the cruelty associated with slavery on the island: one saw a slave stoically receive one hundred lashes from his master; another told of a slave girl beheaded by her jealous mistress; still another

---

10. Edwards, *Historical Survey*, III, 10–11; Saint-Méry, *Description*, I, 102; "Mulattoes of St. Domingo," *American Museum, or Universal Magazine*, XII (1792), 39–40.

11. James Stephen, *The Crisis of the Sugar Colonies* (London, 1802; rpr. New York, 1969), 13; Wimpffen, *Voyage*, 132; Gwendolyn Hall, *Slave Control in Slave Plantation Societies: A Comparison of St. Domingue and Cuba* (Baltimore, 1971). For a comparison of the Code Noir, Las Siete Partidas, and British slave codes, see Elsa Goveia, "The West Indian Slave Laws of the Eighteenth Century," *Revista de Ciencias Sociales*, IV (March, 1960), 75–105.

saw a black fiddler whipped for making a mistake while performing at a dance. These were macabre exceptions, but cruelty in the
form of an unusually high mortality rate was the norm. One reporter explained: "Everything on a West-India plantation wears
the severe aspects of despotism. The tyranny that originates with
the master proceeds through every grade of the black domestics,
and each becomes a tyrant in his turn to those over whom chance
or merit gives him a momentary direction." Imported slaves were
in heavy demand and adequate supply until the time of the revolution. Some 864,000 Africans were imported into St. Domingue
during the eighteenth century. So many were needed because of
the high mortality rate, which was estimated to be 5 to 6 percent per year, not counting the years when major epidemics occurred.[12] The French colonists were preoccupied with achieving
wealth and position, or they were absentee owners, but the result
was the same: they ignored the threat implicit in the wholesale
importation of large numbers of Africans.

One recourse for the slave protesting the arduous and debilitating labor system and the degradation and possible death at the
hands of slave owners was violence. Only an intrepid slave would
dare poison his master or sabotage a free man's property, yet those
actions were frequent enough that whites were constantly aware
of the threat. Another avenue of protest, equally bold, was to run
away to join one of the maroon bands that roamed the mountains
and conducted guerrilla warfare against the planters. These bands
played an important role in the eventual emancipation of the
slaves, for they maintained a tradition of black defiance. Although
limited, these methods of protest kept the whites from controlling the entire colony and served as precedents for action against
the planter class.

Indeed, the continuing introduction of Africans into the West
Indies and the traditions nourished by the maroon bands meant
that black Caribbean societies remained more African than did

12. Wimpffen, *Voyage*, 217–18; [Mary Hassal?], *Secret History or the Horrors
of St. Domingo in a Series of Letters, Written by a Lady at Cape François to
Colonel Burr* (Philadelphia, 1808), 18–19; Philadelphia *Aurora*, March 3, 1792;
Gabriel Debien, "Plantations et esclaves à St. Domingue: Sucrerie Cottineau,"
Notes d'Histoire Coloniale, no. 66. p. 50; Elizabeth Donnan, *Documents Illustrative of the History of the Slave Trade to America* (4 vols.; Washington, D.C.,
1930–35), IV, 47; Philip Curtin, *The Atlantic Slave Trade: A Census* (Madison,
1969), 78–79.

their counterparts on the mainland, particularly in Britain's North American colonies. Residues of African culture, especially in religion, became the common ground for protest against the Europeans in the Caribbean. Voodoo, from the Dahomean word for deity, was one rallying point for black fugitives, and it provided some of the early leaders in the armed struggle against the planter regime.[13] Still, it was the upheaval caused by the revolution in France that afforded slaves the opportunity to rise en masse against the whites, whom they outnumbered by more than ten to one.

In the late eighteenth century, France was paralyzed by social disorder and economic depression. The monarch's ineptitude in handling the nation's serious problems, and a self-serving nobility bent on regaining the powers lost to the Crown over a century's span, exacerbated an already dangerous situation. The recalcitrance of the privileged classes in the face of monarchical power caused Louis XVI to recall the Estates General in 1789. This event influenced St. Domingue profoundly and was largely responsible for what one observer has called "l'anarchie spontanée." Both in France and later in St. Domingue, those who thought that they would be able to control these class rivalries were soon buried by them.

By the 1780s discontent grew in the French West Indies as a result of planters' abhorrence of governmental trade regulations and the mulattoes' disdain for their second-class status. These influential antagonists considered the upcoming meeting of the Estates General an excellent forum for airing their grievances. Some planters opposed having a delegation raise colonial questions in the Estates General. But those who favored such a move sent a group to Paris, one that later allied itself with the plantation owners who lived in France. They organized the Colonial Committee, the aims of which were "to secure home rule . . . and thus guarantee the existence of slavery and [to discuss] how to bring about a further modification of the navigation laws."[14]

13. Hall, *Slave Control*, 69–70; Alfred Metraux, *Voodoo in Haiti*, trans. Hugo Charteris (New York, 1972), 25–57; James, *Black Jacobins*, 86.
14. Mitchell B. Garrett, *The French Colonial Question, 1789–1791* (Ann Arbor, 1916), 5. An excellent study of the struggle between the conservatives and the abolitionists in France during this period is Gabriel Debien, *Les Colons de St. Domingue et la Révolution: Essai sur le Club Massiac* (Paris, 1953).

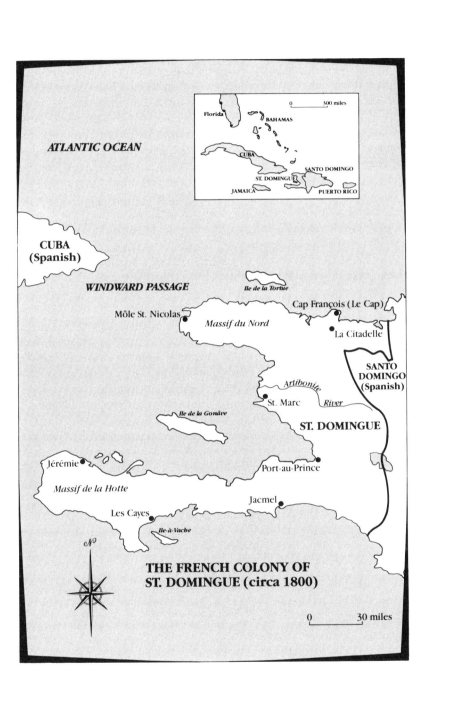

300 miles

ATLANTIC OCEAN

Florida
BAHAMAS
CUBA
SANTO DOMINGO
ST. DOMINGUE
JAMAICA
PUERTO RICO

CUBA
(Spanish)

WINDWARD PASSAGE

Ile de la Tortue

Cap François (Le Cap)

Môle St. Nicolas

Massif du Nord

La Citadelle

SANTO
DOMINGO
(Spanish)

Artibonite

St. Marc   River

Ile de la Gonâve

ST. DOMINGUE

Jérémie

Port-au-Prince

Massif de la Hotte

Jacmel

Les Cayes

Ile-à-Vache

N

**THE FRENCH COLONY OF
ST. DOMINGUE (circa 1800)**

0   30 miles

In opposition, the mulattoes in Paris were supported by the recently organized French abolitionist society, the Société des Amis des Noirs, which saw the question of mulatto rights in St. Domingue as a chance to strike at the slave trade and the planter regime indirectly. The Colonial Committee won its desired seats in the Estates General just in time to take the Tennis Court Oath and to witness the fall of the Bastille. The *grands blancs* then became a reluctant part of a National Assembly that, in August, 1789, promulgated the Declaration of the Rights of Man and thus swept St. Domingue into revolutionary France's struggle for equality. While the planters and the mulattoes spent the next year in Paris maneuvering for an advantage in the Assembly, St. Domingue came close to civil war as the demise of royal authority caused the conservative *grands blancs* and the revolutionary *petits blancs* to vie for power.[15]

The *grands blancs* won a temporary victory over the patriots, but had no time to savor their triumph because they were immediately confronted with a more serious matter: an armed revolt led by a mulatto, Vincent Ogé, recently arrived from France via England and the United States, where he had gained some support. Ogé regarded himself as a spokesman for the rights of the *affranchis*, not for the slaves. In their struggle to gain concessions from the whites, the *affranchis* in St. Domingue were not interested in the rights of slaves; indeed, they were careful to divorce themselves from any antislavery position. Subsequently, the white planters easily aborted Ogé's ill-advised mulatto revolt, and he was executed in March, 1791, the first of many martyrs to the cause of colored freedom in St. Domingue.[16]

Meanwhile, the Jacobins had come to power in France, and their reaction to Ogé's fate furthered the cause of mulatto rights. After almost two years of vacillation, the Assembly, on May 15, 1791,

15. Stoddard, *French Revolution,* 72–79; Ott, *Haitian Revolution,* 39–48; George Brown, "The Origins of Abolition in Santo Domingo," *Journal of Negro History,* XII (1922), 365–76; Shelby McCloy, *The Negro in France* (Lexington, Ky., 1961), Chap. 4, for the role of St. Domingan mulattoes in agitating the colonial question; Philip Curtin, "The Declaration of the Rights of Man in Saint-Domingue, 1788–1791," *Hispanic American Historical Review,* XXX (May, 1950), 157–75.
16. For a detailed account of Ogé's revolt, see Herbert Mills, *The Early Years of the French Revolution in San Domingo* (Ithaca, 1889), 86–90. The Philadelphia *Gazette of the United States,* March 26, 1791, and the *State Gazette of South Carolina* (Columbia), July, 1791, both reported on the revolt.

finally ratified a decree that gave rights of citizenship to a limited number of *affranchis*. Despite the limitations, white colonists in St. Domingue reacted fiercely to any concessions to the *gens de couleur* that implied equality. During the ensuing struggle between the white planters and the mulattoes in the late summer of 1791, the black slaves swept both factions aside to proclaim their own freedom.

The three major divisions of St. Domingan society became involved, each for its own reasons, in the struggle for freedom that had first erupted in the New World a decade earlier in the British colonies of North America. The success of the American Revolution undoubtedly influenced the Creoles in their attempt to wrest St. Domingue from France. Indeed, some of the *affranchis* had fought on the American side against the British in the southern states. During the unsuccessful siege of Savannah in 1779, the Fontages Légion, which included such future black leaders as André Rigaud and the future king of Haiti, Henri Christophe, saved a combined Franco-American army from annihilation by turning back a British counterattack against the retreating allies.[17] An independent United States likewise brought increased trade and contact between the new republicans and the Creoles and slaves of St. Domingue.

Some observers believe that the more educated leaders of the blacks, especially Toussaint Louverture, were familiar with such eighteenth-century egalitarian advocates and authors as the Abbé Raynal and the Abbé Grégoire, who warned of a crisis in the French West Indies unless the colonists stopped abusing the slaves there. The Abbé Grégoire was an influential spokesman for the Société des Amis des Noirs and a champion of mulatto rights in the National Assembly. Grégoire had conferred with Ogé before his journey to martyrdom, and after the May Decree, Grégoire wrote "Lettre aux Citoyens de Couleur" in support of the measure.[18] The actions and affiliations of Grégoire and his antislavery

17. Saint-Méry, *Description*, I, 229–30; Thomas Madiou, *Histoire d'Haiti* (3 vols.; Port-au-Prince, 1847), I, 87; T. G. Steward, "How the Black St. Domingo Legion Saved the Patriot Army in the Siege of Savannah, 1779," *American Negro Academy*, Occasional Papers, no. 5 (Washington, D.C., 1899), 1–15; Alexander A. Lawrence, *Storm Over Savannah: The Story of Count d'Estaing and the Siege of the Town in 1779* (Athens, Ga., 1951), 18, 55, 64, 164.

18. James Redpath, *Toussaint L'Ouverture: Biography and Autobiography* (Boston, 1863; rpr. New York, 1971); Ott, *Haitian Revolution*, 58; Stoddard, *French Revolution*, 138–39; Shelby McCloy, *The Humanitarian Movement in*

colleagues convinced the planters and proprietors that an aboli-tionist conspiracy was afoot to deprive them of their property. In-deed, after the outbreak of the slave rebellion in 1791, the out-raged planter class blamed the Société for inciting the blacks.[19]

While white divisiveness and political machinations contrib-uted to the confusion that led to the revolution in the French West Indies, the greatest influence, invariably underestimated, was the slaves' own desire for freedom. The majority of slaves in St. Do-mingue had been born into freedom in Africa; slavery, no matter how rigid or oppressive, was not likely to make them forget those earlier days of liberty. The maroon bands were symbolic of this refusal to accept the white colonists' world, and masses of slaves slowly came to realize the opportunity that tensions between the white classes and between the whites and the *affranchis* pre-sented to them. The slaves of St. Domingue were not unwilling participants in the colony's growing involvement in the French Revolution.

As reported at the time in American newspapers, the rebellion of blacks in northern St. Domingue in 1791 was a mass movement from the beginning, with black "hordes" overrunning plantations as they rushed out of the mountains toward the principal French stronghold, Le Cap François. The insurrection began with surpris-ing suddenness, and after a month, more than 250 sugar and an untold number of coffee plantations had been destroyed in the Le Cap area alone. The whites fortunate enough to escape were be-sieged in the urban centers; the insurgents and the colonists made unsuccessful forays against one another. The situation quickly deteriorated, and desperate calls for help went out to the British in Jamaica and to the United States, the closest areas that could give quick and substantial aid. According to one contemporary source, confusion was what prohibited any one group from being in com-mand of the situation: "Each port is wishing to destroy the other;

Eighteenth Century France (Lexington, Ky., 1957), 88–89, 105–107; Abbé Henri Grégoire, *Mémoires de Grégoire* . . . (2 vols.; Paris, 1837), I, 396. Grégoire was rumored to have told Ogé that his plan was ill advised. See Thomas Clarkson, *History of the Rise, Progress and Accomplishment of the Abolition of the African Slave Trade* (2 vols.; Philadelphia, 1808), II, 119–20; Ruth F. Necheles, *The Abbé Grégoire, 1787–1831* (Westport, Conn., 1971), 63–64, 76, 93, 97.

19. Clarkson, *History*, II, 95–134; *A Particular Account of the Insurrection of the Negroes of St. Domingo* . . . (London, 1792), 14, 20.

some in favor of the king, others of the nation (Republic), the mulattoes, the free negroes, the slaves, etc. What will be the consequence," he wrote, "God only knows."[20]

Reports reaching the United States reflected the chaos that gripped the island. A ship captain having just arrived from the French West Indies blamed mulattoes for the fire that destroyed a large section of Port-au-Prince; another report said that the same fire had been set by white planters. In either case it was clear that the city of twenty thousand was "a heap of rubbish," and that a great slaughter had taken place, with the "innocent as well as guilty butchered." All accounts of the rebellion spoke of wholesale destruction and carnage. Le Cap was a city of twelve thousand (approximately three thousand of whom were white) with pretensions to being the Paris of the Indies. The unofficial capital of the French West Indies, it had supported a theater and several newspapers. The surrounding countryside was the best agricultural region in the prosperous colony, yet, in September, 1791, "the noble plain adjoining the Cape was covered with ashes, and the surrounding hills, as far as the eye could reach, everywhere presented to us ruins still smoking, and houses and plantations at that moment in flames. It was a sight more terrible than the mind of any man, unaccustomed to such a scene, can easily conceive."[21] Death was as pervasive as destruction, with whites, mulattoes, and slaves all responsible for the cruelest acts against one another. Black prisoners were beaten to death by mobs in Le Cap, and whites—men, women, and children—were indiscriminately broken on the wheel by the black insurgents. Reactions to the barbarity escalated as revenge mixed with racial hatred in the combat's mindless fury. This general chaos could also be personalized, as one survivor recounted to American audiences: "I had a single combat with a large Mondogue Negro. We sparred for some time without wounding ourselves; he was stronger, I was more agile. At last he jumped for the little bottle of rum which I carry slung over my shoulder; happily, by a thrust well placed, I gave him a second mouth, a little beneath the one made by Nature; but I assure you that this time Art surpassed Nature by at least two inches." The whites were fighting for survival, with no immediate

20. Aurora *General Advertiser*, July 24, 26, 1791.
21. Philadelphia *Gazette of the United States*, December 31, 1791, January 7, 8, 1792; Saint-Méry, *Description*, I, 493–97; [Hassal?], *Secret History*, 76–77; Edwards, *Historical Survey*, III, vi–vii, xii. Edwards was an eyewitness.

political goal in mind other than reestablishing order. The mulattoes were willing to side with whoever promised them authority, but they preferred the planter class to the slaves. The blacks lashed out against their enslavement, using as their standard "the body of a white infant impaled upon a stake."[22] To them, nothing short of the destruction of the slave system would suffice.

The first bloodshed aside, the slave revolt initiated a series of complicated actions that over the years brought about the demise of French authority and doomed slavery there. St. Domingue became the focal point of the French Revolution in the Western Hemisphere when, after the Jacobin takeover of France in 1792, the National Assembly decreed full civil rights as Frenchmen for all *gens de couleur* in the colonies. The decree was a compromise for the liberals who really wanted to abolish slavery but could not muster enough support in France. The white planters vehemently opposed the Assembly's move. Jacobin commissioners were sent to St. Domingue to enforce the unpopular decree, but events soon left them and the white planters stranded. Meanwhile, Louis XVI was executed and, in early 1793, France declared war on both England and Spain. That naval war effectively isolated the colonists in St. Domingue. As the rival factions struggled for power in the colony, one of the beleaguered Jacobin commissioners, Léger Sonthonax, was forced to abolish slavery in return for black support against the planter class. Horrified, the planters, who were mostly loyalists, and some mulatto allies sought British intervention on their behalf.[23] The planters believed that their common interest in preserving the slave regime transcended nationalist sentiments. Both Britain, which did fear for its slaveholdings in Jamaica, and Spain, which shared the island of Hispaniola, sent expeditionary

22. Philadelphia *Gazette of the United States*, November 12, 1791; *Maryland Gazette* (Annapolis), January 3, 1793; Althea de Peuch Parham (ed. and trans.), *My Odyssey: Experiences of a Young Refugee from Two Revolutions* (Baton Rouge, 1959), 63; *A Particular Account*, 3.

23. The best modern accounts are Ott, *Haitian Revolution*, and Stoddard, *French Revolution*. The commissioner's action in abolishing slavery was upheld by a surprising unanimous vote in the National Convention in Paris on February 4, 1794 (see Grégoire, *Mémoires*, I, 390–91; Lowell Ragatz, *The Fall of the Planter Class in the British Caribbean, 1763–1833* [New York, 1928], 217, 229). Some French planters who fled the island returned as officers in the British expeditionary force. For British policy in the French West Indies, see David Geggus, *Slavery, War, and Revolution: The British Occupation of St. Domingue, 1793–1798* (Oxford, 1982); and Alfred T. Mahan, *The Influences of Sea Power Upon the French Revolution and Empire, 1793–1812* (2 vols.; New York, 1892), I, 109–13.

forces in late 1793. British troops occupied most of the major seaports in the western and southern provinces, and Spanish troops, including a large number of former slaves from St. Domingue, occupied the eastern part of the war-torn colony. The French army, mostly patriots and *petits blancs*, and under the command of General Etienne Laveaux, was surrounded—it hold only the northern areas around Le Cap. The tenuous French position was saved from eventual collapse in May, 1794, when the black general Toussaint Louverture abandoned his temporary allegiance to the Spanish. Such dramatic shifts in support were common throughout this period. Easily expelling the outnumbered Spanish, Toussaint and his allies conducted a long campaign against the British that eventually led to their leaving the island in May, 1798. British blunders, devastating casualties caused by fever, and Toussaint's skill contributed to the British failure in St. Domingue. To complicate the situation even more, Toussaint emerged as the leader of the French in the north but the mulatto leader André Rigaud controlled the west and the south. This rivalry caused a virtual civil war between former slaves and mulattoes—a color conflict that has not abated in modern times. Toussaint finally defeated Rigaud and after the quick conquest of Spanish Santo Domingo, he claimed control of all Hispaniola in 1801. At this point the shrewd Toussaint still professed loyalty to France, assuring French officials that he was not bent upon an independent St. Domingue. Furthermore, Toussaint was able to restore order to the island, and he reinstated some labor laws (but not slavery) in order to get the plantations producing again. He was conciliatory toward the white planter class because he realized that he needed their expertise and capital to put the economy back together after years of foreign invasion and domination and internecine warfare. Thus was a former slave in control of France's destiny in the West Indies.

Meanwhile, the revolutionary climate in France had undergone a dramatic change as the Directoire and reactionaries gained control of the government and stopped the Reign of Terror. These Thermidoreans were eager to stop the progress of the revolution in the West Indies, but they had been unable to do so because of the wars with Britain and Spain. Furthermore, the sea lanes to the Caribbean were not safe until Napoleon took power in 1799. Napoleon prepared to reestablish control over St. Domingue after his expedition to Egypt, and he was adamant about reestablishing slavery there as well. Napoleon was probably not accustomed to sharing his authority—particulary not with the Black Napoleon. After reimposing slavery in Guadeloupe, Napoleon sent his brother-in-law, General Charles V. E. Leclerc, with an expeditionary force of twenty thousand to St. Domingue in 1802 to take control of the colony from the elusive Toussaint. As instructed by Napoleon, Leclerc tricked Toussaint into his camp, arrested him, and immediately deported him to France, where he died ignobly in a French dungeon in April, 1803. Even with Toussaint out of the way, Leclerc was unable to establish his authority. Several of Toussaint's lieutenants, the vicious Jean Jacques Dessalines and Henri Christophe, resisted Leclerc with the army built by Toussaint. More important, perhaps, was the yellow fever that devastated the French army just as it had the British occupation force. Indeed, Leclerc himself succumbed to the scourge, and the remaining French troops under Donatien Rochambeau withdrew from the island in November, 1804, never to return.[24] Free of European interference, Dessalines, a black general noted for having massacred whites, proclaimed himself the leader of the independent black republic of Haiti on January 1, 1804.

The turmoil in St. Domingue caused many colonists, free persons of color, and slaves to flee to safer shores, particularly to Cuba and Jamaica and to Louisiana and the Atlantic seaboard of the United States. These survivors received aid from Spanish and American authorities, but their presence also caused political problems. Spanish Louisiana, the former French colony, still had many resident Frenchmen. They could create serious trouble should the refugees turn against the king of Spain. In fact, the Spanish had already suppressed one recent revolt by French sympathizers, so they were especially sensitive to the introduction of French revolutionary ideas into their far-flung colonies. Spanish authorities made every effort to keep Jacobins and slaves from St. Domingue out of Louisiana. Only St. Domingan royalists were welcome, since the Spaniards presumed that they would accept and support the Spanish monarchy. Spanish authorities swiftly eliminated any

24. Carl L. Lokke, "The Leclerc Instructions," *Journal of Negro History*, X (1925), 80–98; Colonel Nemours, *Histoire de la Captivité et de la Mort de Toussaint Louverture* (Paris, 1929); Paul Roussier, "Lettres de General Leclerc addressées au Premier Consul et au Ministre de la Marine au Cours de l'Expédition de St.-Domingue," *Revue de l'Histoire des Colonies Français*, XXIV (1936), 102, 162–71, 305.

potentially threatening problems arising from the slave unrest. As early as 1792, the governor-general of Louisiana, the Baron de Carondelet, promulgated a new policy toward slaves largely in response to the news of the massacres in St. Domingue: "From the beginning of the insurrection in Santo Domingo, having been advised of the consequences which might result, I made public a regulation regarding the slaves, on one hand directed to the fact of maintaining them in strong subordination to their masters, and on the other, preventing the owners from inflaming them by severe punishment."[25] This explanation indicates that the Spanish thought the events in St. Domingue were caused by the actions of both the slaves and their masters. The governor also used Spanish galleys to patrol the Mississippi River and other waterways against pro-French sympathizers and refractory Negroes from St. Domingue. By July, 1793, the governor had deported sixty-eight French suspects. In addition, Spanish authorities offered a bounty to French royalist refugees, former planters in St. Domingue, in the United States if they would move to Santo Domingo to boost the ratio of whites to blacks, thereby reducing the threat of another slave revolt. Despite these precautions and inducements, Governor Carondelet had evidence that French agents (patriots) were fomenting revolution in the colony. A secret journal of Jacobin activities in St. Domingue, *La Radateur*, appeared in Spanish Louisiana. A suspected French agent who had fought in St. Domingue, one Jean Pierre Pisgignoux, was arrested as a spy. He was implicated with another undesirable, a French agent named La Chaise, a notorious schemer who had unsuccessfully tried to launch an invasion from the wilds of Kentucky. Officials suspected that both men were attempting to undermine Spanish authority in Louisiana by introducing the ideas of republican government and black emancipation.[26] The same fear was present in all the slave societies on the Caribbean Sea.

25. Despatches of the Spanish Governors, IX, 202 (May 1, 1795) (Typescript in Howard-Tilton Memorial Library, Tulane University, New Orleans); Cabildo Records, May 1, 1795 (Typescript in Louisiana Room, New Orleans Public Library); see Despatches, VII (August 21, 1790), for the governor's very early warning against blacks from the French colonies.
26. Jack D. L. Holmes, *Gayoso: The Life of a Spanish Governor in the Mississippi Valley, 1789–1799* (Baton Rouge, 1965), 163; Frederick J. Turner, "The Origins of Genêt's Projected Attack on Louisiana and the Floridas," *American Historical Review*, III (1898), 667; Despatches, I, 325–43, II, 219–25, IV, 446, V, 221, VIII, 324, IX, 110–18; Ernest Liljegen, "Jacobinism in Spanish Louisiana, 1792–1797," *Louisiana Historical Quarterly*, XXII (1939), 47–97.

In April, 1795, the worst fears of the Spanish were realized when a slave revolt erupted in Pointe Coupée Parish on the Mississippi River more than one hundred miles north of New Orleans. Pointe Coupée's overwhelmingly black population labored in the production of cotton and indigo, and the settlement was vulnerable to revolts because the more heavily garrisoned areas were closer to New Orleans. With an eye to the tragedy in St. Domingue, the authorities moved swiftly to avoid a similar occurrence at Pointe Coupée. Carondelet ordered suspected revolutionaries arrested, including several white Frenchmen. The plot was broken up and twenty-nine of the slave conspirators were either executed or imprisoned, and the Frenchmen were banished. Contemporary accounts and local residents blamed the near tragedy on the influence of St. Domingue on Louisiana's black population. Governor Carondelet reported to his superiors that he had acted quickly because of the massacre that had occurred at Cap François. The governor was convinced that French authorities there had not moved swiftly enough to crush the opposition.[27]

The Pointe Coupée incident underscored the dangerous situation of white slaveholders on the isolated frontier. In fact, Spanish authorities continued to fear French intrusions in their colony—a fear kept alive by the occasional slave conspiracy that was uncovered. Since the struggle in St. Domingue lasted throughout the 1790s, it was easy to identify any pro-French sentiment with radicalism and revolution. Would-be revolutionaries and conspirators sometimes stated that they were following the example of the French by overthrowing their oppressors. One such suspect was a free black tailor who had recently fled from Cap François. He seemed a direct link between the events in St. Domingue and Jacobin attempts to disrupt Spanish rule in Louisiana. Governor Carondelet explained why he had the man banished: "He is a native of the part of Santo Domingo that belongs to the French and

27. Stuart Landry (ed. and trans.), *Voyages to Louisiana by C. C. Robin, 1803– 1805* (2 vols.; New Orleans, 1966), II, 117; Thomas Hutchins, *An Historical Narrative and Topographical Description of Louisiana, and West Florida* (Philadelphia, 1784), 44; Despatches, II, 214–18 (July 30, 1795), V, 247 (June 16, 1795); Jack Holmes, "The Abortive Slave Revolt at Pointe Coupée, Louisiana, 1795," *Louisiana History*, XI (1970), 341–62, is the best account of this little-known attempted revolt; Landry (ed. and trans.), *Voyages*, II, 117; "Paul Alliot's Reflections," in James Robertson (ed.), *Louisiana Under the Rule of Spain, France, and the United States, 1785–1807* . . . (2 vols.; Cleveland, Ohio, 1911), I, 119; Despatches, IX, 110–17; Cabildo Records, May 1, 1795.

is mixed up in all the intrigues and harassments of the French colony, besides being ungovernable and audacious. Having such a character around under the present circumstances in which I am placed, might produce bad results." Such incidents forced the Spanish to consider new measures to ensure that subversion was not imported into Louisiana. The New Orleans Cabildo (town council) discussed the advisability of prohibiting literate blacks, meaning seasoned St. Domingan blacks, from entering the colony. Governor Carondelet decided to take no chances that such a discriminatory policy might fail, however, and he prohibited all importation of blacks until such time as the threat of insurrection no longer existed. The entire colony seemed under siege, as one of New Orleans' most prominent citizens, the Baron Joseph X. Pontalba, remembered: "I can recall when our position in this colony was ever so critical; when we used only to go to bed armed to the teeth. Often then, I would go to sleep with the most sinister thoughts creeping into my mind; taking heed of the dreadful calamities of Saint Domingue." Pontalba's statements could have been made by thousands of other whites who were surrounded by their black bondsmen. The image of St. Domingue was used by public officials and private citizens throughout this period to warn of the potential dangers of a slave population and black emancipation. As Pontalba pointed out, many residents of New Orleans considered owning slaves a liability. The threat of slave revolt retarded the purchase of new slaves, and many slave owners, fearing black retaliation, reduced the number of bondsmen they held.[28]

Colonists looking to improve their economic position were soon complaining to authorities about the severity of restrictions on importing and buying slaves. Furthermore, Louisiana could begin to produce sugar, since that industry in St. Domingue was no longer predominant. Thus, as soon as the immediate danger of slave revolt had subsided, and the situation in St. Domingue eased somewhat, the settlers petitioned the Spanish governor to reinstate the slave trade. Relief finally came in 1800 when the Cabildo consented to the importation of "brute" African slaves from Guinea, but none from the West Indies. Indeed, some councilmen

28. Despatches, II, 226–32, IV, 324; Cabildo Records, April 25, June 20, 1795, February 19, 1796; Despatches, IX, 259–60; Letters of the Baron Joseph X. Pontalba to His Wife, 1796 (Typescript in Louisiana State Museum, New Orleans), 22, 98. Also see "Paul Alliot's Reflections," in Robertson (ed.), Louisiana, I, 113.

still objected to the wholesale importation of blacks, even directly from Africa. The example of St. Domingue was reason enough, they said, to prevent any new slaves from arriving in the colony. Such arguments caused concern, but the economic opportunities of the sugar industry proved more alluring. Louisianians, like slave owners in the American South during the nineteenth century, convinced themselves that the French ideas of *égalité* and *liberté*, and not slavery itself, had caused the problems in the French West Indies. Thus, they reasoned, they should import only ignorant Africans and keep them isolated from the radical ideas that the French so precipitously introduced into slave societies in the New World. The official Spanish interpretation of the slave revolts and the struggle in St. Domingue was evident in the new laws promulgated after the Pointe Coupée affair: "The Inhabitants should pay the greatest attention to the conduct of their slaves, and to maintain them in such a state of contentment, and subordination as may remove from their minds the notions of *acquiring a liberty,* that has caused the effusion of so much blood to those of St. Domingue."[29]

Louisiana was not the only Spanish colony that feared the spread of Jacobinsim to its slave population as a result of the events in St. Domingue. Spain advised its colonies not to intervene in the strife-torn French colony and to beware of importing slaves from there. Nevertheless the governor of Venezuela contributed $400,000 from the Caracas treasury to General Leclerc to aid the French in their efforts to suppress the blacks and reestablish stability and slavery in their Caribbean colonies.[30] By 1800, the Spanish realized that should those efforts fail, "black Jacobinism" would be a far greater threat to their security than their old rival, France, had ever been.

Despite Spanish precautions, slave revolts increased after 1791. One in the Río de la Plata area of Uruguay involved sixty blacks

29. Gayoso did prohibit the sale of any firearms to slaves without written permission. The Proclamation of Don Manuel Gayoso de Lemos, New Orleans, January, 1798, X, 6 (in Howard-Tilton Memorial Library, Tulane); Cabildo Records, August 16, 1800; Holmes, *Gayoso,* 219; Despatches, IX, 187 (emphasis added).

30. Eleazor Cordova-Bello, *La Independencia de Haiti y su Influencia en Hispanoamerica* (Caracas, 1967), 116–23. I am indebted to the late Thomas McGann for calling this source to my attention. Albert De Vidas, "The Foreign Relations of Haiti in Hemispheric Affairs from Independence to Occupation, 1804–1915" (Ph.D. dissertation, New York University, 1971).

who proclaimed an independent republic based on "Liberté, Egalité, et Fraternité." Another occurred at Maracaibo, Venezuela, in
1799 shortly after ships from St. Domingue arrived in the port.
Cuba also attributed some slave revolts to the ever-widening influence of St. Domingan blacks. One uprising that broke out in
the early 1800s in Havana was said to have been led by a rebel who
was inspired by Toussaint Louverture. The British in Jamiaca
must have felt the same sense of insecurity about the implications of the events in St. Domingue.[31]
    Although there was tension between the Creoles and the *penin-
sulares* in the Spanish colonies during this period, just as there
had been between the white planters and the *gens de couleur* in
St. Domingue, the Creoles were cautious about acting on their
desire for independence from Spain. They needed Spanish military protection against slave uprisings. They expressed grave
doubts about introducing liberal concepts to the black popula-
tions of New Spain. Even the revolutionary Venezuelan patriot
Francisco de Miranda was concerned about New World slaves
being unleashed against European despotism in the Caribbean: "I
confess to you that as much as I desire the liberty, and independence of the New World, just so much do I fear anarchy and the
revolutionary system. God forbid that these beautiful countries
should suffer the fate of Saint Domingue, theater of blood and
criminals, under the pretext of establishing liberty; better they
should remain under the barbarous and imbecile oppression of
Spain for another century."[32]
    Spanish worries about free black societies in their midst were
not unfounded. Years later, in 1815–1816, the Liberator of Spanish America, Simón Bolívar, took advantage of the hospitality of
the Haitian president Alexandre Pétion and reorganized his faltering revolutionary movement. Pétion was an ardent supporter, in
part because Bolívar promised that he would abolish slavery when
he liberated the Spanish American mainland. Haiti again played
a role in anti-Spanish activity in the Caribbean in 1830. President

    31. Cordova-Bello, *La Independencia*, 130–51; Hall, *Slave Control*, 55; Geg-
gus, *Slavery*, 88–90.
    32. Francisco de Miranda to [?], August 12, 1798, in Cordova-Bello, *La Indepen-
dencia*, 162–63 (my translation). For a similar example in Mexico during the
Hidalgo Revolt, see Doris Maxim, "The Mexican Nobility at Independence, 1780–
1826" (Ph.D. dissertation, Stanford University, 1971), 203–204.

Jean Pierre Boyer was approached by José Ignacio Basadre, an agent sent by the new Mexican government. Haiti was to be the staging area for an invasion of Cuba, which would lead to a slave revolt there and undermine Spanish authority. Thus, Mexico's independence would be protected. Although the expedition never materialized, the Spanish kept constant vigil against any attempt to repeat the events of St. Domingue.[33]

The American trade in molasses, rum, and slaves with St. Domingue and Europe had always been brisk, even after Britain made it illegal. In addition, St. Domingue supplied the American colonies with most of the coffee they imported. Trade, the proximity of St. Domingue, the flood of refugees to American seaports, and the cultural links between the slaveholding South and the Caribbean meant that Americans were both interested and informally involved in the affairs of the troubled French colony from the beginning. Normal trade relations were disrupted by the hostilities and the great reduction in staple crops, but a new form of trade developed. The United States was interested in continued trade with St. Domingue, but wanted to avoid confrontations with European powers, for that might affect foreign trade elsewhere. Exigencies naturally caused changes in policy, but this goal was uppermost—even in the case, for example, of the destitute refugees who fled to America. Nevertheless, the United States was not a party to the attempts either to restore order in St. Domingue or, later, to restore the former colony to France.[34] The events in St. Domingue spanned the administrations of three American presidents—Washington, Adams, and Jefferson—yet the official policy of noninterference was upheld, their differences notwithstanding.

As a slave-owning patrician, President George Washington was receptive to the French government's request for immediate aid to

33. John Fagg, *Latin America* (New York, 1963), 480; Gerhard Masur, *Simon Bolívar* (Albuquerque, 1948), 192, 194–97, 202–205; José Franco (ed.), *Documentos para la Historia de Mexico Existentes en el Archivo Nacional de Cuba* (10 vols.; Havana, 1961), XCVII; "Correspondencia de Don Jose Ignacio Basadre," in Luis Chavez Orozco (ed.), *Un Esfuerzo de Mexico por la Independencia de Cuba* (Mexico City, 1930), ser. II, no. 32, pp. 195–203.

34. Aurora *General Advertiser*, August 30, 1792. See Rayford Logan, *The Diplomatic Relations of the United States with Haiti, 1776–1891* (Chapel Hill, 1941); Geggus, *Slavery*; Ott, *Haitian Revolution*; and Timothy Matthewson, "Slavery and Diplomacy: The United States and Saint-Domingue, 1791–1793" (Ph.D. dissertation, University of California, Santa Barbara, 1976).

the distressed colonists in St. Domingue shortly after the initial outbreak of hostilities. His secretary of state, who was also a slave owner, Thomas Jefferson authorized piecemeal emergency relief that included a "one thousand stand of arms and other military stores" and $40,000. A delegation from St. Domingue also appealed directly to the United States government without conveying their request through normal diplomatic channels, but the Washington administration, reluctant to deal with an *ad hoc* committee from the West Indies, referred the colonists to the French minister in Philadelphia. It soon was apparent that St. Domingue required more than small-scale philanthropy if order were to be reestablished. Consequently, in December, 1791, the French government officially requested that the monies the United States owed France (as a result of loans during the American Revolution) be sent directly to St. Domingue so necessary provisions could be obtained. The secretary of the treasury, Alexander Hamilton, though a West Indian himself, was an inveterate foe of the French Revolution. He opposed the scheme, since it would bolster the French presence in the Caribbean and might cause problems later if the government of France changed yet again. Hamilton questioned how any future French government might view this indirect fiscal support given the radicals then in power in France. He did concede, however, that some immediate aid was required to keep the colonists from starvation. In spite of his efforts, some $400,000 was finally sent to St. Domingue.[35]

More and more goods had to be imported to keep the colony going, and Americans became involved in supplying foodstuffs and provisions. While the French government was purchasing flour, fish, and other items in the United States, St. Domingans were themselves trading for desperately needed supplies. Opportunistic American merchants on the scene accepted unauthorized promissory notes that the French government would have to honor. The French minister in Philadelphia tried to repudiate

35. Jared Sparks (ed.), *The Writings of George Washington* (12 vols.; Boston, 1834–37), X, 194–95; H. A. Washington (ed.), *The Writings of Thomas Jefferson* (9 vols.; Washington, D.C., 1853–54), III, 303; F. J. Turner (ed.), "Correspondence of the French Ministers to the United States, 1791–1797," *Annual Report of the American Historical Association* (1903), 48–49; Harold Syrett *et al.* (eds.), *The Papers of Alexander Hamilton* (17 vols.; New York, 1972), XIII, 169–73, 443–45; Samuel F. Bemis, "Payment of the French Loans to the United States, 1777–1795," *Current History*, XXIII (1926), 824–31.

these illegal bills issued by the colonists, but abandoned his attempts because of widespread complaints from the American commercial interests conducting the trade. The arrival of a new French minister, the controversial Edmond Genêt, only complicated the situation. Genêt controlled the relief funds and often withheld payment on the bills of exchange. Sometimes he used those funds for other purposes, and he forced the United States treasury to accept his drafts even before the funds were made available to the French. The American government redeemed the bills of exchange irrespective of their authenticity partly for humanitarian reasons and partly to keep St. Domingue a viable commercial market.[36] In this matter, the American government experienced something of the confusion of interests and competing factions that came into play in the French West Indies during the French Revolution.

During the 1790s in America, foreign affairs had a most significant impact upon domestic affairs. Complicating a situation that had no precedent, the French Revolution caused many Americans to support the policies of their former enemy, Great Britain. While the United States was trying to carve out its own independent foreign policy, the changes in Europe and the New World and America's lack of military strength often dictated what could actually be done. With regard to St. Domingue, American policy was based on self-interest: containment of the "insurrectionary" aspects of the events, continued trade, and, eventually, removal of European powers from the scene when it became apparent that the United States would benefit if French interests were not so close to the American continent. After the British and the Spanish invaded in 1793, Jefferson thought that St. Domingue as a colony of France would be the best trading partner; President Washington feared the influence of radical French ideas in North America. Jefferson later changed his position when he realized that an independent St. Domingue would help in his plan for American control of the Mississippi Valley. John Adams thought that Alexander Hamilton was foolish to advocate a joint American and British agreement with the de facto regime of Toussaint, nominally a loyal French official. Yet Adams, during his presi-

36. Turner (ed.), "Correspondence," 131, 139–40; American State Papers: Foreign Relations (6 vols.; Washington, D.C., 1834–61), I, 158; Syrett et al. (eds.), Hamilton Papers, XV, 80–81, 116–17.

dency and the era of quasi wars and alliances, came closest to outright and direct support for Toussaint against the French.[37] In an
age of complicated diplomacy, and on a constantly changing stage,
Adams and Jefferson vied with William Pitt, Napoleon, and
Toussaint in representing their respective countries' interests.

The advent of Toussaint as the central figure in the continuing
drama of St. Domingue gave the United States the opportunity to
negotiate with a single authority, one who had control over the
chaotic colony.[38] As the new commander in chief of the French
armies, this remarkable former slave led a disciplined, battle-
tested army that by 1799 had forced the British and Spanish expeditionary forces from the island. And he outmaneuvered his white
French competitors, Generals Laveaux and Hédouville and Commissioner Sonthonax. For the time being, Toussaint said he was
loyal to France, though St. Domingue was isolated from the
mother country because the wars in Europe kept the French fleet
away from the Caribbean. Toussaint desperately needed supplies
to keep his army in the field against his mulatto rival in the
south, Rigaud, who was the only obstacle to Toussaint's plan to
unite the entire island under black control. He was forced to make
trade concessions to British and American merchants in exchange
for provisions. Toussaint was friendly to the United States because he realized that the rising New World power would play a
vital role in the reconstruction of St. Domingue. The Adams administration went so far as to suggest that Toussaint declare the
colony's independence.[39]

White Americans were willing to trade with Toussaint for several reasons. Federalist merchants were enthusiastic, particularly
after he made genuinely conciliatory offers to white planters and
artisans to help rebuild the colony. Toussaint was conservative in
economic matters. Eager to reestablish the colony as the world's
leading exporter of sugar and coffee, he initiated strict labor laws

37. Turner (ed.), "Correspondence," 74; John C. Fitzpatrick (ed.), The Writings
of George Washington (39 vols.; Washington, D.C., 1931–41), XXXVI, 324; Logan,
Diplomatic Relations, 81–82; Charles F. Adams (ed.), The Works of John Adams
(10 vols.; Boston, 1856), VIII, 634–35.

38. For information on Toussaint, see James, Black Jacobins; George Tyson
(ed.), Toussaint Louverture (Englewood Cliffs, N.J., 1973); and Ott, Haitian Revolution, esp. Chaps. 2, 7.

39. The provisions of the treaty can be found in C. F. Adams (ed.), Works of John
Adams, VIII, 639. Also see "Letters of Toussaint Louverture and of Edward Ste-
vens, 1798–1800," American Historical Review, XVI (October, 1911), 64–101.

to reinvigorate production without the burden of slavery. Since Britain and France were preoccupied with the struggle, an independent St. Domingue seemed a possibility for the first time. After Rigaud's capitulation and the easy conquest of Spanish Santo Domingo, the pragmatic and conservative Toussaint was a valuable ally for the Americans.

Just as important, however, was the effect of Toussaint's rise to power on the diplomatic maneuvering for control of Louisiana and the Mississippi Valley, the heartland of North America. Until the 1790s, Louisiana was a faltering, neglected colony in the French Caribbean that was overshadowed by the fecundity of St. Domingue and the established Yankee trade with the Caribbean. France ceded Louisiana to Spain in 1762 in the wake of the Seven Years' War, but Spain was no more eager to colonize the area than France had been. Not until 1771 did Spanish officials take control from the unwilling but numerically insignificant French colonists there. Louisiana became more interesting only after a lively trade developed with the western American territories, and the possibilities for expansion became more apparent after the American Revolution. An important statement on its potential as a French colony was made in 1789 by the foreign minister to the United States, the Marquis de Moustier: Louisiana could provide the necessary foodstuffs to make the rest of France's Caribbean colonies less reliant upon the contraband trade between St. Domingue and the United States. In arguing his case for the link between Louisiana and French destiny in the Caribbean, Moustier pointed out that politically France would be in a much better position than was Spain for a rapprochement with the Americans. He also favorably compared New Orleans as a military post to some St. Domingan ports. Other French officials began to appreciate the commercial and strategic relationship between St. Domingue and Louisiana—the two colonies were mutually dependent.[40]

Aside from these advantages, Jay's Treaty (1794) brought renewed suggestions from France that Spain retrocede Louisiana to France since St. Domingue would then be less dependent upon

40. E. Wilson Lyon, *Louisiana in French Diplomacy, 1759–1804* (Norman, Okla., 1934), 17–31, 39, 118–19; Ronald Smith, "French Interests in Louisiana: From Choiseul to Napoleon" (Ph.D. dissertation, University of Southern California, 1964), discusses the strategic reasons that France ceded Louisiana to Spain in 1762.

trade with Britain's ally, the United States. Spain offered to do so in 1796, but the French refused because the price seemed too high, and, at this point, they were more concerned with the Mediterranean than with the Caribbean. Napolean later decided that Louisiana was crucial to the resurgence of New France, an idea that followed Moustier's plan for the colony and St. Domingue. In October, 1800, the king of Spain returned Louisiana to French control, though France did not actually take possession of the now-valuable colony until two years later. The First Consul then launched the ill-fated expedition to take back St. Domingue from the Black Napoleon. Leclerc's failure to subjugate the blacks was a factor in Napoleon's decision to sell Louisiana to the United States: without St. Domingue, Louisiana was not important to the French. One American newspaper noted, however, that "if the greatness and increasing prosperity of the United States is indissolubly connected with the complete union of all its parts, no circumstances could be more fatal to that union and prosperity, than the possession of Louisiana by Napoleon."[41]

The vision of the United States as a continental power was only one reason why Americans opposed the French presence in Louisiana. In 1803 a southern newspaper published a document, allegedly of French origin, that discussed the vulnerability of the United States because of its "form of government and the condition and habits of their people. . . . It is a hot-bed for faction and sedition." The "study" also stated the French would retain control of the mouth of the Mississippi in part because of the threat of servile war and Indian attacks within the United States. St. Domingue was the obvious example of how the French could excite factionalism. Furthermore, how could the United States attack the French colony of Louisiana, the author asked, when at any time "a Spartacus or L'Ouverture" might appear behind its lines?[42] The document's authenticity is questionable, but the intent of the editors was not: they wanted to remind the public how important American control of the Mississippi Valley was, and how dangerous it was to have any foreign power, but particularly France, established there. St. Domingue was discussed to impress readers with the dangers of imported French ideas and with the vulnera-

41. Logan, *Diplomatic Relations*, 58–59; Baltimore *Gazette*, reprinted in the Charleston *Courier*, February 14, 1803.
42. Charleston *Courier*, March 11, 12, 18, 19, 1803.

bility of a slave society to foreign influences. The example of St. Domingue became a primary symbol of anti-French sentiment in the southern states.

Napoleon was aware of the increasing hostility to any attempt to control the Mississippi. Selling Louisiana to the United States was one way of gaining American good will before he renewed his war with Great Britain.[43] Toussaint Louverture and his black insurgents became the best hope for eliminating a significant French presence in North America. To Americans, visions of continental powers, diplomacy, and commercial interests took precedence over vague notions of racial antipathy to the black rebels—as long as the United States did not officially have to recognize the success of the former slaves, and someone with Toussaint's temperament was in charge. It was only after his death and Dessalines's massacre of whites that cautious slave owners such as Thomas Jefferson turned against St. Domingue. Americans saw the complicated, long struggle for control of the colony as quite different from the subsequent history of the Republic of Haiti.

43. Meanwhile, Jefferson was skillfully using the plight of St. Domingue to ensure that he acquired Louisiana (see Logan, *Diplomatic Relations*, 118–21). Ott (*Haitian Revolution*, 186) believes that St. Domingue was not as important in Napoleon's decision to sell Louisiana as most historians claim. Yet most of the evidence, including contemporary assessments, does suggest that it was one significant factor.

TWO

ST. DOMINGAN REFUGEES
IN THE LOWER SOUTH

American historians have traditionally emphasized the British antecedents of what Crèvecoeur called "the American, this new man," to the virtual exclusion of such visible ethnic minorities as the Negro, the Chicano, and the American Indian. The cultural contributions of some western European groups have likewise been slighted—the French, for instance, have been largely ignored. France was Britain's long-standing antagonist, constantly threatening the security of the British North American colonies because of its presence on the frontiers. Consequently, most Americans were relieved after the surrender of Canada to the British in 1763. Not even France's vital effort on behalf of the American revolutionaries could shake the Americans from their cultural loyalty to Britain. Americans forsook their erstwhile French allies during the negotiations to end the revolution and signed a separate peace with Britain. The excesses of the French Revolution only exacerbated Francophobia in the United States. To later generations of Americans nurtured on the writings of George Bancroft, the rejection of things French meant that Protestant republicanism was victorious over the twin demons of monarchy and popery. To them, the story of American development was the saga of the Anglo-Saxon, the American of German or British ancestry, in his triumph over the Europeans of Mediterranean descent, the French and the Spanish, and their allies, the hostile Indians.

But in the Mississippi Valley, especially in Louisiana, French Creole influence antedated that of the British and survived after the Americans took over. While it is generally recognized that French cultural influences were significant in early Louisiana, the role of the St. Domingan refugees in maintaining that unique cultural identity has never been properly acknowledged. With their help, Louisiana became the cultural center of the Gulf states and gave the area an excitement that denies the traditional characterization of antebellum southern society as moribund.

The diaspora caused by the French Revolution scattered refugees over several continents, but the majority came to America. Saint-Méry, a prominent refugee who settled in Philadelphia, estimated that about 25,000 Frenchmen in the United States had come from the French West Indian colonies. Because of the length of the insurrection in St. Domingue, refugee migration was uneven. Individuals fled throughout the thirteen-year-long fighting, and several large migrations coincided with key events. In the summer of 1793, for example, General François Galbaud was ousted by Jacobins. Escorted by eight warships, Galbaud arrived off the coast of Norfolk, Virginia, with an armada of 137 vessels carrying several thousand colonists, chiefly royalist planters who did not support the cause of mulatto equality.[1]

Ironically, other Frenchmen, especially absentee landowners, arrived in St. Domingue, seeking refuge from the terror in France. Many hoped to keep their property from being confiscated or destroyed. As conditions seemed to stabilize, especially after the British occupied the southern and western parts of the colony and Toussaint came to power in the north, more refugees returned. Those who remained were confident that the worst was over and that their property was secure. There had always been some planters who had refused to assess the potential dangers realistically, and they were convinced that blacks never posed a threat to whites. Thus, there was a large number of whites still on the island when the ultimate collapse of the planter regime occurred in 1803–1804.[2]

That event caused the second large migration of refugees—in this case, survivors. After the death of Toussaint, the ruthless Dessalines struggled against the remnants of Leclerc's expeditionary force. Both the French and the black insurgents were brutal during the last days of the conflict. Americans at home could read

1. M. L. E. Moreau de Saint-Méry, *Journey in the United States*, ed. and trans. Kenneth Roberts (New York, 1947), 265; also see Francis Childs, *French Refugees in the United States* (Baltimore, 1940); *Virginia Chronicle* (Alexandria), July 13, 1791; Norfolk and Portsmouth *General Advertiser*, July 13, 1793; Newport *Mercury*, July 30, 1793; Philadelphia *Gazette of the United States*, August 17, 28, 1793. For an additional study of the subject of this chapter, see Winston C. Babb, "French Refugees from Saint Domingue to the Southern United States, 1791–1810" (Ph.D. dissertation, University of Virginia, 1954).

2. François Perrin du Lac, *Voyages dans les deux Louisianes* (Lyon, 1805), 3; Emile Provost Papers (Louisiana State Archives, Baton Rouge) contains a letter dated "16 Germinal, 11th year [1803]" that illustrates the business-as-usual attitude of many colonists.

all the gory details, which, given how frequently such accounts were published, proved fascinating, if not horrifying: "A passage boat . . . with 44 souls on board, was taken by one of those [Negro] barges, and every soul murdered. The women they put to the ignominious torture of boring out their eyes with a corkscrew, in ripping up the bellies of those with child, and exposing the unborn infants to the eyes of their expiring mothers."[3] The whites had their own devices. On a ship called a "stifler," a large number of blacks were put in the hold and suffocated when brimstone was burned overhead. The bodies of the several hundred blacks floated in the harbor of Le Cap for days. Such wholesale massacre of prisoners was characteristic of warfare that was tainted with racial hatred. The French army imported two hundred bloodhounds from Cuba to ferret out and kill any black foolish or unfortunate enough not to flee to the hills surrounding the white stronghold at Le Cap.[4]

Dessalines's military success and the ravages of yellow fever eliminated most of the French expeditionary force and thus removed the last hope of protection for the white colonists. Dessalines distrusted the French and all whites, and, like most subsequent leaders of early-nineteenth-century Haiti, he feared that the French would attempt to take back the island. Unlike Toussaint, Dessalines chose to kill all whites as the best way to ensure Haiti's future. Claiming an end to the conflict, Dessalines invited the remaining whites to come forward to receive a pardon and a security guarantee. Those who had not escaped to other countries received their pardons and everlasting peace at one and the same time. Not a white was left in Haiti after these massacres.[5] It was at this time that many Americans drew their images of Haiti and of what black emancipation might bring. Unfortunately for the future of the Republic of Haiti, Dessalines managed to destroy more than the white "devil": he also eliminated technical expertise,

3. *Virginia Gazette and General Advertiser* (Williamsburg), December 11, 1802; Alexandria (Va.) *Advertiser and Commercial Intelligencer*, January 15, 1803.

4. Washington *Federalist*, December 13, 1801; *Virginia Gazette and General Advertiser* (Williamsburg), December 29, 1802; Alexandria (Va.) *Advertiser and Commercial Intelligencer*, December 29, 1802; Charleston *Courier*, March 14, 16, 1802.

5. Richmond *Enquirer*, May 19, 1804, June 11, 1806; Raleigh (N.C.) *Minerva and Anti-Jacobin*, June 18, 1804.

commercial connections, and any semblance of a productive economy. Born in bloodshed and destruction, Haiti quickly became a
subsistence culture that was ostracized by most nations of the
Americas and that endured years of wasteful civil war between
rival mulatto and black leaders.

The last mass migration, then, fled St. Domingue for good. Unlike the earlier groups, these refugees had no identifiable political,
economic, or social characteristics. Rather, everyone white—
grand blanc, petit blanc, royalist or republican, slaveholder or
not—fled the blacks' retaliation. Perhaps one-half of the approximately 20,000 colonists still on the island escaped the carnage;
contemporary newspaper accounts estimated that more than
100,000 whites and some 60,000 blacks lost their lives in the
thirteen-year struggle.[6]

Not all the refugees were white. Many free persons of color who
had allied themselves with the dominant planter class also chose
to quit the island after the collapse of French authority. And a
number of slaves accompanied their masters on their desperate
flight. Some slaves chose service to their masters rather than
chance the outcome of the rebellion. One slave woman, Berna-
dine, was so faithful to her owner that she swam out to the ship
that was taking him into exile. She remained with her master's
family during their stay in Cuba, and when they were forced to
leave, she voluntarily accompanied them to Louisiana. After his
death, she filed a lawsuit against his executor and won the freedom she had been promised by the grateful family. A Mr. Labatut
of Tortuga, an island off the northern coast of Haiti, wanted his
slave freed because she had followed him in his "precipitate re-
treat in the recesses of the forests." Many slaves likely thought
that the best way to attain their freedom was to serve their owners
faithfully during those trying times.[7]

6. Modern scholars have been somewhat confused about the nature of the migrations. Howard M. Jones (*America and French Culture* [Chapel Hill, 1927], 116)
incorrectly assumed that the refugees were all monarchists; Winthrop Jordan
(*White Over Black: American Attitudes Towards the Negro, 1550–1812* [Chapel
Hill, 1968], 380) erred in assuming that most of the refugees went to Virginia.
These assumptions result from looking only at the initial refugee movement in
the early 1790s. (Nevertheless, Jordan's treatment of St. Domingue and its influence on America is one of the best). Also see the Charleston *Courier,* June 20,
1803.

7. Helen T. Catterall (ed.), *Judicial Cases Concerning American Slavery and
the Negro* (4 vols.; Washington, D.C., 1932), III, 483. Also see passes dated June 24,
1803, in De La Vergne Family Papers, Howard-Tilton Memorial Library, Tulane

The St. Domingan refugees were bound together in a strange land by their Creole culture and by the harrowing violence in St. Domingue. The white colonists, once the proud rulers of a caste system in the wealthiest European colony in the New World, arrived at American ports with vivid memories of their horrifying experiences. The following account was not uncommon: "Dr. Chazel's wife's grandmother lived near Port-au-Prince. Her husband had been seized by a party of insurrectionary blacks, and while she was seated in the verandah of her dwelling sometimes afterwards his head was suddenly thrown in her lap by some of the men who were passing by. She escaped afterwards with her only son, and while walking across a stream she looked at her reflection in the water and saw that her hair which was brown a few days before had become completely white." Besides those killed outright during the long insurrection, some whites died on the often arduous journey to safety, and a few ended their torment by committing suicide. Death was a constant threat, and many colonists had incredible tales to relate to thrill-hungry Americans. One family endured a private siege:

> One night they heard the insurrectionists coming! With all haste and their children in their arms, they ran for the block house; a few neighbors had gathered at their house and ran with them for refuge. The negroes saw them running and made a rush to intercept them. Mr. La Chicotte ran in last and closed the heavy door, a negro thrust in his arm to prevent it from shutting. Mr. La Chicotte with great presence of mind chopped of the hand with his sword. They were besieged there for many hours in a terrible state of terror. . . . Mr. La Chicotte received a mortal wound and died in the blockhouse.[8]

Nor did the colonists' tribulations end when they reached the United States, Cuba, or Jamaica. Many found themselves victims

---

University, New Orleans. The *South Carolina Gazette and Daily Advertiser* (Columbia), July 6, 1793, reported that of some ninety-nine passengers, approximately two-thirds were blacks or mulattoes. *Louisiana Courier* (New Orleans), July 4, August 1, 1810; Jane Campbell, "San Domingo Refugees in Philadelphia, Compiled from the Original d'Orlic-Rodrigue Papers," *Records of the American Catholic Historical Society*, XXVIII (July, 1917), 108.

8. "Copy of some loose papers found among the Manigault Papers in the handwriting of Dr. Gabriel Manigault, October 25, 1888," *South Carolina Historical and Genealogical Magazine*, XL (1939), 20; *Columbia Mirror and Alexandria Gazette* (Va.), September 10, 1799; Saint-Méry, *Journey*, 177; [?] to De Bordes, August, 1806, in De Bordes Family Papers, Troy H. Middleton Library, Louisiana State University, Baton Rouge; [?] to Amelie Drouillard, September 12, 1808, in Jean-Baptiste Drouillard Papers, *ibid.*

of the conflict in Europe: British authorities jailed those who arrived in Jamaica, and the Spanish declared the exiles personae non gratae several years after they had been in Cuba. Other refugees escaped St. Domingue with their possessions, only to have them stolen by privateers who sailed the Caribbean. For those who eventually reached safety, the question of livelihood was not easily solved. Luckily, many received support from fellow Frenchmen in the United States until they could get settled. However, the French foreign ministers in Philadelphia during this period were less eager to become involved with the West Indian refugees, whose loyalty to and support for the French Revolution were lukewarm at best.[9]

Americans initially gave the refugees a warm welcome. During the early years of the French Revolution, they were sympathetic toward the cause of "Liberté, Egalité, et Fraternité" because it reminded them, rhetorically at least, of their recent struggle against the tyranny of Britain. Local citizens' groups, state legislatures, and eventually the federal government all answered the call for hospitality and philanthropy. A Virginia newspaper spoke of the refugees who arrived with General Galbaud: "The situation of these distressed people may be more easily conceived than depicted; the husband bemoaning the loss of a wife—the wife, the loss of her husband, and hapless children, in a strange land, bathed in tears for the loss of both." These emotional descriptions were followed by patriotic statements: "Let the sympathizing heart of every American, view with compassion the accumulated distress, of those unfortunate fellow men, who were not long ago, nurtured in the lap of ease, affluence and plenty, now reduced almost to the wretched state of penury. . . . The man who would hold his assistance, under these circumstances, we hope, does not reside in America."[10] Effective in raising funds to help the refugees, these appeals also dramatized the "horrors" of St. Domingue in such a way as to create an erroneous impression of the cause of suffering. In the popular opinion, such terrifying occurrences were the natural consequences of a slave society in transition.

9. James Achille de Caradeuc, Mémoir (Typescript in Southern Historical Collection, University of North Carolina, Chapel Hill), 16–17.

10. T. Lothrop Stoddard, The French Revolution in San Domingo (Boston, 1914), 239–40; Aurora General Advertiser, July 30, 1791; Virginia Chronicle (Alexandria) and Norfolk and Portsmouth General Advertiser, July 13, 1793; Charleston City Gazette, July 1, 1793; Courrier de la Louisiane (New Orleans), May 26, 1909.

In March, 1794, the federal government appropriated $15,000, emergency funds for the refugees. And on March 7, Congress voted a "remission of the duties arising on the tonnage of sundry French vessels which have taken refuge in ports of the United States." This act provided that ship captains had to prove that they were forced to leave Hispaniola and thus were not engaged in normal trade between the United States and the islands. This temporary easing of the customs laws allowed the refugees to bring their salvaged possessions into the country without penalty. It did not affect the duties on imports or commercial transactions with the West Indies.[11]

Nor did local government neglect the refugees. Virginia put $2,000 at the disposal of the mayor of Norfolk to relieve temporarily crowded conditions there. New York's governor John Jay initiated a similar gift. Charleston, South Carolina, provided $12,500 and temporary housing; Baltimore donated almost that amount. Eleemosynary organizations throughout the country extended aid and solicited contributions. In Louisiana, citizens as far away as the frontier post of Natchitoches responded to a benevolent society's appeals for shelter for the victims. French travelers marveled at the generosity of Americans, especially in the areas that bore the brunt of the unexpected migration: Philadephia, Norfolk, Baltimore, Charleston, and New Orleans.[12]

The sudden influx of such large numbers of needy refugees, however, meant that lodging was scarce. More than one hundred were living in a house in New York and were entirely dependent upon contributions from the locals. In addition, some of the poorer exiles complained that those who had escaped with possessions or a source of wealth were taking advantage of charitable subscriptions they did not really need. Still others were too proud or embittered by their experiences to receive the aid graciously, no doubt because they were accustomed to being the providers and not the recipients of charity.[13]

11. *Courrier de la Louisiane* (New Orleans), May 26, 1909.
12. *Public Acts of Congress passed at the 1st session of the Third Congress* (2 vols.; Washington, D.C., 1794), I, Appendix, 1417–19.
13. *House and Senate Journals of the State of Virginia*, November 5, 10, 19, 1793; *Columbia Mirror and Alexandria Gazette* (Va.), November 12, 1796; *Philadelphia Gazette of the United States*, July 24, September 11, 1793, April 12, 26, 1794; *Courrier de la Louisiane* (New Orleans), July 24, 1809; Childs, *French Refugees*, 65, 87–90; Saint-Méry, *Journey*, 35, 50, 79, 153; Charles Fraser, *Reminiscences of Charleston* (Charleston, 1854), 44; Jeffrey Brackett, *The Negro in Mary-*

Americans' response to the St. Domingans often depended on public sentiment toward France and what was happening both on the Continent and in the islands. As American acceptance of the French Revolution changed to ultimate horror, Frenchmen were less welcome and less trusted. For instance, outspoken aliens who criticized the government or vehemently defended Jacobinism were arrested or deported during the Adams administration. This official skepticism pervaded the daily lives of the refugees as well, since landlords singled them out for higher rents. The specter of a race war had caused many St. Domingan patriots who were loyal to the revolution in France to flee the carnage in St. Domingue, but the American government was more comfortable with the planters, who came to the United States with their conservatism intact. Thus, public aid quickly dwindled as a result of the political climate. Most of the refugees were self-sufficient by the time the contributions were no longer forthcoming. Wealthy St. Domingans looked to France to indemnify them for their personal losses, some of which amounted to vast fortunes. But France did not make even a partial settlement until the late 1820s, and that climaxed a prolonged round of diplomatic discussions on France's formally recognizing Haiti as an independent nation.[14]

Political refugees seldom leave a permanent mark on the culture of the host country. A case in point involves those who came to the United States, seeking refuge from the French Revolution. Many of them eventually returned to France, and those who did not had every opportunity to assimilate quickly because they were mostly white, skilled, educated persons, to whom citizenship was readily available. In most places where the refugees stayed on, they intermarried, learned to speak English, and virtu-

land (Baltimore, 1889), 96; Baltimore *Daily Advertiser*, July 13, 1793; South Carolina House Resolutions, 1793, no. 5 (in South Carolina Archives, Columbia); François, Duc de La Rochefoucauld-Liancourt, *Voyages dans les Etats-Unis* (4 vols.; Paris, 1799), I, 1–4, II, 4, IV, 36. Also see Richard Blau to [?], July 13, 1793, Letterbook of Richard Blau (MS in Richard Blau Papers; Earl G. Severn Library, College of William and Mary, Williamsburg), 167–68.

    14. La Rochefoucauld-Liancourt, *Voyages*, II, 253, 274; Constantine Volney, *View of America* (Philadelphia, 1804), xvi–xvii. For a schedule of the indemnities, see *Etat Retaillé des Liquidations par la commission chargée de repartir l'indemnité attribuée aux anciens colons de St. Domingue . . .* (Paris, 1829). Copies in the New Orleans Public Library and in Howard-Tilton Memorial Library, Tulane.

ally vanished as a distinct cultural group. Generally, the refugees from the French West Indies who settled in the antebellum South had the greatest influence on American life. The distinctiveness of Creole culture in the lower Mississippi Valley, in the Gulf states, and around Charleston and Savannah can be traced to those who fled from St. Domingue.

Louisiana was the most desirable region in North America for the Creole refugees to reconstruct their shattered lives. Not only was it accessible and its population sympathetic, but the former French colony was the major repository of Gallic culture in the United States. Charleston was attractive as well—there was a French Huguenot community—but most people in the city spoke no French and Catholicism was not the predominant religion. Refugees also settled along the Atlantic seaboard from Boston and New York to Savannah, along the Gulf coast, and along the Mississippi up to St. Louis.[15] Baltimore was popular with some refugees because of its Catholic community.

Although relatively few St. Domingans reached the upper Mississippi, their influence on vernacular architecture was significant. Many houses in early-nineteenth-century Illinois were built to eclectic designs that combined Canadian and West Indian traditions. These dwellings displayed such distinctively West Indian features as a large porch or gallery around the house to keep it cool, a ground floor that was raised on stilts for the same purpose, and casement windows that swung inward on hinges. The wall construction was typically West Indian: *poteaux en terre*, that is, vertical wood siding was covered with clay or mud. This method was used in northern Haiti. Furthermore, as folklorist John Vlach has convincingly argued, the most pervasive southern architectural style—the shotgun—is another link with St. Domingue. This distinctive style of house is found throughout New Orleans

15. Philadelphia was the favorite gathering place of refugees from France. For a short time, the refugees who swamped Norfolk gave a quality of French life to the seaport (see Mrs. Anne Ritson, *A Poetical Picture of America, Being Observations Made, During a Residence of Several Years at Alexandria and Norfolk . . .* [London, 1809], 146–47; and Thomas J. Wertenbaker, *Norfolk: Historic Southern Port* [Durham, 1931], 88–89). There were several prominent St. Domingan families who settled in St. Louis and in Maryland (see Dorothy G. Holland, "St. Louis Families from the French West Indies," in John F. McDermott [ed.], *The French in the Mississippi Valley* [Urbana, 1965], 41–46; and Walter C. Hartridge, "The Refugees from the Island of St. Domingo in Maryland," *Maryland Historical Magazine*, XXXVIII [June, 1943], 103–22).

and the river towns such as Vicksburg and Memphis, as well as in more remote areas of the rural South. This rectangular frame house is usually one room wide and several rooms deep and has doors at both ends. These buildings are identical (even down to the dimensions) to houses found throughout Haiti. According to Vlach, the style was introduced into the Mississippi Valley by black Haitian artisans fleeing St. Domingue. Simple, inexpensive to build, and suitable for small lots, such dwellings could accommodate large numbers of people. The shotgun house is one of the enduring symbols of both New Orleans and the rural South. It also represents one of the greatest influences of black Haitians on American culture.[16]

Because of its demography and history, only Louisiana afforded the St. Domingans the opportunity to attain success as a group without having to assimilate into the dominant culture. The whites quickly moved into positions of authority and influence. The free blacks found that the laws and attitudes concerning them were more lenient than in other slave states. The slaves not only followed their masters but were quickly given many of the same tasks they had had before, since in topography and climate Louisiana resembled the sugar-growing areas of St. Domingue.

The crucial factor in the St. Domingans' influence on Louisiana was their sheer numbers. In 1791, before the influx of refugees, New Orleans had 4,446 inhabitants, excluding the Spanish military garrison. Of these, approximately 1,900 were whites, 750 free Negroes, and 1,800 slaves, and fewer than one-half of the family heads had French surnames. By 1797 the population of New Orleans had climbed to 8,056 and included 3,948 whites, 1,335 free Negroes, and 2,773 slaves. Although it is impossible to arrive at a definite number, St. Domingan refugees added substantially to this dramatic increase. After the United States acquired Louisiana, Governor William C. C. Claiborne in a letter to the American secretary of state James Monroe characterized the immigration

16. Frederick L. Billon (ed.), *Annals of St. Louis in Its Early Days Under the French and Spanish Dominations* (St. Louis, 1886), 81–82; Georges Henri Victor Collot, *A Journey in North America*, trans. J. Christian Bay (2 vols.; Paris, 1826); Charles Peterson, "The Houses of French St. Louis," in McDermott (ed.), *The French in the Mississippi Valley*, 17–40; Charles E. Peterson, *Colonial St. Louis: Building a Creole Capital* (St. Louis, 1949). See John Vlach, "Sources of the Shotgun House: African and Caribbean Antecedents for Afro-American Architecture" (Ph.D. dissertation, Indiana University, 1975).

from the French West Indies as "considerable." The immigration from 1791 to 1808 aside, a group large enough to almost double the number of French-speaking persons in New Orleans arrived by way of Cuba between May and August of 1809. Governor Claiborne reported that 5,754 St. Domingan refugees entered the territory—approximately 1,887 whites, 2,060 free Negroes, and 2,113 slaves.[17] Because few of these refugees left the New Orleans area, they represent the largest single migration into the Louisiana Territory since its colonization.

These refugees had fled to southeastern Cuba or to Havana during the Dessalines campaign of 1803. Despite hardships, they managed to establish themselves as planters and merchants in Cuba. A Mr. Basil, for example, built a lucrative coffee plantation on an estate that had thirty-eight slaves. The French exiles in this remote part of Cuba also established churches and schools. Some found conditions agreeable enough to become naturalized Spanish citizens. But when Napoleon invaded Spain in 1808, the Spanish government ordered the expulsion of all former French colonists from Cuba.[18] The hapless St. Domingans had to undergo their second uprooting in less than five years.

The refugees had to arrange for their own passage. One group chartered an American brig, the *Fair American*, to take them to New Orleans. According to the contract, the captain was to provide food and water sufficient for the fourteen-day voyage. He was also to secure permission from American authorities to disembark the group, both whites and blacks, within ten days of their arrival. The cost was $3,200, paid to Captain Coffin in advance. Assurances of safe entry were risky because ship captains bringing St. Domingan exiles and their slaves could be imprisoned for

17. Census of the City of New Orleans, 1791, and "Population de la Louisiane en l'année 1797," both in Charles Thompson Papers, Middleton Library, LSU; W. C. C. Claiborne to James Madison, January 23, 1802, and Claiborne to Robert Smith, n.d., both in Dunbar Rowland (ed.), *Official Letter Books of W. C. C. Claiborne* (6 vols.; Jackson, Miss., 1917), I, 38, IV, 408–409. Also see Luis M. Perez, "French Refugees in New Orleans in 1809," *Publications of the Southern Historical Association*, IX (1905), 293–310.

18. *Courrier de la Louisiane* (New Orleans), May 22, 24, 1809, October 17, 1810; Perez, "French Refugees," 293–94; Stephen Frontis, "Memories of my life written by myself" (Typescript in Frontis Papers, Southern Historical Collection, University of North Carolina, Chapel Hill; [?] to Jean-Baptiste Drouillard, April 11, 1807, in Drouillard Papers; Eliza Williams Chotard, "Autobiography," 1868 (MS in Southern Historical Collection).

violating the federal statutes against the slave trade after 1808. Under the same laws, the owners of the slaves were subject to penalties and forfeiting their property. Then southern legislators introduced a bill into Congress that specifically exempted those St. Domingans who came from Cuba. Supporters of this legislation denied that the proposal was designed to encourage an increase in the number of slaves in the South; rather, they contended that the measure would achieve quite the opposite end, since the slaves impounded by customs officials under the current law could not leave or be exported. The act passed in June, 1809, with several amendments to ensure that only those who suffered deportation by the Spanish authorities in Cuba would benefit from the exemption.[19]

The arrival of these St. Domingans in Louisiana was timely, if accidental: American migration to the territory was increasing; without these new French immigrants, Louisianians of French background would have undoubtedly been overwhelmed by Anglo-Americans. The St. Domingans were the major contributing factor to the resilience of French Creole culture in the next twenty years or so; for example, French was still the official language of the New Orleans City Council for twenty-five years after the Americans took over the government of the territory, and Gallic names were still chosen for new streets in New Orleans until the early 1820s.[20]

The St. Domingan refugees established an impressive record of rebuilding their lives after their harrowing experiences, financial losses, and physical dislocations. A modest number of refugees were incapable of providing for their own care—widows, orphans, and the elderly—and had to rely primarily upon charity. Nevertheless, the majority of the émigrés had valuable skills to offer the

19. Contract, May 5, 1809, in Peters-Lastrapes-Lemonier Papers, Howard-Tilton Memorial Library, Tulane; *Annals of Congress*, 11th Cong., 1st Sess., 39–42, 322, 461–66; *Public Statutes at Large of the United States of America* (4 vols.; Boston, 1845), Vol. II, Chap. VIII, pp. 549–50. For additional petitions for remission of duties, see *Annals*, 11th Cong., 2nd Sess., 738, 906, 1009, 1197, 1208–10, 1215–16.

20. Minutes de Conseil de Ville (Typescripts in New Orleans Public Library); Archie Arnaud, "The Social and Historical Significance of the Names of Streets in New Orleans" (M.A. thesis, Xavier University, 1936), 10–12, 27. One traveler to New Orleans, John Winthrop, complained to a friend in 1814 that he had learned the French language "by force" (see Everett Brown, "Letters from Louisiana," *Mississippi Valley Historical Review*, XI [1924], 577).

expanding society they found in the United States. Mayor James Mather of New Orleans reported that within three months of their arrival in Louisiana, two-thirds of the white male refugees were gainfully employed as cabinetmakers, bakers, upholsterers, glaziers, and planters. The pattern was the same elsewhere, though some who had been well placed in St. Domingue now found themselves having to do mundane chores.[21] Many of those who brought their slaves with them were able to live by hiring their slaves out to Americans; others went into the countryside and continued to plant as they had in the West Indies.

The majority of the refugees were not white. While the slave states were accustomed to having slaves accompany their masters, the arrival of such a large number of free blacks was quite unusual. About two thousand free blacks came to New Orleans in the 1809 migration, doubling the free black population there and giving the city its highest percentage of free nonwhites (50 percent) in its history. One fascinating and unique feature of New Orleans society that seldom went unnoticed by visitors was the key role played by these so-called Creoles of color, a subculture that was a close-knit ethnic minority in between the whites and the free blacks. While the law treated them simply as free blacks, they distinguished themselves from their black counterparts primarily by their lighter skin color, their Caucasian features, and their family background. Most of them had come from families that had forgotten the sting of slavery but not their kinship with the planter class. By the early nineteenth century, and particularly in the New Orleans area, the term Creole came to imply miscegenation. Born of the West Indian custom of *plaçage,* a planter taking a mulatto mistress, Creoles enjoyed a special status in the minds of whites. Creole free women of color acquired unofficial acceptance in New Orleans by participating in the famous quadroon balls and as mistresses to white men. Americans romanticized Creole women as representing their emotional images of the tropics—dark, exotic, and beautiful. St. Domingan Creoles of color, male and female, quickly became leaders in the free black community because of their long-standing tradition of liberty and their education. Their influence was apparent well into the twen-

21. James Mather to Claiborne, August 7, 1809, in Rowland (ed.), *Letter Books of Claiborne,* IV, 404–405; *Courrier de la France et des Colonies* (Philadelphia), October 21, 1795.

tieth century, and they were distinguished from the other blacks by their looks, language, church affiliation, and occupations. They gave Louisiana and, to a lesser extent, Charleston a unique four-tiered caste system similar to that of St. Domingue before its demise.[22]

These Creoles enjoyed extraordinary status in Louisiana because they spoke and wrote good French or patois, were devoutly Catholic, and were better educated than were free blacks elsewhere. Some even sent their children to Paris to be educated. The Black Code of Louisiana, introduced in the French colony as early as 1724, allowed greater legal flexibility and stability for blacks than existed in the English colonies. For instance, in 1803, Governor Claiborne wrote to President Jefferson that Creoles of color were armed members of the militia. One of the most distinguished units in Andrew Jackson's forces that fought against the British in the rather peripheral battle of New Orleans in 1815 was a battalion of St. Domingan free men of color led by a mulatto, a Captain Savary.[23]

St. Domingan free blacks were employed in most of the journeymen trades in New Orleans as a result of apprenticeships that often called for formal education as part of the indenture contract. A free Creole from Port-au-Prince, Jacques Daniel St. Erman, was apprenticed to an important New Orleans architectural firm as a

22. Clarence E. Carter (ed.), *The Territorial Papers of the United States* (26 vols.; New York, 1934–62), IX, 174; Joseph G. Tregle, "Early New Orleans Society: A Reappraisal," *Journal of Southern History*, XVIII (1952), 20–39, gives a much-needed revision of the meaning of the quadroon balls, which were romanticized by travelers and local writers alike; Ronald Wingfield, "The Creoles of Color: A Study of a New Orleans Subculture" (M.A. thesis, Louisiana State University, 1960), 65, 72, 76–77, 167, 178–179, 203–204, 217–19. Wingfield found that about one-third of the surnames of his subjects were names also evident in Haiti. In 1843, three St. Domingan women of color are said to have founded St. Mary's Academy in New Orleans; however, I was unable to obtain permission to see the source that was quoted (Sister Mary Francis Borgia, "A History of the Sisters of the Holy Family in New Orleans" [M.A. thesis, Xavier University, 1931]). Also see Laura Foner, "The Free People of Color in Louisiana and St. Domingue: A Comparative Portrait of Two Three-Caste Societies," *Journal of Social History*, III (Summer, 1970), 406–30.

23. Annie L. West-Stahl, "The Free Negro in Ante-bellum Louisiana," *Louisiana Historical Quarterly*, XXV (1942), 357, 378. Also see *Le Code Noir, ou Recueil des Règlements* . . . (Paris, 1767); and Louis Casimir Moreau-Lislet and Henry Carleton (trans.), *The Laws of Las Siete Partidas* . . . (2 vols.; New Orleans, 1820); Carter (ed.), *Territorial Papers*, IX, 18; Bernard Marigny, *Réflexions sur la Campgane de Général André Jackson, en Louisiane, en 1814 et 1815* (New Orleans, 1848), 24–26.

brick mason. The three-year contract called for the employer to teach St. Erman construction and drawing in their spare time. Jean Louis Moreau, a fourteen-year-old Creole orphan from St. Domingue, accepted an apprenticeship with a free black cabinetmaker for five years. Under the terms of the contract, the boy's aunt would provide his clothing and expenses, and the cabinetmaker would teach Moreau his trade and support Moreau's efforts to learn to read at night school. The indenture records show that almost every skilled craft in New Orleans had St. Domingan free black youths as apprentices: tinsmithing, carpentry, shoemaking, saddle-making, bricklaying, blacksmithing, printing, tailoring, goldsmithing, hairdressing, and making "fashionable articles." J. D. B. De Bow's compendium of statistics for the Seventh Federal Census, though notoriously inaccurate in some areas, indicated correctly that free blacks continued to serve New Orleans well throughout the antebellum period: in 1850 they accounted for 355 carpenters, 278 masons, 80 tailors, and 92 shoemakers. Several of these free black apprentices were fortunate enough to become self-employed after their tenure as journeymen. Honoré Besson, a free quadroon from Cap François, who in 1811 had indentured himself as a turner for seven years, was a self-employed painter by the 1830s. Similarly, St. Domingan François Degré (or Degrey) was self-supporting as a carpenter.[24] Local records in Charleston and Savannah indicate that those urban areas had a like number of St. Domingan free black tradesman in their midst.

Not all the free black émigrés who came to the United States from St. Domingue were able to prosper. The confusion caused by events left some blacks on American shores with little or no proof that they were free. The Black Codes notwithstanding, free blacks in the antebellum South lived under the threat of enslavement should circumstances go against them. Blacks had to be vigilant to guard their freedom. In one court case, for example, Adelaide Metayer petitioned the Louisiana state court for her freedom under a Spanish law that required the manumission of any slave

24. Contracts, January 24, July 3, 1811, March 9, 1812, Indentures, Mayor's Office, July 12, 1809–November, 1814, all in City Archives, New Orleans Public Library; also see Frederick L. Olmsted, *A Journey in the Seaboard States* (New York, 1856), 637; J. D. B. De Bow (ed.), *Statistical View of the United States . . . Beginning with 1790 . . .* (Washington, D.C., 1854), 80–81; *New Orleans City Directory for 1831*, pp. 28, 54.

who had lived in freedom for twenty years in the absence of her owner. After a lower court disallowed her claim that residence in St. Domingue constituted living in freedom, an appeals court overturned the decision and granted her freedom with the reasoning that the French had abolished slavery in St. Domingue more than twenty years ago. Another case involved a free man of color named McPherson who had been born free in St. Domingue, but had been sold into slavery after he reached Alexandria, Virginia. The courts upheld his suit for freedom, and remunerated him in cash for his stolen services.[25]

As the expatriate groups developed into more permanent communities, institutions that served their particular needs played an important role. None was more vital to the continued existence of the St. Domingan refugee community than the establishment of French-language newspapers. These newspapers helped preserve the language pattern so fundamental to the Creoles' cultural identity, and they devoted many more pages to European affairs than did most American papers, especially to the relations between France and the Republic of Haiti. They also were the focal point for advertising and announcements. Without these instruments of cultural cohesion, French Creole culture could not have retained its influence in the affairs of Louisiana for so long.

Several St. Domingans had operated newspapers in the colony before the revolt, and they put this experience to good use in Louisiana. The *Affiches Américaines,* for example, was well established in Le Cap before the revolution. Émigrés transferred the publication of the *Journal des Révolutions de la Partie Française de St. Domingue* from Le Cap to Philadelphia, the headquarters of émigrés from France itself. Another journal from St. Domingue, the *Courrier Français,* was smuggled into Spanish Louisiana in an effort to excite French descendants there to rebel against Spanish authority. These newspapers, edited by St. Domingans, represented French culture's most conspicuous presence in the New World. Médéric Louis Elie Moreau de Saint-Méry, erstwhile colonial representative from Martinique to the Estates General and author of several authoritative volumes on the history of Hispaniola, published the Philadelphia French-language newspapers

25. Catterall (ed.), *Judicial Cases,* II, 506, 514–15, III, 497.

and used his bookstore as a distribution point. The bookstore was also a gathering place for those who had fled the revolution, both in France and in the French West Indies. A member of the American Philosophical Society, Saint-Méry occasionally entertained other prominent émigrés such as the Duc de La Rochefoucauld-Liancourt and Talleyrand.[26]

These French newspapers made their most lasting contributions to the French community in Louisiana. Virtually all of them were edited by St. Domingans throughout the antebellum period. The first in an impressive tradition and the only French-language newspaper published during the Spanish period was the *Moniteur de la Louisiane,* founded by Louis Declot of St. Domingue in 1794, but edited by Jean-Baptiste LeSueur Fontaine. Fontaine had been an accomplished artistic director of the Comédie du Cap, and he was active in the French theater in New Orleans. Under Fontaine, the *Moniteur* became the official state paper of the Spanish regime in 1797; Fontaine remained its editor and part-time publisher until his death in 1814.[27]

The *Moniteur* was New Orleans' only newspaper until two St. Domingan master printers, Jean Renard and Claudius Beleurgey, started *Le Télégraphe* in 1803. Beleurgey's wanderings in the publishing business were typical. In Port-au-Prince he published *Le Républicain et Affiches Américaines,* but within a year he was in Charleston producing *La Patriote François.* Next Beleurgey moved to Georgetown, South Carolina, for a stint with the *Gazette,* and finally he arrived at New Orleans to edit *Le Télégraphe* for eight years.[28]

The newspapers Beleurgey edited in the United States were short-lived when compared with New Orleans' most important

26. Saint Méry, *Journey,* 206, 177; George Winship, "French Newspapers in the United States from 1790–1800," *Proceedings and Papers of the Bibliographical Society of America,* XIV (1920), 83–109; Despatches of the Spanish Governors, I, 325–40 (1793) (Typescript in Howard-Tilton Memorial Library, Tulane University, New Orleans).

27. Minutes of the Cabildo, November 10, 1797 (Typescript in New Orleans Public Library). Jack Holmes, "Louisiana in 1795: The Earliest Extant Issue of the Moniteur . . . ," *Louisiana History,* VII (1966), 133–51; Jack Holmes, "The Two Series of the Moniteur . . . ," *Bulletin of the New York Public Library,* LXIV (1960), 323–28; *Louisiana Gazette* (New Orleans), July 7, 1814; William Beer, "Moniteur de la Louisiane, New Orleans, 1794," *Proceedings and Papers of the Bibliographical Society of America,* XIV (1920), 127–31.

28. Samuel Marino, "Early French-Language Newspapers in New Orleans," *Louisiana History,* VII (1966), 311–13.

antebellum papers, the *Bee* (*L'Abeille de la Nouvelle Orleans*) and the *Louisiana Courier* (*Courrier de la Louisiane*), first published only in French and then quickly expanded to include a mirror English-language section. Both the founders and editors were St. Domingans, François Delaup of the *Bee* and J. C. de Saint-Romes of the *Courier*. The most controversial of the St. Domingan newspapermen was Jean Leclerc, who founded a lively paper, *L'Ami des Lois*, in 1809 after an apprenticeship with the other French newspapers in New Orleans. Outspoken, Leclerc soon became embroiled in a dispute with a rival suitor for a lady's favor, ridiculing the man in his paper to the point that the man sued to have the publisher desist. Judge François Xavier Martin, renowned as an early-nineteenth-century historian of Louisiana, also became the object of Leclerc's scorn: Leclerc referred to him in print as an "imbecile in robe." This local *cause célèbre* turned on the issue of freedom of the press. Judge Martin found no humor in Leclerc's actions and imposed a ten-day jail sentence and a hundred-dollar fine. Although he enjoyed community support, the eccentric Leclerc sold the newspaper after ten years, and local gossip no doubt diminished as a consequence.[29]

The St. Domingan editors and publishers exhibited a remarkable influence on the early history of Louisiana: their French-language newspapers kept Creole traditions alive in the face of an American cultural onslaught that absorbed all but the most tenacious subcultures. Indeed, the gradual dissipation of Creole culture after the Civil War was due in part to, and was partly symptomatic of, the disappearance of these pioneering journals published by energetic and experienced St. Domingans.

Education provided St. Domingans another opportunity to exert a continuing influence upon several generations of young southerners. Newspapers in all the major United States ports were replete with advertisements by St. Domingan refugees who sought to make a living as tutors of French, mathematics, social arts, or other disciplines. Teachers were scarce in Charleston, but thirteen of them were St. Domingans. Madame Anne-Marie Talvande,

29. Edward L. Tinker, *Les Ecrits de Langue Française en Louisiane en XIXe Siècle: Essais Biographiques et Bibliographiques* (Paris, 1932), 113, 277–84; John Kendall, "The Foreign Language Press of New Orleans," *Louisiana Historical Quarterly*, XII (1929), 366–68. Issues of *L'Ami des Lois* are in the New Orleans Public Library. The controversy occurred in the spring of 1811.

a St. Domingan, established an academy that soon gained a reputation throughout the South for offering "ladies of dignity [a] liberal education of the old sort." Other St. Domingans opened a similar school in Natchez, Mississippi, in 1810. During the administration of Thomas Jefferson, French manners became the fashion in polite society, and St. Domingans taught Americans the art of fencing, music, and dance. Several southern colleges added French to their curriculums.[30]

Educational opportunities were limited during the Spanish domination in Louisiana—less than one-half the colony's population was literate when the United States took control. There were no colleges, and the one public school taught children in Spanish only. After the Louisiana Territory was organized, Governor Claiborne expressed concern about the lack of education in the region. The legislature authorized, at Claiborne's suggestion, a rudimentary public school system, and a *collège* in Orleans Parish. Six years laters the same body provided $15,000 for the construction of the Collège d'Orléans, with an annual $3,000 appropriation for operating expenses. The city administration's extensive publicity campaign was successful: the inhabitants of New Orleans recognized the value of education in a democratic society.[31]

The Collège d'Orléans opened its doors in 1812 with a St. Domingan, Jules d'Avezac, as its first president. Other St. Domingans were involved: James Pitot and Louis Moreau-Lislet were trustees, and other educated émigrés were either instructors or pupils. The City Council had provided a full scholarship for one

30. De Caradeuc, Mémoire, 40; J. G. Rosengarten, *French Colonies and Exiles in the United States* (Philadelphia, 1907), 94; Eola Willis, *The Charleston Stage in the XVIII Century with Social Settings of the Time* (Columbia, S.C., 1924), 235; Robert Gourdin, *Mémoire*, 24, quoted in Rosser Taylor, *Antebellum South Carolina: A Social and Cultural History* (Chapel Hill, 1942), 112; Chotard, "Autobiography," 18; Jones, *America*, 194–95, 201, 289.

31. Carter (ed.), *Territorial Papers*, IX, 38; D. K. Djork, "Documents Relating to the Establishment of Schools in Louisiana, 1771," *Mississippi Valley Historical Review*, XI (1925), 561–69; Rowland (ed.), *Letter Books of Claiborne*, I, 326–27; "An Act to Institute a University in the Territory of Orleans," April 19, 1805, *Acts Passed at the First Session of the Legislature of the Territory of Orleans, 1804–1805* (New Orleans, 1805); "An Act to Institute a University in the Territory of Orleans," April 9, 1811, in *Acts Passed at the Third Session of the Legislature . . . 1810–1811* (New Orleans, 1811); Martin Riley, "The Development of Education in Louisiana," *Louisiana Historical Quarterly*, XIX (1936), 623–31; *Courrier de la Louisiane* (New Orleans), January 7, 1811; Minutes of the Cabildo, February 18, 1809, March 17, December 12, 1810.

pupil out of each twenty-five enrolled, and ten students were granted tuition waivers. Competition was brisk for the coveted fellowships, and St. Domingans were well represented since children of refugee families, especially school-aged children of widows, were given preference.[32]

The Collège d'Orléans educated several men who later become prominent in Louisiana society and made significant contributions to the development of a sense of the distinctiveness of Creole culture. There were, for example, the author François Dominique Rouquette and a poet, Tullius Saint-Ceran, whose family came from St. Domingue. But the most famous pupil was undoubtedly the Creole historian and lawyer, Charles Etienne Arthur Gayarré. Gayarré's impressions of his student days were vividly captured in his autobiographical novel *Fernando de Lemos*, in which he revealed the intensely personal influence the St. Domingan instructors had upon him. According to Gayarré, d'Avezac was a "highly polished gentleman of the old school," something also said of Gayarré in his later life. Since d'Avezac stayed but a short time, his successor and fellow émigré, Rochefort, professor of literature and Latin, had a great influence on Gayarré. Rochefort's habit of adopting certain deserving young scholars as privileged students, giving them access to his apartment and large library, as well as daily personal contact, afforded Gayarré the opportunity to develop a mentor-student relationship with his professor. Years later, Gayarré visited the aristocratic Rochefort on his deathbed, and the old scholar reminded him, "You are my work—never forget it." Gayarré claimed that he remained true to that charge throughout his life. Rochefort would have recognized his influence on Gayarré and probably have given his approval to the romantic nineteenth-century histories of Louisiana and Creole culture that Gayarré produced. Gayarré, called by historian Clement Eaton the "South's greatest historian," was responsible for initiating scholarly interest in Louisiana culture. Further, Gayarré founded the Louisiana Historical Society, which, during

32. Sidney Villers, "The Enterprising Career of Don Pablo Lanusse in Colonial New Orleans and a genealogy of his descendants," *Genesis*, II (1963), Chap. VII, p. 244; Tinker, *Les Écrits*, 4, 20; Minutes of the Cabildo, May 29, 1811, June 6, 1812; letter dated June, 1813, copy in New Orleans Municipal Records, City Archives, New Orleans Public Library.

his twenty-eight year presidency, began its collection of historical documents.

Internal strife beset the Collège, but it continued to educate the youth of New Orleans until the 1820s when it closed, partly because of the controversial hiring of an old Jacobin, Joseph Lakanal. Lakanal's name had appeared on the order to execute Louis XVI, and New Orleans residents did not approve of having their sons educated by a regicide. By the time the Collège's first president died in 1831, French-style academies no longer played an exclusive role in the New Orleans education system. Like the French-language newspapers, the Collège d'Orleans fostered a sense of community, giving the Creoles a base from which to develop culturally in Louisiana.[33]

One of the most prominent Catholic educators in the United States was another St. Domingan refugee, Louis Guillaume Valentine Du Bourg. From his arrival in Baltimore in 1794 until his departure for France in 1825, Du Bourg dedicated himself to establishing educational institutions and furthering Catholicism in the United States. Du Bourg obtained the favor of America's first Catholic bishop, John Carroll, while attending a Sulpician seminary in Baltimore, and Bishop Carroll subsequently appointed Du Bourg to the presidency of Georgetown College, where he served from 1796 to 1798. After a short sojourn in Havana, Cuba, Du Bourg returned to Baltimore and founded Saint Mary's Academy, an institution that enrolled mostly the children of St. Domingan refugees. Du Bourg also ministered to the needs of the black refugees from St. Domingue. In 1812, Bishop Carroll sent the capable educator to New Orleans as an administrator; however, his clash with the popular Capuchin Antonio de Sedella (Père Antoine) and his dislike for New Orleans resulted in negligible accomplishments there. Undaunted, Du Bourg made a pilgrimage to Rome, where he was consecrated bishop of "Louisiana and the Floridas" in 1815. The new bishop was personally responsible for having his see located in St. Louis instead of New Orleans, where a cathedral already stood. In St. Louis, then a fledgling river town, he su-

33. See Charles Gayarré, *Fernando de Lemos* (Philadelphia, 1872), Chaps. 1, 2, and pp. 400–404; John H. Nelson, "Charles Gayarré, Historian and Romancer," *Sewanee Review*, XXXIII (1925), 427–38; Clement Eaton, *The Waning of the Old South Civilization* (Athens, Ga., 1968), 53–78.

pervised the construction of a magnificent brick cathedral and furnished it with works of art and religious treasures from Europe. He also founded St. Louis Academy, later to become St. Louis University, one of the largest Catholic schools in the country. Among Du Bourg's numerous other important ecclesiastical tasks, he worked to establish a seminary in Louisiana and to convert the nearby Indians. In 1825 he resigned his position and returned to France, where he died an archbishop in 1833. Du Bourg gave the Catholic church a presence and vitality it had lacked in the Mississippi Valley. His efforts, along with those of numerous parishioners from St. Domingue, contributed to the growth of Catholicism in America.[34]

As a group, the St. Domingans who came to Louisiana between 1791 and 1809 were better trained and educated than were the inhabitants of the Louisiana Territory. Many of them became exemplary citizens in a remarkably short time. Their influence on politics, public service, and agriculture in Louisiana ensured that the state would have a Creole flair for years to come.

Immigrants in America in the 1790s exerted more influence on domestic affairs than at any other time in American history. The early St. Domingan political refugees were royalists who became associated with Federalist policies, especially in Charleston, South Carolina, a Federalist stronghold. Conversely, later St. Domingans included those who joined Jacobin clubs that sprang up along the northeastern seaboard, such as the Colons de St. Domingue Réfugiés aux Etat-Unis in Philadelphia. These refugees were loyal to the principles of the French Revolution, though they thought that the French West Indies, a society based on caste of color, was hardly appropriate for such radical notions as *égalité*.[35] These political groups responded to the events of the French Revolution, and most

34. This brief biography of Du Bourg was taken from several sources: *Missouri Gazette* (St. Louis), October 18, 1820; John Pacton, "Notes on St. Louis (1821)," in John F. McDermott (ed.), *The Early Histories of St. Louis* (St. Louis, 1952), 65–66; William B. Faherty, "The Personality and Influence of William Valentine Du Bourg . . . ," in John F. McDermott (ed.), *Frenchmen and French Ways in the Mississippi Valley* (Urbana, 1969), 43–55. Louis Hue Girardin, a St. Domingan, was the president of Baltimore College and the first president of the Maryland Academy of Science and Literature (see Annie L. Sioussat, *Old Baltimore* [New York, 1931], 133–34).

35. Rayford Logan, *The Diplomatic Relations of the United States with Haiti, 1776–1891* (Chapel Hill, 1941), 45–47. Jones, *America*, discusses French influ-

of them died out as the revolution ran its course. Few of these refugees along the eastern seaboard actually ran for or held public office and none of their issues survived the Napoleonic years. The situation was quite different in Louisiana, since the political refugees were also émigrés looking to establish roots in their new home. The large number of permanent émigrés in Louisiana and the remnants of the resident French population gave the St. Domingans a unique opportunity to build a polity. Most of the successful St. Domingans spoke English, but it was not necessary to learn the host language to become involved in politics in Louisiana. In fact, speaking French was often an advantage. Initially the St. Domingans found no reason to gravitate toward political groups based on French nationality. However, as more Americans poured into the territory, an inevitable clash of cultures developed that lasted until the Americans finally won control over local politics in the late 1840s. The Americans wanted the French language abolished for official proceedings, control over the militia, and change from Louisiana's civil code, based on the Napoleonic Code, to a legal system founded upon English common law, as in other American states. In New Orleans, municipal government was reorganized to minimize the power of the French political faction. One pro-American newspaper described the opposing faction as "composed of foreign Frenchmen, and refugees from St. Domingue, together with a few active recruits of the city. It is sowing seeds of discord and dissension in the city, well organized for their purposes; some of them high in office and in our councils." Although the Americans lost the battle to abolish the civil code, which was radically democratic in many of its aspects, they eventually won control over Louisiana's political life, thus initiating what the *Bee* called "despotism of faction"—boss rule in New Orleans.[36]

---

ence in American politics during this period, as do most biographies of Washington, Jefferson, Adams, and Hamilton. Also see Childs, *French Refugees*, 141–59.

36. Joseph Tregle, "Political Reinforcement of Ethnic Dominance in Lower Louisiana, 1812–1845," in Lucius Ellsworth (ed.), *The Americanization of the Gulf Coast, 1803–1850* (Pensacola, 1972), 78–87; Albert Fossier, *New Orleans: The Glamour Period* (3 vols.; New Orleans, 1957), III, 101; Jones, *America*, 117; *Louisiana Gazette* (New Orleans), June 22, 1824; William Hoe, "Municipal History of New Orleans," *Johns Hopkins Studies in History and Political Science* (Baltimore, 1889), 15–16; New Orleans *Bee*, March 15, 1854.

St. Domingans were involved in the politics of Louisiana from its beginnings as an American territory. The first mayor of American New Orleans was James Pitot, an exile from St. Domingue who arrived in New Orleans in 1796. He soon became a partner in a profitable importing firm. Pitot quickly professed loyalty to the new American administration when he took over, and he participated in a merchants' petition to Governor Claiborne, expressing the desire that New Orleans be governed by free-trade policies. In a secret dispatch, "Characterizations of New Orleans Residents," sent by General James Wilkinson to President Thomas Jefferson, Pitot was described as a "merchant tolerably well informed . . . and of pretty good morals," a considerable compliment in view of the general's comments about the morals of most French Creoles. Pitot was elected to the New Orleans City Council in 1804, and Claiborne shortly thereafter approved his elevation by the council to the office of mayor. During his tenure, most of the essential functions of municipal government in New Orleans were established. He presided over the incorporation of the City of New Orleans and its environs, the census of 1805, the first elections, and various improvements in municipal services, such as voluntary police protection and better sidewalks and street paving. Pitot resigned as mayor in 1805 but was appointed a justice of the parish court three months later. He also served as president of the Orleans Navigation Company, which was responsible for maintaining the vital canal between Lake Pontchartrain and the Mississippi River, and as director of the New Orleans Insurance Company. Pitot was defeated in 1811 in a second bid for the mayor's office, primarily because of his connection with the navigation company. This very successful New Orleans businessman and local politician died in 1831.[37]

Louis Casimir Moreau-Lislet was another émigré prominent in the political affairs of the Louisiana Territory. Born in 1767 in Dondon, near Cap François, he fled the rebellion to set up a law practice in New Orleans sometime around the turn of the century. Moreau-Lislet's rise was uncommonly fast for an immigrant, even in America. In 1805 he began his lifelong involvement in politics

37. Henry Pitot, *James Pitot (1761–1831): A Documentary Study* (New Orleans, 1968), 30–32, 79–83, 158, 252; Register, Civil Appointments, in Carter (ed.), *Territorial Papers*, IX, 598–99, 603, *Moniteur de la Louisiane* (New Orleans), February 14, April 29, 1807.

as the official interpreter for the territory; by 1809 he was a member of the Parish Assembly, which was concerned with construction of a levee along the Mississippi River, a project he supported. He represented the city in lawsuits concerning the Land Bureau and related land disputes as well.[38]

Moreau-Lislet's most important contribution was his work on Louisiana's civil and penal codes, which to this day distinguish Louisiana from the rest of the Union. On March 11, 1808, the Louisiana State Legislature adopted a digest of civil laws that had been prepared by the aspiring St. Domingan jurist and a colleague. His later revision, the Civil Code of 1812, ensured that Louisiana would be governed by laws based on the Napoleonic Code and not English common law. In 1820, Moreau-Lislet and another colleague co-edited and translated from the Spanish two volumes of Las Siete Partidas, the codification of Roman and Spanish law concerning blacks and slavery that was used throughout Latin America. In 1825 he and two other colleagues revised the Civil Code of the State of Louisiana for adoption by the state as its legal code.[39]

Moreau-Lislet, a New Orleans city judge in his early career, served in the state legislature as a representative and as a senator in seven sessions between 1816 and 1828. He also helped train a younger breed of lawyers; Pierre Soulé, a student who read law in his office, became a partner in his firm and was prominent as a United States senator and a diplomat.[40]

Among other St. Domingans who participated in the political life of Louisiana was J. F. Canonge, who served as a justice in the district criminal court, the last court of appeals in Louisiana at that time. He was also a member of the Louisiana militia. He was a director of the Louisiana State Bank, along with his fellow St. Domingan, the merchant Amable Charbonnet. Canonge's chil-

38. Carter (ed.), *Territorial Papers*, IX, 603; *Moniteur de la Louisiane* (New Orleans), June 24, 1809; J. G. Baroncelli, *Une Colonie Française en Louisiane* (New Orleans, 1909), 133; Alcée Fortier, *A History of Louisiana* (4 vols.; New York, 1904), III, 59; Robert Pascal, "A Recent Discovery: A Copy of the Digest of the Civil Laws of 1808 with marginal source references in Moreau-Lislet's Hand," *Louisiana History*, VII (1966), 249–51.

39. Records and Deliberations of the Cabildo, II (June 27, 1810), 205 (Typescript in New Orleans Public Library); Moreau-Lislet and Carleton (trans.), *The Laws of Las Siete Partidas*; *Courrier de la Louisiane* (New Orleans), December 6, 13, 1832.

40. Fossier, *New Orleans*, III, 505; Leon Soulé, *Notice sur Pierre Soulé, Avocat à la Nouvelle Orleans, Senateur de la Louisiane à Washington* (Toulouse, 1901), copy in New Orleans Public Library.

dren distinguished themselves in Louisiana: Alphonse became an attorney, and Placide was manager of the French Opera, a writer of comédies, and a respected critic. Thomas Theard and his son, Paul-Emile, held various political offices in local and state government. Pierre Dormenon was a parish judge and later a state representative from Pointe Coupée. Augustin Dominique Tureaud also became a parish judge.[41]

Besides participating in politics, St. Domingans contributed significantly to the agricultural development of Louisiana, especially in transplanting successful sugar production into the underdeveloped territory. St. Domingue had been, by the middle of the eighteenth century, the world's largest producer and exporter of sugar and was justifiably called the Pearl of the Antilles. The slave rebellion and the European wars in the Caribbean destroyed the industry. The sugar shortage in the Western world, resulting in higher prices and unfulfilled demand, encouraged the development of sugar production in Louisiana and Cuba.

In the 1750s, Jesuits and other concerned colonists had unsuccessfully tried to transplant sugarcane seeds from St. Domingue to Louisiana. The first profitable cultivation of sugarcane did not occur until 1795 when a French planter, Etienne de Boré, gambled his resources on large-scale sugar production. Twenty years later, some two hundred sugar plantations, stretching across lower Louisiana from Pointe Coupée to Plaquemines Parish, were using Boré's methods. While Boré's experiment was duly acknowledged, his venture might never have been started, and certainly might not have been successful, had it not been for an experienced St. Domingan sugar producer, Antoine Morin, who supervised Boré's efforts. Further, refugees from the slave rebellion included knowledgeable managers, overseers, and workers. They helped reduce the risks of failure in a nascent industry that required large capital outlays and production on a massive scale. These St. Domingans were in high demand. One refugee advertising his services as a sugar refiner stated that he hoped that "28 years of experience . . . would enable him to merit the confidence of employers." Louisiana historians have tended to acknowledge the whites' role in

41. For information on the Canonge family, see Grace King, Creole Families of New Orleans (New York, 1921), 392–93; Stanley Arthur, Old Families of Louisiana (New Orleans, 1931); and New Orleans City Directory for 1832, pp. 198, 216; Catterall (ed.), Judicial Cases, III, 446.

developing the sugar industry, but they have not considered the equally important contributions of the slaves whose labor determined the outcome of the harvest. St. Domingans brought semi-skilled slaves into Louisiana to work the cane fields and others to tend the kettles during the crucial cooking process. Black St. Domingans ensured that sugar became the primary economic asset in lower Louisiana. In addition, many of the planters from St. Domingue were able to move into the parishes surrounding New Orleans to cultivate sugar themselves. Newspaper advertisements indicated that local entrepreneurs were hiring out slaves at twelve dollars a head to help the émigrés start planting again. One such St. Domingan planter was Paul Mathias Anatole Peychaud, whose plantations in St. Tammany Parish extended over 2,240 acres worked by twenty slaves.[42]

Southerners regarded the St. Domingans as good cultivators, and though the refugees did not have as great an impact on other areas as they did on Louisiana, they did improve the indigo yield in South Carolina by introducing chemical agents. Furthermore, James Achille de Caradeuc, son of the St. Domingan French general who settled on Cedar Hill plantation in Saint Thomas Parish, South Carolina, was a pioneer in cultivating grapes for domestic wines in the Charleston area before the Civil War. In Maryland, St. Domingans were known for their fine gardens and especially for their roses.[43]

The émigrés were involved in other aspects of daily life as well. Physicians were scarce in the antebellum South, especially those experienced in diagnosing and treating yellow fever. St. Domingue had long been associated with the spread of that dread disease, originally called "mal de Siam" because it was believed to have been brought to the West Indies by French ships that came from

42. Pierre Clément de Laussat, *Memoirs of My Life* . . . , trans. Sister Agnes-Josephine Postwa, ed., Robert D. Bush (Baton Rouge, 1978), 81–84; Collot, *A Journey*, II, 168–76; Thomas Ashe, *Travels in America* (London, 1809), 301. Also see J. Carlyle Sitterson, *Sugar Country: The Cane Sugar Industry in the South, 1753–1950* (Lexington, Ky., 1953), 3–12; John G. Clark, *New Orleans, 1718–1812: An Economic History* (Baton Rouge, 1970), 217–19; *Louisiana Courier*, June 23, July 21, 28, October 9, 1809; Succession Inventory, February 20, 1835, in New Orleans Court Archives, New Orleans Public Library.

43. Saint-Méry, *Journey*, 76; Henry Brackenridge, *Views of Louisiana* (2 vols.; Baltimore, 1817), II, 124; La Rochefoucauld-Liancourt, *Voyages*, IV, 140–41; de Caradeuc, *Mémoire*, 36; Edith Bevon, "Gardens and Gardening in Early Maryland," *Maryland Historical Magazine*, XLV (1950), 269.

the Far East. One of the largest outbreaks of yellow fever in the United States occurred in Philadelphia in 1793 after the arrival of six hundred St. Domingan refugees. Ports along the eastern seaboard, especially Norfolk, Virginia, closed their harbors or quarantined ships from St. Domingue.[44] Besides fearing the importation of yellow fever from the French West Indies, medical authorities such as Dr. Benjamin Rush suspected that the disease was of miasmic origin. This theory blamed the fever on morbific materials stagnating in swamps. Louisiana, a low-country region with plenty of backwater bayous along the Mississippi River basin, was thought to be one of the unhealthiest places in America. One observer described the climate: "A vast alluvion of vegetable mould, and decaying remains of animals, and of countless myriads of animalcula, afforded a fruitful hot-bed of corruption, quickened by the operation of a powerful sun, and teeming with the generations of sickness and death." At the center of this hapless, sickly place was the populace of New Orleans, forever alert for any signs of an outbreak of the "saffron scourge." Doctors were known to overdiagnose yellow fever in an attempt to cover up their own shortcomings as healers; they could point with pride to a recovered patient and escape blame for losing a patient to the dread malady. Merchants were equally self-serving: they were anxious to keep all accounts of yellow fever out of the newspapers because of the effect an outbreak would have on business. The late summer and early fall, when yellow fever always struck, brought renewed anxiety to the city.[45]

Because of New Orleans' practically annual siege of yellow fever, the city appreciated anyone who helped treat the disease.

44. C. C. Robin, *Voyages dans l'intérieur de la Louisiane, de la Floride Occidentale, et dans les Isles de la Martinique et de Saint-Domingue, pendant les Années 1802, 1803, 1804, 1805, et 1806* (3 vols.; Paris, 1802), I, 145; John Duffy (ed.), *The Rudolph Matas History of Medicine in Louisiana* (2 vols.; Baton Rouge, 1958, 1962), I, 11; Chevalier de Pontgibaud, *A French Volunteer in the War of Independence*, trans. and ed. Robert B. Douglas (Paris, 1897), 56; *Calendar of the State Papers of Virginia* (Richmond, 1886), VI, 1; Richard Bayley, *An Account of the Epidemic Fever . . . in New York . . .* (Philadelphia, 1796); *Virginia Gazette and General Advertiser* (Williamsburg), June 26, July 3, 1802.
45. Jabez Heustis, *Physical Observations and Medical Tracts . . .* (New York, 1817), 39. See Anne Carrigan, "Saffron Scourge: A History of Yellow Fever in Louisiana" (Ph.D. dissertation, Louisiana State University, 1960); and John Duffy, *Sword of Pestilence: The New Orleans Yellow Fever Epidemic of 1853* (Baton Rouge, 1966).

Refugee doctors such as Christian Miltenberger received their li-
censes to practice from the municipal medical examiners as
quickly as possible. Although Miltenberger was trained as a surgeon, he treated yellow fever extensively and kept detailed case
histories. In a Cap François hospital under the supervision of a
renowned Paris surgeon, Dr. Arthaus, he served for the British
garrison at Tiburon in southern St. Domingue in 1796. Such service was not uncommon among the French planters who supported the British occupation against the French radicals and their
black allies. Since yellow fever devastated the unseasoned British
troops, Miltenberger must have seen a great many of its victims.
The mayor of New Orleans put this experience to good use when
he appointed Miltenberger to supervise indigent health care for
his district. Miltenberger delivered a paper before the Medical Society of New Orleans in 1819, arguing the theory that yellow fever
was not a contagious disease. His success as a physician was apparent not only in the testimonials by grateful patients but in his
wealth and standing in the New Orleans community. An active
Mason, he was president of a commission to raise funds for the
construction of a Masonic hospital in the city. In 1822, Miltenberger went into partnership with Madame Joseph Baylé, who
owned a sugar plantation in Plaquemines Parish. The merger
joined 320 acres of her land with 120 acres of his. Eighteen slaves
supervised by the doctor's nephew labored on the Habitation
Sucrerie. Three years later, Miltenberger bought out Madame
Baylé. He also owned real estate in New Orleans, where he rented
out his buildings and lived in comfortable ease in a large French
Quarter home. Following the pattern of many St. Domingan refugees who lived in America but did not want to sever their ties
with France completely, Miltenberger sent his son Aristide to
Paris to be educated. Aristide received his college degree there but
returned to New Orleans to become an accountant and a proprie-
tor of a commercial firm.[46]

Christian Miltenberger was only one of several experienced St.

46. Biographical data, Will Book, IV, 285, miscellaneous letters (March 22,
1804, September 20, 1817, April 3, 1820), all in Civil District Archives, Orleans
Parish, New Orleans Public Library; [?] to C. Miltenberger, August 28, 1820, December 9, 1822, and Bills and Receipts, April, 1826, all in Christian Miltenberger
Papers, Southern Historical Collection. Also see letters of February 29, March 11,
12, 29, April 29, May 30, August 18, 1828, February 4, 1829.

Domingan physicians who settled permanently in New Orleans. The Lemonier brothers, Yves and René, were both surgeons from near Aux Cayes in southern St. Domingue. Their careers were similar to Miltenberger's, and they too were active Masons who had large families and developed considerable estates. Yves's son, Yves René, carried on the family tradition by becoming a physician himself. Jean-Charles Faget, a descendant of a St. Domingan refugee, became a prominent doctor in New Orleans, and one who published widely on yellow fever. Faget and another son of a St. Domingan, Octave Huard, studied medicine in Paris before returning to their native Louisiana. Huard also strongly advocated preserving the French language in Louisiana, and he published *De l'Utilité de la Langue Française aux Etats-Unis* (New Orleans, 1882), a treatise defending his position. These physicians helped provide New Orleans residents some of the best medical care available at that time.[47]

The St. Domingans—journalists, educators, doctors, and businessmen—were involved in the social life of New Orleans. They were the first to introduce Freemasonry to Louisiana. Firmly established in St. Domingue before the rebellion, Freemasonry was an important adjunct to the commercial and social ties of the émigrés. The first Masonic lodges in Louisiana were organized in the 1790s, and St. Domingans played important roles in their founding. These early lodges languished under Spanish rule in Louisiana, but after the United States assumed control of the territory, the St. Domingans, under the leadership of Moreau-Lislet, resurrected the movement. They were leaders in Louisiana Freemasonry because of their longer membership in the fraternal order.[48]

According to music historian Henry Kmen, the French Opera in New Orleans in the nineteenth century was just as important as was the development of jazz in the twentieth century, making New Orleans "undeniably the musical capital of America" during the first half of the nineteenth century. Yet most students of the

47. Peters-Lastrapes-Lemonier Papers. In Baltimore, the Pierre Chotard family had five generations of doctors.
48. James Scot, *Outline of the Rise and Progress of Freemasonry in Louisiana* . . . (New Orleans, 1873), 4–9, 11, 15–19, 22, 88–89; Edwin Gayle, *History of Freemasonry of Louisiana* (New Orleans, 1932), 756–61.

antebellum South ignore this rich aspect of its culture, primarily because they focus on the English antecedents of southern life.[49] Actually the arts in the antebellum South received an immediate boost as soon as experienced St. Domingan actors, actresses, singers, dancers, and stage entrepreneurs began arriving in Baltimore, Charleston, Savannah, and New Orleans.

By the late eighteenth century, St. Domingue had developed a remarkable reputation in the Caribbean for French comedy, opera, and drama. The Haitian scholar Jean Fouchard has traced the names of more than three hundred artists. In 1791, the year in which the first outbreaks of slave revolt occurred, there were more than 150 theatrical performances in St. Domingue, including Molière's comedy *Tartuffe*, Grétry's opera *Richard Coeur-de-Lion*, and a drama by Beaumarchais, *Les Deux Amis*. Theater continued during the period when Toussaint Louverture controlled the colony, though more contemporary and popular productions were mounted, such as *Héros Africain*, obviously created to celebrate the new status and accomplishments of African culture in the colony and to signal the beginning of the Théâtre Haïtien in place of the Comédie du Cap.

Until recently, Louisiana historians accepted the popular notion that the first theater in New Orleans was built by St. Domingan refugees in 1791. Current scholarship, however, has traced the first theater's founding to Jean-Marie Henry and Louis-Alexandre Henry, brothers from Paris who attempted to introduce theater in New Orleans in 1792. Nevertheless, St. Domingans did play a vital role in the eventual development of the theater and related arts in New Orleans and lent support to such enterprises elsewhere because St. Domingan upper-class refugees were a theatergoing group. Even among the French refugees in Santiago de Cuba, there was sufficient interest to support a theater during their four-year exile.[50]

49. Henry Kmen, "The Music of New Orleans," in Hodding Carter (ed.), *The Past as Prelude: New Orleans, 1718–1968* (New Orleans, 1968), 210. For examples of this neglect, see James Dormon, *Theater in the Antebellum South, 1815–1861* (Chapel Hill, 1967); and Albert Stoutamire, *Music of the Old South: Colony to Confederacy* (Rutherford, N.J., 1972). Dorman assumes—I think, incorrectly—that Richmond was the cultural center of the Old South.

50. René J. LeGardeur, *The First New Orleans Theater, 1792–1803* (New Orleans, 1963), is a careful study that revises the old thesis. However, Jean Fouchard, in *Artistes et Répertoires des Scènes de St. Domingue* (Port-au-Prince, 1900), 45,

In 1793 after the Henry brothers' theater opened in New Orleans, a Madame Durosier, quite likely the wife or relative of a famous St. Domingan actor, took over and introduced quadroons, a practice in St. Domingue theaters. By 1795, artists from St. Domingue were conspicuous in local theatrical productions. Visitors frequently commented on the rapid development of the theater in New Orleans: "The troupe . . . was composed of a half dozen actors and actresses . . . who had formerly been connected with the theater in Cap Français, in the island of St. Domingue, and who, since the revolution in that island, had taken refuge in Louisiana."[51]

When the New Orleans theater hired the impresario-engineer Barthélemy Lafon, he organized a troupe of regular, salaried artists, among them some of the most distinguished in St. Domingue. One was Jean-Baptiste LeSueur Fontaine, editor of the *Moniteur de la Louisiane*, who had been the director of the famed theater in Cap François. Fontaine was successful enough to leave an estate worth $22,000 to his sister in Paris. Closely associated with Fontaine, and considered by contemporaries the most distinguished actress in St. Domingue, was Madame Marsan, a world-traveled performer whose versatility made her one of the most popular artists of the early Louisiana stage. Both Fontaine and Marsan and several St. Domingans of lesser stature were under contract to Lafon, who paid them a monthly salary. Theatrical activity continued sporadically in New Orleans until 1803, when city authorities closed the theater because of the dilapidated state of the building. However, in 1804, another St. Domingan, Jean-Baptiste Fournier, remodeled and reopened the theater, which, according to Governor Claiborne, achieved great popularity.[52]

---

mentions one "Henri" who could have been one of the Henry brothers. Also see Berquin-Duvallon, *Vue de la Colonie Espagnole . . .* (Paris, 1803), 29–30. [Mary Hassal?], *Secret History or the Horrors of St. Domingo in a Series of Letters, Written by a Lady at Cape François to Colonel Burr* (Philadelphia, 1808), 156–57; Fouchard, *Artistes et Répertoires;* M. L. E. Moreau de Saint-Méry, *Description Topographique, Physique, Civile, Politique et Historique de la Partie Française de l'Isle Saint-Domingue* (3 vols.; Philadelphia, 1797), I, 343, 359–66, II, 985–86; Duracine Vanal, *Histoire de la Littérature Haïtienne à l'Ame Noir* (Port-au-Prince, 1933), 241–43.

51. LeGardeur, *First New Orleans Theater,* 10–11; Jean L. Fouchard, *Le Théâtre à St. Domingue* (Port-au-Prince, 1955), 345–49; Robin, *Voyages,* II, 200–201; Berquin-Duvallon, *Vue de la Colonie Espagnole,* 29–30.

52. *Louisiana Gazette* (New Orleans), and New Orleans *Advertiser,* July 6, 1814; LeGardeur, *First New Orleans Theater,* 38–40; Will Book, II, 120–24, in Civil District Archives, Orleans Parish; Fouchard, *Artistes et Répertoires;* 56–59,

However, the central figure in the development of a permanent French theater in New Orleans was Louis Tabary, an educated French colonist who was forced by economic ruin in St. Domingue to resort to theatrical management. He created and managed what was called "le spectacle de la rue St. Pierre," a loosely organized group of artists who performed there at the turn of the century. The "spectacle" was discontinued in 1807, but the location served for other theatrical productions. Some amateur actors under the guidance of François de Saint Just, a professional St. Domingan actor, opened the Théâtre Saint Pierre in September, 1808. The theater closed in 1810, and Saint Just retired from the stage but offered his services as a dance master and tutor to the citizens of New Orleans. In late 1807, Tabary became the first director of the elegant Théâtre Saint Philippe, which seated seven hundred people; adults paid one dollar and blacks and children paid fifty cents (free blacks had to sit in the balcony). The size and popularity of this theater, and the continuing efforts of so many St. Domingan artists, indicate the central role that these activities had in the social life of New Orleans.[53]

The ubiquitous Tabary had plans to build another theater on Orleans Street. It finally opened in 1809, under the guidance of backers who were financially more secure than Tabary was. Still, he could be credited with initiating the plans for the theater that was to become the pride of New Orleans. The opening of the Théâtre d'Orléans in November, 1809, marked the beginning of continuous French opera and drama throughout the nineteenth century. The original building was destroyed by fire, but a new one was opened in 1817 by another St. Domingan theater impresario, John Davis. This edifice, a magnificently appointed structure like the Théâtre Saint Philippe, housed the French Opera until 1859.

139–41; *Moniteur de la Louisiane,* March 4, 1807; LeGardeur, *First New Orleans Theater,* 23–26, 29; Minutes de Conseil de Ville, December 12, 20, 1803, August 16, 1804; Rowland (ed.), *Letter Books of Claiborne,* II, 35.

53. Louis Tabary, "Early New Orleans letter," July 13, 1805, in Howard-Tilton Memorial Library, Tulane; Nellie W. Price, "Le Spectacle de la Rue St. Pierre," *Louisiana Historical Quarterly,* VI (1918), 215–23; Harry Loeb, "The Opera in New Orleans," *Publications of the Louisiana Historical Society,* LXX (1916–17), 30–31; Henry A. Kmen, *Music in New Orleans: The Formative Years, 1791–1841* (Baton Rouge, 1966), 62–92; *Courrier de la Louisiane* (New Orleans), December 12, 1810; J. G. Baroncelli, *Le Théâtre Français à la Nouvelle Orleans* (New Orleans, 1906), 13–21; *New Orleans Bee,* February 2, 1831; Sylvie Chevally, "Le Théâtre d'Orléans en Tournée dans les Villes du Nord," *Comptes Rendus de l'Athénée Louisianais* (New Orleans, 1955), 27–71.

In that year the most elaborate building of all opened. It was de-
signed by John Gallier, the architect responsible for most of the
Greek Revival structures in New Orleans. Over the years, the
Théâtre d'Orléans was the center for opera in the South. Renowned artists, such as Felix Bernier de Maligny ("Aristippe"),
the Talma of America, performed productions of works by William
Shakespeare and James Fenimore Cooper; Julia Calvé, a talented
French opera singer who married a manager of the theater, Charles
Boudouquié, sang the lead in *The Barber of Seville;* and the Swed-
ish Nightingale, the popular Jenny Lind, performed before packed
audiences. The building was also the site of political meetings and
important social functions such as that honoring the visiting
Marquis de Lafayette.[54]

John Davis was responsible for other social activities that have
come to be identified with Creole culture in New Orleans. A
shrewd businessman, he lured personnel from Paris to staff his
theater, and he brought a French chef, Louis Boudro, to serve his
patrons Continental and Creole dishes. Thus began a tradition
that has brought New Orleans a well-deserved culinary reputation
in the United States. One exotic ingredient used in Creole cooking is filé, made from ground sassafras, and popularized in Louisiana by white and black St. Domingans.[55]

The St. Domingans' efforts on behalf of the French theater in
New Orleans indirectly benefited the development of English-
language theatrical productions in the city. James H. Caldwell
brought a company to New Orleans in 1819 that quickly became
popular with the fast-growing American population. Caldwell's
success was due in part to his being allowed to use the St. Philip
Theater on the three nights the French did not perform. The established theater had so conditioned the public to good stage productions that many theatergoing French patrons supported the
American company as well. Having established New Orleans as a

54. Baroncelli, *Le Théâtre,* 24–25; André Lafarque, "Opera in New Orleans in
Days of Yore," *Louisiana Historical Quarterly,* XXIX (1946), 600–671; Kmen, *Music in New Orleans,* 218–20; Lucile Gafford, "Material Conditions in the Theaters
of New Orleans Before the Civil War" (M.A. thesis, University of Chicago, 1955),
3–7; Sylvie Chevally, "Aristippe, le Talma de l'Amérique," *Revue de la Société
d'Histoire du Théâtre,* II (1951), 185–90.
55. Phil Johnson, "Good-Time Town," in Carter (ed.), *Past as Prelude,* 253; Ver-
non Loggins, *Where the Word Ends: The Life of Louis Moreau Gottschalk* (Baton
Rouge, 1958), 4–7.

theater town, the French company launched successful tours of the North, beginning with a well-received opening in New York City in 1827.[56] Charleston was the other major cultural center of the antebellum South that developed a successful French theater, again due to support and aid from St. Domingans. While French drama and opera had been performed in Charleston before this period, it was during the spring of 1794 that, as Charles Fraser remembered, "the great increase of French population in Charleston and their national fondness for theatrical amusements, led to the establishment of a French theater . . . with a good company of comedians, pantomimists, rope dancers, etc." However, the American Charleston Theater company looked askance at this development—particularly after three St. Domingan refugees, musicians already under contract to the American company, petitioned to perform with the new French group when they were not otherwise engaged. Although they pled poverty because of their flight from St. Domingue, the musicians were turned down. However, a *modus vivendi* soon developed: the two rival groups played on alternate nights so as to complement rather than compete with each other. The French theater was opened in April, 1794, in a brick building on Church Street under the management of Alexandre Placide, a celebrated rope dancer and comedian from St. Domingue. Placide was an astute businessman, and the French theater prospered. For his patrons, there were opera, dancing, rope dancing, and charity balls, several of which were excellent money-makers. He married Charlotte Wrighten, a local performer, and together they became impresarios of the Charleston stage. They eventually took over management of the American Charleston Theater as well.[57]

An obvious example of a native American influenced by the events of St. Domingue was the composer and pianist Louis Moreau Gottschalk. Born in New Orleans into a family that had a strong St. Domingan link, he was named after his uncle, Louis

56. Karl Bernhard, Duke of Saxe-Weimar-Eisenach, *Travels Through North Carolina During the Years 1825–1826* (New York, 1828), 59–60; Noah Ludlow, *Dramatic Life As I Found It* (St. Louis, 1880), 140–43; Johnnie A. Perkins, "Dramatic Productions in New Orleans from 1817–1861" (M.A. thesis, Louisiana State University, 1929); Kmen, *Music in New Orleans*, Chap. 4.

57. Fraser, *Reminiscences of Charleston*, 4; Charleston *City Gazette*, April 12, 1794; Willis, *Charleston Stage*, 209–12, 245, 252–53, 256, 276, 334–35; 464; Fouchard, *Artistes et Répertoires*, 70–71.

Moreau-Lislet. Gottschalk grew up in a New Orleans that could accurately be described as exotic, a blend of American, French, Spanish, and Creole, in white, brown, and black tones. Because of his background and his contact with slaves in the city—even as an observer of the slave dances and songs on Congo Square—he was sensitive to the evidence and influence of Caribbean culture in his region. Gottschalk's piano compositions emulated the exciting, hybrid sounds that he heard around the square: they made him the most distinctive, and perhaps the most popular, American musician at that time. To his European admirers, who flocked to hear his concerts while he was on tour there, he was a "pianiste compositeur louisianais," an artist from the New World who represented what they thought a young American was all about. As Parisians saw it, he was a Creole "noble savage." The titles of his works illustrated his blending Afro-American themes into a new, exotic mixture: "Bamboula, danse de nègres," "La Vavanne, ballade créole," "Le Bananier, chanson nègre," and "Le Mancenillier, ballade créole." Gottschalk expressed his feelings about the macabre events in St. Domingue when, on a voyage from Cuba to the Virgin Islands, the high mountains of Haiti came into view: "Everything, and more especially the name of St. Domingo seemed to speak to my imagination by recalling to me the bloody episodes of the insurrection, so closely associated with my childhood memories. When very young, I never tired of hearing my grandmother relate the terrible strife that our family, like all the rest of the colonists, had to sustain at this epoch; the narrative of the massacre at the Cape, the combat fought . . . by my great-grandfather against the Negroes." No doubt such scenes were described endlessly by the descendants of the former colonists—the children gathered around the fire, their imaginations stirred by tales of adventure and horror about their deceased relatives. Gottschalk went on to explain his emotional involvement with those morbid events: "Can anyone be astonished that the mere name of St. Domingo awakens somber memories in me, or that I could not help feeling an indescribable sentiment of melancholy while for the first time beholding this fatal land, with which so many grievous recollections are associated." And yet Gottschalk indicated he understood why the blacks revolted against slavery to claim their rights as free men. Perhaps his empathy related to his acknowledged debt to the blacks he saw perform in the square and on the streets of New Orleans. He knew that some of them had come from St. Domingue as well.[58] Gottschalk was one of the first white artists to take black music and dance seriously. "Bananier" (Banana Tree) was taken from the Creole song "En Avan' Grenadier" (Go Forward, Soldier), one of the many sung by blacks in New Orleans; a "bamboula" was the name of a small drum in St. Domingue that was made of bamboo and that blacks used on Congo Square. Gottschalk's most enduring contribution to American culture was not his once-popular piano pieces as much as his pioneer role in recognizing the possibilities that black culture had to offer the dominant white one.

A local Louisiana musician of lesser stature was Henri Fourrier, who also wrote music incorporating French Caribbean, particularly Haitian, rhythms and sounds in his work. In 1859, Fourrier published a series of piano pieces with titles referring to Haitian personages—"Proclamation de Soulouque aux Haïtiens" (Soulouque, as Faustin I, had been emperor of Haiti), for example, and "Les Amours de Duc de Marmelade" (a member of the Haitian court). Taken together, these St. Domingan artists profoundly influenced the cultural life of New Orleans. Their energies in establishing the theater were laudatory, and it is understandable that New Orleans would be the first American urban area to blend white and black art forms into a hybrid, one that subsequently engendered the most distinctive genre of American vernacular music and dance.[59]

58. Louis M. Gottschalk, *Notes of a Pianist* (1881; rpr. New York, 1964), 10–11; Loggins, *Where the Word Ends*; Gilbert Chase, *America's Music: From the Pilgrim to the Present* (New York, 1955); Wilfrid Mellers, *Music in a New Found Land* (New York, 1965), 239–61. For another good example of this attitude, see C. Vann Woodward (ed.), *Mary Chesnut's Civil War* (New Haven, 1981), 211. Mrs. Chesnut attended an academy in Charleston run by a St. Domingan refugee, Madame Anne-Marie Talvande, and she claimed to have had the St. Domingo stories "indelibly printed" on her mind.

59. Gottschalk, *Notes*, 12–13; Saint-Méry, *Description*, I, 63. Some of Gottschalk's pieces were named after St. Domingue black dances (see Clara Gottschalk Peterson, *Creole Songs From New Orleans in Negro Dialect* [New Orleans, 1902]; sheet music available in the Louisiana Room, Middleton Library, LSU). Jefferson Davis paid tribute to the Creole culture in his 1882 address, on behalf of the Southern Historical Society, at the Opera House (see Dunbar Rowland [ed.], *Jefferson Davis, Constitutionalist: His Letters, Papers and Speeches* [10 vols.; Jackson, Miss., 1923], IX, 162–64).

Because free blacks and slaves were proscribed in St. Domingue and continued as second-class citizens in the slaveholding sections of the United States, their contributions to antebellum society were dutifully ignored or purposefully misattributed by unsympathetic whites in the nineteenth century. Written evidence by blacks was rare, so historians and folklorists often have to rely on biased accounts by whites who were not very reliable when it came to evaluating the activities of blacks. If slaves were childlike, free blacks were even more an anomaly, as the missionary Timothy Flint said: "The heaviest scourge of New Orleans is its multitudes of free blacks and colored people. They wallow in debauchery, are quarrelsome and saucy, and commit crime in proportion to slaves as a hundred to one." Even rarer than a reliable white observer was a black man who was successful in that southern white world. One such was Victor Sejour, the son of Juan François Louis Victor Sejour Marcou, a free man of color who fled St. Domingue and established a prosperous cleaning and dyeing business on Chartres Street in the French Quarter. Victor's parents sent him to Paris to be educated because they were convinced he had talent. The publication of his short ode "Le Retour de Napoléon" (1841) brought the young Louisiana mulatto to the attention of the Parisian literati and to a friendship with another mulatto, Alexandre Dumas. Sejour's most famous work was a dramatic version of *Richard III*, one of more than twenty of his melodramas that were presented on the Paris stage. His only treatment of an American theme was *Les Volontaires de 1814* (1862), a dramatization of the Battle of New Orleans, in which a regiment of St. Domingan blacks had participated. Although Parisian audiences eventually tired of Sejour's melodramas, he returned to New Orleans only once to visit his parents. Sejour, like some other black writers later, chose to remain in Paris, where he died in relative obscurity in 1874, rather than return to life in a slave-owning society.[60]

60. Felix Flugel (ed.), "A Voyage Down the Mississippi in 1817," *Louisiana Historical Quarterly*, XII (1924), 432; Timothy Flint, *Recollections of the Last Ten Years, Passed in Occasional Residences and Journeys in the Valley of the Mississippi* (Boston, 1826), 343; Tinker, *Les Ecrits*, 427–30; New Orleans *Annual Advertiser for 1832* (New Orleans, 1832), 119; Charles Rousseve, *The Negro in Louisiana* (New Orleans, 1937), 82–91; *Dictionary of American Biography*, VIII, 565–66.

Blacks also introduced Caribbean folk patterns into lower Louisiana that caused the development of a distinctive slave culture.
French colonialism and the Catholic church were the dominant
influences on both whites and blacks in the French West Indies;
however, the slaves, many of them recently come from Africa,
drew heavily upon that heritage as well. Louisiana's proximity to
and cultural affinity with the French West Indies, and the large
number of freshly imported slaves and rather bland Catholicism,
allowed the slave community to maintain more a semblance of
African culture than was possible in Britain's North American
colonies after the American Revolution. As the first staging area
for slaves taken from Africa, the West Indies was the repository of
African culture in the New World north of Brazil. St. Domingue
was certainly no exception to this observation: both Saint-Méry
in the eighteenth century and anthropologist Melville Herskovits
in the twentieth century found ample evidence of Africanisms—
religious beliefs, cultural artifacts, and folktales—in Haitian society. Many of these important elements were found in isolated
communities on offshore islands and in Louisiana, and account
for the unique character of the black communities in these areas.
Charles Schultz, an early-nineteenth-century visitor to New Orleans, was struck by the apparent independent and foreign culture
that blacks had evolved: "They [the slaves] have their own national music, consisting for the most part of a long kind of narrow
drum of various sizes . . . three or four of which make a band. The
principle [sic] dancers or leaders are dressed in a variety of wild
and savage fashions, always ornamented with a number of tails of
the smaller wild animals." These impromptu slave gatherings
usually took place in a vacant lot, but in 1817 the New Orleans
City Council required that the mayor designate an area for such
festivities. The principal meeting place of slaves until dusk on
Sundays was unofficially called "Congo Square" (now Beauregard
Square) and was located on the edge of a swamp just across Ram-
part Street from the French Quarter. *Congo* was probably the correct word for the area, since the mixture of urban slaves, Creoles
from the West Indies, and free blacks produced the most vibrant
black subculture in the antebellum South—a subculture at times
unrecognized by white southerners because of its antecedents in
cultural forms that they had never seen or appreciated. It was here

that blacks shared their experiences and a few whites such as Louis M. Gottschalk had the opportunity to observe black culture firsthand and to be influenced by it.[61] The cement for this cultural integrity was language, and in the Americas the Creole language joined the hybrid cultural patterns of the West Indies into an intelligible experience. Until recently the standard assessment was that Creole was a "corrupted" brand of a traditional European language, a patois that resulted from the slaves' trying to copy their white masters' language. The patois in the West Indies depended upon whether the masters were English, French, Spanish, or Dutch. Actually, each of these "Creoles" is a vital, fully syntaxed language whose relationship to the prevalent European tongue approximates that of the romance languages to Latin. In the case of St. Domingue, seventeenth-century French buccaneers introduced a Norman dialect to the Antilles that developed in relative isolation from France and combined with Indian and Spanish words to form a Creole language, the lingua franca by the mid-eighteenth century. Slaves introduced many Africanisms into the language, both of vocabulary and of style. The repetition of words for emphasis and the exaggerated use of onomatopoeia were common to African and Creole dialects.[62] This language base facilitated the assimilation of slaves of different tribes into their new environment and may have had something to do with the much greater incidence of unified slave actions, such as maroonage and slave revolts, in the West Indies as opposed to the American South.

A number of Haitian influences appear in Louisiana's songs,

61. Melville J. Herskovits, *Life in a Haitian Valley* (New York, 1937); Schultz quoted in John Blassingame, *The Slave Community: Plantation Life in the Antebellum South* (New York, 1972), 30; Lawrence W. Levine, *Black Culture and Black Consciousness: Afro-American Folk Thought from Slavery to Freedom* (New York, 1977); William Wells Brown, *My Southern Home; Or, the South and Its People* (Boston, 1880), 121–23; Minutes de Conseil de Ville, October 15, 1817; Brown was a black eyewitness to such dancing (see *My Southern Home*).

62. James Leyburn, *The Haitian People* (New Haven, 1941), Chap. 18; Edith Efron, "French and Creole Patois in Haiti," in David Lowenthal and Labros Comitas (eds.), *Consequences of Class and Color: West Indian Perspectives* (New York, 1973), 215–17; Jean Baptiste Romain, "Haiti, Louisiane et la Francophonie," *Revue de Louisiane*, I (Winter, 1972), 98–99. For scholars who discuss more African influences in the development of Creole, see David DeCamp, "Introduction: The Study of Pidgin and Creole Languages," and Albert Valdman, "The Language Situation in Haiti," both in Dell Hymes (ed.), *Pidginization and Creolization of Languages* (Cambridge, Mass., 1971), 13–42, 61–64.

dances, and folk religion. These aspects of black folk culture are the very ones that best withstood white domination, perhaps, as Lawrence Levine observes, because they were the most like whites' folk patterns. Whites often commented that blacks liked to sing—only they rarely listened to or understood the meaning of that singing. Harold Courlander, the distinguished scholar of black and Haitian folk music, has pointed out the similarities between some songs from Congo Square and traditional Haitian folk songs. These ditties begin with a repeated couplet that introduces the idea of the song, which is then developed in a limited way around the couplet. This structure is basic to blues singing as well. The Louisiana author and student of Creole culture, George Cable, collected several black songs from Congo Square, and one of them, "Belle Layotte," illustrates the point:

> I have searched the entire coast
> And found no equal to beautiful Layotte
> I have searched the entire coast
> And found no equal to beautiful Layotte
> I have searched the entire colony
> Since (the time of) Monsieur Pierre Sonist
> And not found a griffone like her,
> Comparable to my beautiful Layotte.

In another Louisiana Creole song, Cable noted the reference to a geographical phenomenon very uncharacteristic of Louisiana. But "M'alle haut montagn samie" refers to the high mountains of Haiti.[63]

Whites in the antebellum South usually understood something of dance's central place in the slaves' lives, though they dismissed it as mere entertainment. Furthermore, they viewed the seemingly frenzied motions, unusual regalia, and the drums as vestiges of a half-civilized people whom they had rescued from the Dark Continent. For whites, the drum was particularly symbolic of African savagery. As late as the American intervention in Haiti in the 1920s, Americans campaigned to eradicate drums from the island. The Haitian and other dances by Louisiana blacks seemed to whites to be lewd and more for the participant than the observer.

63. Harold Courlander, *Negro Folk Music, U.S.A.* (New York, 1963), Chap. 8; George Cable, "The Dance in Congo Place," *Century Magazine*, XXXI (February, 1886), 521; George Cable, "Creole Slave Songs," *Century Magazine*, XXXI (April, 1886), 812.

Often the dances had religious significance or mocked the whites; in either case, they were central to slave culture. Blacks gathering to socialize exacerbated white fears of slave plots. With the exotic rhythms of drums, group dances conjured up nightmares of slave frenzy and potential rebellion. A comparison of reports of these dances suggests that Haitian influences in Louisiana's slave community were strong. Many of the dances that Moreau de Saint-Méry saw in St. Domingue just prior to the revolution were also performed by free blacks and slaves in Congo Square some ten years later. The calinda, for example, was a dance of African origin that by the late eighteenth century featured such European concepts as matching partners. Cable referred to it as "a sort of vehement cotillion" when he saw it danced in Congo Square. Another dance brought to New Orleans by black St. Domingans was the bamboula. Most of the musical instruments that blacks used on these occasions, such as the drums and the banjo, originated in Africa but came into Louisiana through the West Indies. As Courlander has pointed out, none of the instruments used in American black communities were crude adaptations of more sophisticated instruments, nor were they simple substitutes. Instead, they were traditional instruments with historical antecedents in Africa. For instance, Cable described what he thought was a crude, makeshift device called a marimba, a combination reed-and-string instrument. Actually it was the same as the marimbula, a thumb piano used in Haiti ever since slaves introduced it from Africa.[64]

Whites believed that blacks' savage and barbaric acts should be blamed on the St. Domingan slaves, since whites were quite aware of the connection with the African slave trade. It was in the lack

64. Harold Courlander, The Drum and the Hoe: Life and Lore of the Haitian People (Berkeley, 1960), 190; Saint-Méry, Description, I, 54–63; M. L. E. Moreau de Saint-Méry, De la Dance . . . (Parma, 1803); Althea de Peuch Parham (ed. and trans.), My Odyssey: Experiences of a Young Refugee from Two Revolutions (Baton Rouge, 1959), 26; Baroncelli, Une Colonie, 119–20; Cable, "Dance in Congo Place," 529. For the argument that these ritual dances of the early nineteenth century had a profound impact upon contemporary social dances, see John O. Anderson, "New Orleans Voodoo Ritual Dance and Its 20th Century Survivals," Southern Folklore Quarterly, XXIII–XXIV (1959–60), 135–43. Also see Marshall Sterns, Jazz Dance: The Story of American Vernacular Dance (New York, 1968), 11–34. Compare Cable, "Dance in Congo Place," Courlander, Drum and the Hoe, 83 (illustration), 201, and Benjamin Latrobe's drawings in his Impressions Respecting New Orleans: Diary and Sketches, 1818–1820, ed. Samuel Wilson, Jr. (New York, 1951).

of religious decorum that whites most feared slaves from the West Indies. Benjamin Hunt, a mid-nineteenth-century scholar of Haiti, described some slaves on the eve of their coming to America: "Le Cap might also have seemed in its last French days to have been covered with African sod, which had borne with it, all its native products . . . little disturbed by the transfer. Hence, Vaudouism, a serpent worship went on almost as little checked by public regulation, or softened by contact with Christian civilization, as if the slaves, who practiced it, were still in their native Whidah."[65] No better statement of St. Domingue slave society's fear of Africanism can be found.

Vodun, the Dahomean word for deity or spirit, was a folk religion of the African slaves who came to St. Domingue. They mixed a composite of their own West African heritage with the weak Catholicism of their masters to form a set of beliefs and practices that we call "voodoo." Like most of West African life, voodoo was an amalgam of European and African experiences that resulted in a new synthesis. It is a spiritualism that guides and comforts the peasants of Haiti to this day. Ancestor worship is important in vodun, and spirits are viewed as a combination of good and evil. Consequently, there is no heaven or hell for the vodum worshiper, only spirits that must be kept appeased if one is to continue in the struggle for life. One misconception about this folk religion is centered on black magic, which is the alleged ability to put a curse on one's enemies. Hungans, the priests of vodun, work to maintain the balance between good and evil by placating the spirits when they seem upset; they do not curse individuals, the popular perception of voodoo doctors notwithstanding. Like many practitioners of folk medicine, the hungans were, and are, adept herbalists, soothsayers, and exorcists, serving as natural healers and amateur psychologists for the peasants. Animal sacrifice has been known to occur at times, to appease the spirits. Voodoo as a folk religion in the West Indies was not the same thing as the conjuring that was so prevalent in southern black culture. While some blacks used the word *voodoo* or *hoodoo*, the context was quite different, though these folk activities had many of the

65. Benjamin Hunt, "The Haytians," 1877 (MS in Boston Public Library). A similar account is in William W. Harvey, *Sketches of Hayti: From the Expulsion of the French to the Death of Christophe* (New York, 1827).

same aims, if not the same traditions. But those elements of voodoo that existed in black southern society retained little of their original force. The voodoo queens of New Orleans were Sanité Dédé, a free woman of color from St. Domingue, and Marie Laveau, whose tomb in St. Louis Cemetery No. 1 still bears her followers' markings. They were more valuable to their community as conjure women and do not represent traditional voodoo priestesses. Both in New Orleans and Haiti today, the tourist can see voodoo ceremonies—spectacles staged to entertain nonbelievers more than to give meaning to the participants' lives. Unfortunately, there are also those who peddle voodoo paraphernalia—powders, charms, gris-gris dolls (to cast spells)—that represents the degradation of the folk traditions that are an everyday part of peasant life in Haiti.[66]

Voodoo played a shadowy role in the initial stages of the slave revolt in St. Domingue if only because it gave the slaves a common bond and perhaps some sense of power in the belief that the spirits were on their side. Whites always looked upon black rituals as both primitive and potentially savage. Until recently, white Christians associated human sacrifice and cannibalism with such "pagan" rites as voodoo. Saint-Méry mentioned some incidents of reported cannibalism in St. Domingue in the late eighteenth century, and Americans throughout the nineteenth century associ-

66. I use *vodun* for the folk religion of Haiti, and *voodoo* for its American counterpart, though the latter is sometimes seen as *hoodoo*. The best accounts of vodun are Leyburn, *Haitian People*; Herskovits, *Life in a Haitian Valley*; and Alfred Metraux, *Voodoo in Haiti*, trans. Hugo Charteris (New York, 1972). There has always been speculation about the role of vodun in the Haitian Revolution. See "Un Document sur les Rites des Nègres à St. Domingue," *Revue de l'Histoire des Colonies Français*, XVII (1929), 72–76; George Simpson, "Belief System of Haitian Vodoun," *American Anthropologist*, XXXVII (1945), 35–39; New Orleans *Commercial Bulletin*, July 5, 1869; New Orleans *Daily Picayune*, June 17, 1881, April 11, 1886; Zora Neale Hurston, "Hoodoo in America," *Journal of American Folk-Lore*, XLIV (1931), 318; Blake Touchstone, "Voodoo in New Orleans," *Louisiana History*, XII (1972), 371–86; Hortense Powdermaker, *After Freedom* . . . (New York, 1939), for incidents of conjuring and voodoo in a southern town; Levine, *Black Culture*, 56, 72, 80. Also see Richard M. Dorson, "How the Hoodoo Doctor Works," in Dorson (ed.), *American Negro Folktales* (New York, 1957), 193–95; Newbell N. Puckett, *Folk Beliefs of the Southern Negroes* (Chapel Hill, 1926), 302–304; and Norman Yetman (ed.), *Life Under the Peculiar Institution: Selections from the Slave Narrative Collection* (New York, 1970), 53, 63, 115–16, 189–90, 251, 258; Bernice Webb, "A Study of Voodoo Mailorder Advertising in Louisiana," *Revue de Louisiane*, II (Summer, 1973), 65–71; Ron Fimrite, "Pinning Down the Voodoo Ball," *Sports Illustrated*, August 27, 1973.

ated it with voodoo. Popularized accounts told of child-stealing for the purpose of human sacrifice; the child was a "goat without horns," in the dramatists' words. The debate raged on, unresolved; but no one knowledgeable about Haitian affairs has ever witnessed either human sacrifice or cannibalism in connection with religious practices.[67]

White southerners were ever watchful, fearing that black gatherings and any nocturnal ceremonies would breed black mischief and perhaps even slave plots that would lead to violence. In New Orleans, participants in alleged voodoo gatherings were prosecuted by the authorities under statutes that controlled unlawful assembly, meaning clandestine black gatherings. In the summer of 1850 a New Orleans newspaper reported that many Negroes gathered at the Recorder's Office to hear what happened to "several voluminous females who . . . had been arrested the evening before in a house in Conti St. whilst performing the ceremonies and mysteries of Voodooism. It was also rumored that the police had made a razzin [sic] of the instruments and symbols used in the dark rites. Betsy Toledaro, stout middle aged free colored women was called up as the chief witness of the society, as she called it. . . . The officers stated that they had often noticed slaves entering the house in numbers and had heard singing."[68] As was not the case in vodun ceremonies in Haiti, women in New Orleans seemed to have the leading role as mambo. The next summer a story of twenty colored women "engaged in the mysterious rites of Voudou" was reported in the newspapers. When arrested, these women, one of whom was naked, were "dancing at the time around a fowl, a toad's head and other articles which are considered indispensable to the proper observations of the ceremonies." Another nighttime meeting was reported when a police officer at midnight "discovered a *voudou* assemblage. . . . Five disreputable

67. William W. Newell, "Myths of Voodoo Worship and Child Sacrifice in Hayti," *Journal of American Folk-Lore*, I (1888), 16–30; Saint-Méry, *Description*, I, 53, 63. For an example of how proslavery advocates considered voodoo evidence of African savagery, see John Campbell, *Free Negroism; Or, Results of Emancipation in the North and the West India Islands* (New York, 1862), 12; and David Christy, *A Lecture on African Civilization* (Columbus, Ohio, 1853), 7–11 (reprinted in Christy's *Ethiopia: Her Gloom and Glory* [Cincinnati, Ohio, 1857], 71–72).

68. New Orleans *Daily Picayune*, July 1, 1850; New Orleans *True Delta*, June 29, August 27, 1850, November 3, 1854.

free women of color were lying in a state of nudity within a chalked circle on the floor mumbling some nonsensical incantations. A cauldron of water containing a large snake, was boiling in the fireplace, and a table was spread with roasted oysters, hard boiled eggs, and liquor, of which free indulgence had been made. One of these women had been supported lately by an implicated party in the great forgery case; and she had got up this voudou incantation to spirit him out of the scrape."[69] Because there were no potentially dangerous black males involved in these incidents, the authorities apparently treated them as nuisances that only reinforced their feelings about black culture; namely, that blacks were inherently lewd and pagan and would revert if left to their own devices. The public was quick to blame any bizarre or unexplained event on the "mysteries of voodoo." In New Orleans during the Civil War, a news item under the headline "The Voodoo Again!" reported that a body found in a vacant lot had been "thrown from the garret window of a shanty occupied by Voodoos." The body, sawed in half from the head down through the center to the feet, was badly decayed. The excitement over this strangely mutilated corpse subsided after it was learned that a boy discovered the cadaver in a vacant medical shop and sold it to a black women for ten cents. Out of curiosity, she mummified the body, but got rid of it when vermin took over.[70]

Taken together, the traditions of folk culture that the St. Domingans brought with them seemed to blend in new ways. In Louisiana, blacks had more options, the Christian church was more accessible, and New Orleans and its environs meant that the rural folk religion of Haiti, vodun, had little relevance for them.

Had it not been for the influx of survivors of the rebellion in St. Domingue, French Creole culture in Louisiana would not have developed to the extent that it did, affecting both the Gulf coast area and beyond. As a group, the St. Domingans were the single most influential Gallic element in Louisiana, and perhaps in all of

69. New Orleans *Bee*, July 25, 1851, October 15, 1860. On another occasion forty naked women were arrested (see the New Orleans *Daily Picayune*, July 31, August 1, 1863).

70. New Orleans *Bee*, October 22, 1860. Also see New Orleans *Daily Picayune*, October 3, 1863; and Lafcadio Hearn, *An American Miscellany* (2 vols.; New York, 1924), II, 201–208.

American society. The French minister Laussat noted at the time: "I imagine that Saint-Domingue was, of all our colonies in the Antilles, the one whose mentality and customs influenced Louisiana the most. Frequent intercourse existed between the two. Even today when the Negroes, having become independent, have chased us from Haiti, exiles from the island prefer Louisiana as refuge."[71] These refugees were better educated and more skilled than the native Louisianians were, and they quickly became a dominant force in the French-speaking community, preserving their heritage through French-language newspapers, laws, education systems, and social groupings. They almost completely dominated the Creoles of color, an important subculture that gave New Orleans some of its unique aspects. Louisiana benefited economically from the sugar industry that was introduced to the region by white and black St. Domingans. They were responsible for the cultural flowering of New Orleans and, to some extent, of Charleston. New Orleans as a cultural center compared favorably with any city in antebellum America. St. Domingans, white and black, were responsible for introducing a Gallic-African pattern into the United States. The cultural foundations became institutionalized in new, indigenous forms: theater, architecture, folk religion, dance, and music. If the lower South was the northern extremity of Caribbean culture, and I suggest that it was in many ways, the St. Domingans were a link between the American South and the West Indies.

71. Laussat, *Memoirs of My Life*, 55.

THREE

TOUSSAINT'S IMAGE IN ANTEBELLUM AMERICA

Henry Adams' observation is as valid today as when he made it almost a century ago: "The story of Toussaint Louverture has been told almost as often as that of Napoleon, but not in connection with the history of the United States although he exercised on their history an influence as decisive as that of any European ruler." Toussaint has become a footnote to American history, and that seems an irony given the primacy his contemporaries accorded him both inside and outside the United States during the late 1790s and early 1800s. More than anyone else, Toussaint personified for Americans the bewildering events in the French West Indies that had such important consequences. Even after General Leclerc finally captured Toussaint, he warned Napoleon that "the man has fanaticized this country to such a degree that his appearance would set everything once more aflame."[1]

Leclerc's concern was prophetic: Toussaint died in 1803, but Napoleon's hopes for a French empire in America went forever unfulfilled. His soldiers were decimated by yellow fever and defeated by Toussaint's army. Napoleon turned his attention elsewhere, selling the faltering colony of Louisiana to the United States in the meantime. Toussaint thus helped change the course of the history of the Americas and perhaps the map of the United States as well. While most Americans viscerally disapproved of rebelling slaves violently overthrowing a white European power, they still displayed a genuine admiration for Toussaint Louverture, a man with whom all factions could identify and for quite different reasons.

St. Domingue was a partisan issue in the United States because domestic policies and foreign affairs were inextricably interwoven in the early days of the Republic. The American trade with St. Domingue was extensive, ranging from lumber, food, and fish to manufactured goods, gunpowder, and arms. Anxious to continue and expand this trade, American Federalists saw that Toussaint

1. Henry Adams, *History of the United States During the First Administration of Thomas Jefferson* (New York, 1889), 378; Leclerc quoted in George Tyson, Jr. (ed.), *Toussaint Louverture* (Englewood Cliffs, N.J., 1973).

represented the instrument for disassociating St. Domingue's trade policies from revolutionary France. Even though the British expeditionary force collapsed in 1798, having been unable to take possession of the island, the Federalist merchants did not find it difficult to switch their hopes to Toussaint, who helped defeat the British.[2]

The Jeffersonian Republicans were caught in a dilemma because their pro-French and antiblack attitudes were in conflict with American national interests. By itself, Louisiana was not a viable possession for France unless the colony could maintain control and become as agriculturally productive as St. Domingue has been; yet French control of St. Domingue depended upon subduing Toussaint and reestablishing slavery, as Napoleon did in Guadeloupe and Martinique. In this curious way, President Jefferson found himself at least partially reliant upon a former slave in revolt against France to secure American interests in both the Mississippi Valley and the Caribbean. The president made no meaningful attempts to hinder American merchants supplying the rebels until the fate of St. Domingue had been decided. Only then did Jefferson yield to French pressure for an embargo on St. Domingue.[3]

Southern editors, aware of Toussaint's role in freeing Louisiana for American expansion to the southwest, paid tribute to his military prowess and, in spite of his color, referred to him with the same propriety as northern newspapers did. For instance, one southern tabloid acknowledged that Toussaint "must be a man of no inconsiderable talent, since he has both conceived and executed so great a project as that of rescuing his unhappy country from the miseries with which it was afflicted by the tyranny of France." And this from a southern newspaper referring to a rebellious former slave. Southern Federalists especially admired his military accomplishments; in his struggle against the oppression of his people, they portrayed him as the Caribbean counterpart of George Washington—wise, talented, and in the vanguard, yet ever

2. See Rayford Logan, *The Diplomatic Relations of the United States with Haiti, 1776–1891* (Chapel Hill, 1941), 118–21; Adams, *History*, 378–94; Thomas Ott, *The Haitian Revolution, 1789–1804* (Knoxville, 1973); and David Geggus, *Slavery, War, and Revolution: The British Occupation of St. Domingue, 1793–1798* (Oxford, 1982).

3. Linda Kerber, *Federalists in Dissent: Image and Ideology in Jeffersonian America* (Ithaca, 1970), 23–66.

cautious not to lose control of the volatile situation. In a strong essay supporting the deposed black general after his capture by the French, one editor noted that "in every point of view Toussaint is an interesting character. To those who consider him an advocate of an oppressed people, his discomfiture will be a source of regret. . . . Even as the leader of a revolt, his conduct as far as has been correctly developed, evidences powers of mind, which in higher stations would exhort admiration." Southerners admired Toussaint's ability to control the revolution, restore law and order in the war-torn colony, and forcibly return the former slaves to the plantations to work as a free labor force.[4]

Aware of Toussaint's support in America, French authorities tried to garner sympathy for their cause. They published in American newspapers an official explanation of Toussaint's arrest and his being sent to France: Leclerc accused Toussaint of complicity in the massacre of whites and of plotting to move the colony toward independence from France.[5] Also printed for American audiences was Napoleon's appeal to the blacks in which he vowed, disingenuously as it turned out, not to reinstate slavery in St. Domingue. Refusing to believe that Toussaint was responsible for the carnage that the French blamed on him, one Virginia editor who frequently wrote about the affairs of St. Domingue defended the black general's conduct: "Toussaint, before the arrival of the French army could not by the most rancorous of his enemies, be accused with having spilt the blood of the innocent; he could not be reproached with requisitions and robberies, such as have marked the progress of General Leclerc. We have been told that he was a monster, and that he has committed the most wanton cruelties, but where are the proofs of this?" Southerners were surprisingly anxious to give the black general the benefit of the doubt. If his demise were not enough to heighten anti-French sentiment in the United States, several southern newspapers editorialized about

4. *Columbia Mirror and Alexandria Gazette* (Va.), May 25, 1799; *Virginia Gazette and General Advertiser* (Williamsburg), April 17, 1802; *Alexandria* (Va.) *Advertiser and Commercial Intelligencer*, June 28, 1802. Others made the same point. See Louis M. Gottschalk, *Notes of a Pianist* (1881; rpr. New York, 1964), 13; and Moncure Conway, *The Rejected Stone* (Boston, 1862), 123.

5. *Virginia Gazette and General Advertiser* (Williamsburg), July 17, 1802; *Moniteur de la Louisiane* (New Orleans), August 14, October 9, 1802. See Alexandria (Va.) *Advertiser and Commercial Intelligencer*, July 15, 1802, for the American reaction.

the indignities perpetrated by the French upon Toussaint's family. In an unusually long, front-page article, the Richmond *Enquirer* excoriated the French for defiling womanhood in the person of Madame Toussaint. Taken to France but immediately separated from her family, Madame Toussaint, a St. Domingan black, was said to be pregnant but lost her child after she was tortured. The compassionate writer reported that her body was living proof of what she had endured: Her left arm was useless, and she "has no less than 44 wounds in different parts of her body. Pieces of flesh have been torn from her breast, as with hot irons, together with nails of her toes!" To emphasize his point, the editor claimed sarcastically that Madame Toussaint was "a living witness to the humanity and honor of the tender Emperor of the French, the august chief of the French Legion of Honor." Madame stayed in France and died in poverty at the age of seventy-four in May, 1816.[6]

Americans who were proslavery or antislavery were willing to abandon their racial stereotypes when it was to their advantage to do so. Toussaint Louverture's fate became a rallying cry for those American Federalists who wished to discredit the French, in view of the excesses of the French Revolution and their own desire for increased commerce with the French West Indies. Even southern slave owners were more anti-French than anti-Negro: the French threat to their expansionist plans in the Mississippi Valley was immediate. Furthermore, they admired Toussaint's conservative tactics after assuming power, particularly his attempt to stabilize the work force and his treatment of white planters. They praised a former slave who stood up to one of the strongest powers in Europe. Toussaint Louverture's success was a victory of the New World over the Old.

The death of Toussaint and Napoleon's preoccupation with affairs in Europe did nothing to reduce the literature on the black general. Throughout the antebellum period, Americans read and discussed the meaning of his life, but this fascination cannot be explained solely in terms of his role in diverting the French from the northern Caribbean. As the slavery controversy gained emotional

6. *Virginia Gazette and General Advertiser* (Williamsburg), July 3, 1802; Richmond *Enquirer*, January 15, 1805; *Louisiana Gazette* (New Orleans) reprinted the same story on March 5, 1805. Madame Toussaint, of course, was not pregnant, but it is important that the newspaper exaggerated in that way.

intensity in the early nineteenth century, Toussaint became an important symbol of stability and reason in a world seemingly dominated by anger, passion, and the threat of violence. Southern apologists for slavery, northern antislavery advocates, and free black abolitionists all relied upon Toussaint to reassure themselves. That he was a black man, and a former slave, only deepened their resolve to seek solace in what they thought he stood for.

One of the first of many biographies appeared in 1804 shortly after his death. *The Life and Achievement of Toussaint Louverture* was probably of English origin. Most later accounts follow the basic pattern set by this anonymous document that praised the former slave as a hardworking and faithful servant before the revolution. The author pointedly held Toussaint up as an example for freedmen and slaves because he was not motivated by racial hatred or by revenge when circumstances put him in control of the destiny of whites in St. Domingue: "He uniformly prevailed with his countrymen to spare the lives of their masters, and other white persons in their employ, first exhibiting an example of the most grateful and dignified sentiment, in embracing his late master, and with bended knees and tears supplicating his departure from his habitation, manfully and religiously promising him a safe escort."[7] Not only was he forgiving and solicitous of his former master, he made extraordinary efforts to ensure that his master's property was returned to him without loss. In fact, Toussaint saw that if St. Domingue was going to prosper after the end of slavery, white resources and know-how would be needed to restore the economy of the war-torn island. Compared with other actors on this stage, he did strive for stability and for having all constituencies—white, brown, and black—recognize that their future depended upon mutual cooperation. In the last pages of these filiopietistic biographies, the hero's mantle was draped over Toussaint as he wrote his last noble thoughts to his followers from his death cell. The image was of a man of dignity and Christian resignation about his fate at the hands of the deceitful French. White Americans looking at the carnage associated with the "horrors of St. Domingo" sighed their relief at the thought that Toussaint, first among the blacks, was a moderate peacemaker. Toussaint reassured them that race war need not be inevitable in a multiracial

7. *The Life and Achievement of Toussaint Louverture* (N.p., 1804), 7.

society, so long as strong men prevailed to keep the former slaves in line.

To southerners, Toussaint thought like a white man. One of the most popular arguments used by slavery apologists was that blacks would not work unless they were forced to do so. Further, slavery was necessary to keep the work force producing on the farms and plantations as well as to keep blacks from taking revenge upon their former masters. To illustrate this point, southerners were fond of comparing the impressive prerevolutionary sugar and coffee production in St. Domingue using slave labor and the dramatic decline in agricultural production after slavery was abolished, Toussaint was removed, and the free blacks controlled their own destinies. To southerners, black Haiti symbolized economic decay and ruin.[8] White planters claimed that blacks were incapable of civilization, supporting the argument with evidence from Toussaint's policy. In the midst of the turmoil in October, 1800, Toussaint did initiate a tough forced-labor policy under martial law that required blacks to return to the fields. Slavery apologists pointed out both the wisdom and efficacy of this policy, initiated by a former slave who knew his people and the situation well.

One of the South's leading spokesmen for slavery, Thomas R. Dew of the College of William and Mary, was convinced that only Toussaint's harsh law against idleness saved Haiti from total ruin. It was true that staple-crop production did rise because there were enough working plantations with sufficient white planters, black laborers, and commercial agents left to carry on. Zaphaniah Kingsley, a Florida planter known for his humanitarian schemes, agreed with Dew that Toussaint was able to reestablish agricultural output because of his "patriarchal restraint." The southern apologist George Fitzhugh, no spokesman for black talent, conceded that "the free Negroes of Haiti were all well governed under Toussaint Louverture but this meant strict military surveillance, compulsory labor, and severe penalties for deserting their farms." In a similar statement, which suggested that even the black general knew that he had to force blacks to labor in the fields, eccentric southern agriculturist Edmund Ruffin remarked: "The black general Toussaint, (the only truly great man yet known of the negro

8. See, for example, *Commercial Review*, V (May–June, 1848), 498–99; or *De Bow's Review*, XVI (1854), 276.

race), who, after suppressing the civil war, assumed and exercised despotic and severe authority, compelled the former slaves to return to the plantations, and to labor, under military coercion, and severe punishment for disobedience." The leading journal of the South, *De Bow's Review*, carried yet another article stressing this aspect of Toussaint's accomplishments: "Toussaint Louverture . . . set the negroes to work, and even recalled some planters and the overseer even, under whom he had been a slave, to manage the estates and to compel the negroes to work. In every respect he was more humane, reasonable, and discreet than the white fanatics sent there from France, and only fell because he was less tricky and faithless than his French friends, and was inferior in deceit to the generals of the great Napoleon."[9] There was a hint in this statement, as in all the anti-French writings by antebellum slavery advocates, that it was unbelievable that the French dared to introduce black freedom and equality into the Caribbean. Slavery apologists had no use for the French or their radical ideology.

Proslavery spokesmen, reassured by Toussaint's example, were willing to give him unqualified praise. As Eric Foner has pointed out, the planter classes of all these slave societies were primarily concerned about the stability of their labor force, both before and after freedom. It was that concern that led American planters to praise a black slave-rebellion leader.[10]

Toussaint's southern reputation benefited from the moderate tone of his administration compared with that set by his successors, particularly the infamous Jean Jacques Dessalines, who, in a widely publicized maneuver, ordered all the remaining whites massacred. Dessalines had good reason not to trust either the planters or the French; however, his action also made practically

9. Thomas R. Dew, *An Essay on Slavery* (Richmond, 1849), 82, 87–88; Zaphaniah Kingsley, *A Treatise on the Patriarchal, or Co-Operative System of Society As It Exists . . . Under the Name of Slavery* (1829; rpr. Freeport, N.Y., 1970), 8; George Fitzhugh, "What's To Be Done With The Negroes?" Richmond *Enquirer*, May 2, 1851; Edmund Ruffin, *The Political Economy of Slavery* (Richmond, 1857), 17; "Practical Effects of Emancipation," *De Bow's Review*, XV (1855), 597. For a northern racist view that is similar, see Louis Schade, *Appeal to the Common Sense and Patriotism of People of the United States . . .* (Washington, D.C., 1860), 39.

10. See Eric Foner, *Nothing But Freedom: Emancipation and Its Legacy* (Baton Rouge, 1983), for an excellent comparison of the reaction to emancipation in the West Indies, the United States, and modern Africa.

impossible the resurrection of stable agricultural production. The destruction of the planter class, in its economic sense, caused Haiti to lapse into a subsistence economy. This situation was further aggravated by debilitating civil wars between mulattoes and blacks in the young republic. To Americans, Dessalines was the sinister figure representing a long line of violent, vengeful rulers; Toussaint represented stability and forgiveness. Several journals carried a story in which Dessalines was a man of "wild and flighty mind" who killed whites on sight. In this fictional and emotional account, Dessalines captured Toussaint's former master after Toussaint had helped him escape. Toussaint pleaded for his former master's life, but Dessalines replied, "He must perish because he is white. His color is his guilt." Dessalines then killed the planter, and a grief-stricken Toussaint resigned from the army. Dessalines was then accused of betraying Toussaint to the French, and of ordering that all whites be slain. He was finally assassinated by his own men, who rejoiced that "the tyrant is no more!"[11] Toussaint was the tragic man of principle, a positive image that did not change throughout the antebellum period; Dessalines was a monster, an early-nineteenth-century version of Richard Wright's angry black man, Bigger Thomas. As time passed and the memory of St. Domingue dimmed, Americans were willing to evaluate leaders only in terms of these two paradigms. Ironically, southerners accepted Toussaint into their pantheon of heroes because they saw the father of black independence in the Caribbean and perhaps in all the New World as a primary symbol for maintaining slavery in the Americas.

Antislavery spokesmen were anxious to prove that without slavery blacks were capable of living meaningful lives and contributing to the advancement of society. In their attempt to counter the argument that slavery was the best means of keeping blacks productive, the abolitionists predictably focused on Toussaint as the most conspicuous black man in the world at the turn of the century. Toussaint was in a position to decisively influence the history of the Americas in a way that startled most whites. His abrupt fall from power in St. Domingue only enhanced the image

11. "Dessalines and Toussaint L'Ouverture: An Episode in the History of Haiti," *Daguerreotype*, II (Boston, 1848), 369–75.

of him as a martyred savior of his people.[12] As early as 1802 the opponents of slavery were using his life as a symbol to promote abolition. The Reverend Alexander McLeod, pastor of a Presbyterian church in New York, wrote a religious tract against slavery in which he answered those who claimed that slavery was necessary to keep blacks functioning in society. He stated that the inferiority of blacks had been "greatly exaggerated," and he noted that "the courage and skill of the negroes in war will no longer be disputed, after their transactions in St. Domingo." McLeod argued that "great must be his prejudice who can deny to the black Toussaint the qualifications of a warrior and a statesman."[13]

The rise of militant abolitionism in the North during the 1830s resulted in antislavery advocates' sustained interest in what Toussaint's life symbolized. Like some southern Federalists, abolitionists developed a strong analogy between the struggle for freedom that brought Toussaint to the fore in the Caribbean and the circumstances that lifted George Washington to the leadership of Britain's rebelling North American colonies a decade earlier. Shortly after Washington's birthday celebration in 1832, and at a time when Washington was being apotheosized as a national hero, William Lloyd Garrison printed a dialogue in which, after eulogistic greetings from Toussaint to Washington, the American father of independence replied: "Why when we released ourselves from oppression, did we continue oppression! Toussaint! That my example and acquiescence sanctioned this, is the bitterest recollection of my life on earth." Washington then expressed guilt over slavery and he praised Toussaint's efforts to ameliorate the condition of blacks: "Yet in . . . [Haiti] your race are free, and enjoy with the blessings of freedom that increasing light and knowledge which give it its true value, and they may now show to the world that the despised African race have immortal souls, are rational beings." Washington concluded with a plea for citizens to cast off slavery so that all Americans might live up to the ideals of the American Revolution. Author and black abolitionist William Wells Brown also used the comparison between Toussaint and

12. Several authors referred to Toussaint as "god-like." One was J. Theodore Holly, *A Vindication of the Capacity of the Negro Race* (New Haven, 1857), 52. Holly's title aptly describes Toussaint's major influence on black thought. Others compared him favorably with Napoleon (for example, see E. Quincy to H. A. Chapman, February 25, 1840, in Weston Sisters Family Papers, Boston Public Library).

13. Alexander McLeod, *Negro Slavery Unjustified* (New York, 1802), 21–22.

Washington, but he tersely dismissed the analogy: "Toussaint liberated his countrymen; Washington enslaved a portion of his."[14] To both Garrison and Brown, it was Haiti—and not the United States—that lived up to the American ideal of freedom.

The Washington of St. Domingo was also presented to the American public as living proof that blacks were inaccurately depicted as inferior to whites in mental and moral capacity. One enthusiast claimed that "though perfectly black, he was unquestionably one of the greatest and best men of his age." Those whites who used Toussaint's life as a refutation of black inferiority always emphasized his blackness. He was not a mulatto, and they undoubtedly did not want to detract from his achievements by having it said that he had "white blood" in him. New England reformer David Lee Child wrote that Toussaint was a precious example because the "white man's blood ran not in his veins, but the milk of kindness was around his heart." In a similar vein the *Anti-Slavery Record,* an abolitionist newspaper, ran a short piece that argued its thematic title, "TOUSSAINT LOUVERTURE NEVER BROKE HIS WORD." Later an article in the same journal maintained that the "results of his powerful intellect, undaunted courage and generous philanthropy, could not be hid." Other attributes of this romanticized Toussaint included his dedication to hard work and his temperate and modest character. Often these interpretations lead us to believe that he was a good New Englander, imbued with the Protestant ethic and Christian temperance. In sum, the numerous articles that appeared in antislavery literature in the antebellum period agreed with the *New York Mechanic and Concord People's Advocate* (1842) that "the name of Toussaint Louverture . . . is entitled to a high rank in the rolls of history, and, . . . it will be as familiar as the name of Bolivar and Washington."[15]

14. William Lloyd Garrison, "Some Remarks on the Former and Present State of St. Domingo and Hayti," *Liberator,* March 10, 1832; William Wells Brown, *The Black Man, His Antecedents, His Genius and His Achievements* (New York, 1863), 105; J. Dennis Harris, *A Summer on the Border of the Caribbean Sea* (New York, 1860), 115.

15. Lydia M. Child, *The Antislavery Catechism* (Newburyport, Mass., 1835), 28–29; also see *An Appeal to the Women of the Nominally Free States, Issued by an Anti-Slavery Convention of American Women* (Boston, 1838), 33; David Lee Child, *The Despotism of Freedom; Or, The Tyranny and Cruelty of American Republican Slave-Masters* (Boston, 1833), 68; *Anti-Slavery Record,* December, 1835, pp. 151–52, December, 1837, p. 6; *New York Mechanic* quoted in Philip S. Foner, *History of Black Americans: From Africa to the Emergence of the Cotton Kingdom* (New York, 1975), 439.

The literati, like the activists, were attracted to Toussaint. Several times during the antebellum period, journals serialized the history of St. Domingue and Haiti. In one long article in the *Knickerbocker* in 1841, the author took note that the black chief was still used as an exemplar to his race, his specific reference being to the biography by the popular English author Harriet Martineau: "'Toussaint L'Ouverture has been recently held up to the world as possessing more virtues than were ever before bestowed on any human being. No wonder Miss Martineau is so enthusiastic in her love for the race, if she believes Toussaint to have been as she has painted him in 'The Hour and the Man.'" Several poets also immortalized his life. John Greenleaf Whittier, politically involved with the movement to abolish slavery, wrote some of his best poems on that issue. One was a tribute to Louverture:

> Everywhere thy name shall be
> Redeemed from color's infamy
> And men shall learn to speak of thee
> As one of earth's greatest spirits, born
> In serviture and nursed in scorn
> Casting aside the weary weight
> And fetters of its slow estate
> In that strong majesty of soul
> Which knows no color, tongue, or clime,
> Which still hath spurned the base control
> of tyrants, through all time.

Toussaint had always been a favorite of the English, perhaps because they admired his leadership during their occupation of St. Domingue, and certainly because he eventually succeeded against Napoleon. In 1802, shortly before Toussaint's death, William Wordsworth wrote a sonnet that was later widely circulated among American abolitionists and reprinted in their publications throughout the antebellum period:

> Toussaint, thou most unhappy man of men!
> Whether the whistling rustic tends his plough
> Within thy hearing, or thou liest now
> Buried in some deep dungeon's earless den—
> O, miserable chieftain! Where and when
> Wilt thou find patience? Yet die not; do thou
> Wear rather in thy bonds a cheerful brow;
> Though fallen thyself, never to rise again,
> Live and take comfort. Thou has left behind

Powers that will work for thee: air, earth, and skies;
There's not breathing of the common wind
That will forget thee; thou hast great allies;
Thy friends are exultations, agonies,
And love, and man's unconquerable mind.[16]

Lydia Maria Child, the wife of reformer David Child, was an author and an abolitionist in her own right who was a consistent champion of Toussaint. Born in Massachusetts in the same year that Wordsworth wrote his sonnet to the imprisoned Toussaint, Child championed black freedom and equality through her writings from the mid-1830s to the end of the Civil War. The longest of her several pieces on Toussaint was in *The Freedman's Book* (1865), in which she attempted to trace the black general's lineage back to a noble African chief. She suggested that Toussaint's good morals and his desire to acquire knowledge foreshadowed his dignity as a great leader. Her romantic narrative of Toussaint's background was certainly apocryphal. She also used the long-lived rumor that Toussaint had become aware of his mission to liberate the Negroes in the West Indies by reading the Abbé Raynal, the eighteenth-century French humanist who had predicted that a courageous chief would one day come to free the blacks. Toussaint, to the antebellum abolitionists, was clearly the Moses and the deliverance from slavery in the Old Testament, which Lawrence Levine suggests was so central to black folklore. Child imbued Toussaint with values that illustrated her own conviction that the righteous do indeed triumph. Her Toussaint was a living parable of the message that Harriet Beecher Stowe had so forcefully expressed in *Uncle Tom's Cabin*. This Christ-like figure, forced to join the black insurgents, rejected violence for healing the wounded—"an office," according to Child, "for which he was well qualifed by his tender disposition and knowledge of medicinal plants." She, like many of his southern admirers, praised Toussaint because he was "never in a bloodthirsty spirit"; his motto was "no retaliation." Revealing another of her interests, Child made much of the point that "no trait in the character of

16. "Life in Haiti," *Knickerbocker*, XVIII (December, 1841), 491; Whittier's poem is reprinted in Lydia M. Child, *The Freedman's Book* (Boston, 1865), 53, and in Beard's English biography of Toussaint; Wordsworth's poem is reprinted in Lydia M. Child, *An Appeal in Favor of That Class of Americans Called Africans* (New York, 1836), 177–78. Lamartine wrote a play about Toussaint and Victor Hugo's first novel, *Bar-Jargal*, was about St. Domingue and the black revolution.

Toussaint . . . was stronger than his domestic affections." She claimed that his moral character was even more worthy of admiration than was his intellectual acuity: "What can be more beautiful than his unchanging gratitude to his benefactor, his warm attachment to his family, his highminded sacrifice of personal feeling to the public good." Child's story ends with Toussaint's treacherous betrayal by Napoleon (Judas?) and his martyr's death, which she calls "slow murder." To Child, then, Toussaint was a pacifist and family man of great integrity, a grateful former slave, a reluctant warrior who was more concerned with healing than destroying, and an honest Christian who was deceived by a dishonorable man. Child embellished the meager known facts of his life; her story extolled the virtues of a good Christian life. Nevertheless, her fiction had an ecumenical message for all Americans concerned about the treatment of blacks in the United States: "Well may . . . the United States take pride in Toussaint Louverture, as the man who made an opening of freedom for his oppressed race, and the greatness of his character and achievements proved the capabilities of Black Men."[17]

During the Civil War many antislavery sympathizers were anxious to defend the right of Negroes to join the armed forces to fight for their own freedom. They argued that blacks were capable of fighting bravely and of accepting discipline. They published several accounts of Toussaint's military exploits that characterized the black general as an accomplished war leader and strategist, not as a "reluctant" soldier. James Redpath, a white man who often championed black causes, edited and published a biography in 1863 that stressed the military success of Toussaint and his black troops. This volume was essentially a reprint of the biography by Beard published ten years earlier, but Redpath added a section to the pirated work to emphasize the accomplishments of black soldiers. Abolitionist orator Wendell Phillips also gave speeches and wrote a pamphlet on Toussaint, *The Hero of Hayti*, in which he stressed the physical strength and courage of blacks

17. Child, *The Freedman's Book*, 46–48 (though she did criticize Toussaint's forced-labor policy); Child, *An Appeal*, 83, 198. Also see A. Mott, *Biographical Sketches . . .* (New York, 1838), 133–36; and W. C. Blake, *The History of Slavery and the Slave Trade* (Columbus, Ohio, 1859), 268–72. The *Anti-Slavery Record*, December, 1835, also stressed Toussaint's honesty; Ralph Waldo Emerson shared the view that Toussaint was a symbol of black regeneration (see Edward W. Emerson [ed.], *The Journals of Ralph W. Emerson* [10 vols.; Boston, 1911], VI, 532–33).

in combat. Phillips admonished those who doubted the Negro's courage to "go to Hayti, and stand on those fifty thousand graves of the best soldiers France ever had, and ask them what they think of the negro's sword." And to emphasize Toussaint's remarkable character, Phillips placed him in the company of exalted white warriors:

> I would call him Cromwell, but Cromwell was only a soldier, and the state he founded went down with him into his grave. I would call him Washington, but the great Virginian held slaves. This man risked his empire rather than permit the slave-trade in the humblest village of his dominions.
>
> You think me a fanatic to-night, for you read history, not with your eyes, but with your prejudices. But fifty years hence, when Truth gets a hearing, the Muse of History will put Phocion for the Greek, and Brutus for the Roman, Hampden [for] English, Fayette for France, choose Washington as the bright consummate flower of our earlier civilization, and John Brown the ripe fruit of our noonday, then dipping her pen in the sunlight, will write in the clear blue, above them all, the name of the soldier, the statesman, the martyr TOUSSAINT L'OUVERTURE.[18]

Most of the abolitionist literature of this period that used the name and image of Toussaint was as romantic and hyperbolic as this speech, and usually had the same conclusion—namely, that the black general was as great as any leader in history.

Although both white and black abolitionists portrayed Toussaint as larger than life, they emphasized different aspects of his character. They were all impressed by his mercurial rise from humble origins and his status as one of the most important figures in the history of the Americas. Whites, however, stressed Toussaint's racial moderation and temperance; blacks admired his qualities as a Spartacus who threw off the yoke of oppression. If whites saw him as Jesus, blacks saw him as Moses, leading his people out of slavery and into freedom. Toussaint and the history of Haiti provided black Americans with a model to combat the charges of inferiority leveled at them by whites in the North and the South.

18. James Redpath, *Toussaint Louverture: Biography and Autobiography* (Boston, 1863; rpr. New York, 1971); Wendell Phillips, *The Hero of Hayti*, is reprinted in Charles D. Warner (ed.), *A Library of the World's Greatest Literature* (New York, 1897), XXIX, 11413ff.; also see *Anti-Slavery Record*, November, 1837, pp. 138–41, 174–75; Wendell Phillips, *Speeches, Lectures and Letters* (New York, 1968), 491, 493–94.

Haiti was the only specific example of black national freedom available to them, and they gained self-esteem and pride from Toussaint's accomplishments and even from the existence of the black republic. One black lecturer said, "There appeared as a spirit of peace, the patriot, the father, the benefactor of mankind, Toussaint Louverture."[19] With Toussaint, the blacks had a positive image that was both known and renowned by whites as well. Toussaint was not only the topic of lecturers, his name appeared in clubs in the black community and in military groups during the Civil War. It would be difficult to overestimate Toussaint's impact on a generation of free blacks growing up in the United States during the antebellum period. Young John Browne Russwurm, one of Bowdoin College's first black graduates (and one of the first black college graduates in the United States) and later a prominent editor in the black community, pointed out that the Haitians "have acquired a new existence—their powers have been developed: a career of glory and happiness unfolds itself before them." The editor of *Freedom's Journal* reiterated what most blacks thought of Toussaint and the Haitian Revolution when he declared emphatically that "the establishment of the Republic of Haiti after years of sanguinary warfare, its subsequent progress in all the arts of civilization . . . prove that blacks are capable."[20]

Using Haiti as their hope, more militant blacks saw the ominous meanings that the black insurrection and Toussaint's rise had for their struggle against slavery and discrimination in the United States. To David Walker, the fiery pamphleteer whose *Appeal to the Colored Citizens of the World* (1829) aroused sectional feelings over the slavery issue because of his outspoken advocacy of violence, Haiti proved that "a groveling servile and abject submission to the lash of tyrants . . . are [sic] not natural elements of

19. Earl E. Thorpe suggests that Toussaint, Denmark Vesey, and Nat Turner were "significant others" for blacks in the antebellum period (see his *The Old South: A Psychohistory* [Durham, 1972], 166. Also see James McCune Smith, *A Lecture on the Haytian Revolution, with a Sketch of the Character of Toussaint Louverture* (New York, 1841), 9. Compare this black's appraisal with ones such as William Jay's "Inquiry into the Character and Tendency of the American Colonization and American Anti-Slavery Societies," in *Miscellaneous Writings of Slavery* (Boston, 1853), 177–85, and Child's *An Appeal*, 83.

20. Philip Foner (ed.), "John Browne Russwurm: A Document," *Journal of Negro History*, LIV (1969), 393–97; *Freedom's Journal*, March 16, 1827. For other examples, see *Liberator*, August 6, September 3, 1831; *Colored American*, June 9, 1838; *Anti-Slavery Reporter*, June–November, 1833.

the blacks."[21] Giving notice to whites that blacks were no longer content with being pushed around, a mysterious letter written from Boston to southerners in Southampton County, Virginia, after the Nat Turner revolt warned that blacks were taking lessons from Haiti and "know how to use the knife, bludgeon, and the torch with effect—may the genius of Toussaint stimulate them to unremitting exertion." The letter, perhaps the most blunt that southern whites ever received advocating the overthrow of the slave system, was full of allusions to black retribution and to Haiti's role in provoking violence against that system. Henry Highland Garnet continued the tradition among militant blacks of associating Toussaint with slave resistance in a controversial and contentious speech before a black convention in Buffalo, New York, in 1843. Garnet linked Toussaint with Denmark Vesey and Nat Turner, and in his "Address to the Slaves of the United States," he exhorted the slaves to "let your motto be resistance! resistance! resistance!" This link between slave resistance and the Haitian example was made by George Vashon, a graduate of Oberlin College and a lawyer and teacher in the black community in Ohio and New York, who spent a year in Haiti and upon his return wrote a poem commemorating Vincent Ogé, an early Haitian revolutionary:

> Thy name with that of L'Ouverture
> And the noble souls that stood
> With both of you, in times of blood
> Will to be the tyrant's fear—
> Will live, the sinking soul to cheer.

Rather than stay permanently in Haiti, Vashon and other black militants chose to fight their battle in the United States, drawing inspiration from their model, Toussaint, and their spiritual fatherland in the New World, Haiti. The Reverend J. Theodore Holly, a consistent advocate of Haitian emigration, recognized the role of the black republic: "Our brethren of Hayti, who stand in the vanguard of the race, have already made a name and a fame for us, that is as imperishable as the world's history. They exercise

21. Herbert Aptheker, *One Continual Cry: David Walker's Appeal to the Colored Citizens of the World (1829–1830)* (New York, 1965), 83. Walker followed the events in Haiti closely (see *Freedom's Journal*, December 19, 1828; and *An Address Delivered Before the General Colored Association of Boston* [Boston, 1830]).

sovereign authority over an island that in natural advantages is the Eden of America."[22]

Perhaps the best example of the meaning of Toussaint Louverture and the Haitian Revolution to black Americans was revealed in the work of William Wells Brown, the most prominent black novelist of the antebellum period. Born into slavery in Kentucky, Brown escaped and became one of the most active spokesmen for black rights during the mid-nineteenth century. Brown was steeped in the history of Haiti. In an essay, "St. Domingo: Its Revolution and Its Patriots," Brown warned whites that slavery would someday come to haunt them: "Who knows but that a Toussaint . . . may some day appear in the Southern States of this Union?" Brown linked the destiny of the southern slaveholding states with that of the West Indies in much the same manner that Jefferson had some fifty years earlier. He predicted ominously that "the day is not far distant when the revolution of St. Domingo will be reenacted in South Carolina and Louisiana."[23] Brown's familiarity with the history of Haiti and its leaders was evident in a much-needed volume that was aptly titled *The Black Man, His Antecedents, His Genius and His Achievements* (1863), a collection of biographical sketches of prominent blacks intended to bolster black morale and to influence white attitudes about black soldiers during the Civil War. The only non-American subjects were the seven Haitian leaders he praised, beginning with a tribute to Toussaint in which he stressed that blacks were capable of controlling their own destinies and were determined to do so.

Seldom has a symbol become so important to disparate groups in American society as Toussaint was in antebellum America.

22. Ira Berlin (ed.), "After Nat Turner: A Letter from the North," *Journal of Negro History*, LV (1970), 146; Henry Highland Garnet, "An Address to the Slaves of the United States," in Carter G. Woodson (ed.), *Negro Orators and Their Orations* (Washington, D.C., 1925), 157; Holly, *Vindication*, 39 (Vashon's poem), 44. Also see *Freedom's Journal*, June 1, 1827; and Charles Burleigh, "Slavery and the North," in *Anti-Slavery Tracts: Second Series*, no. 10 (New York, 1855), 16. For examples of Haiti's influence on an individual, see John Mercer Langston, *From the Virginia Plantation to the National Capital* (Hartford, Conn., 1894), 355; and Mott, *Biographical Sketches*, 61, 315–16. A modern example of how Toussaint captured the imagination of blacks can be seen in the work of black artist Jacob Lawrence, whose Toussaint L'Ouverture series, consisting of forty-one tempera paintings, was exhibited at the 1940 Chicago Negro Exposition and was praised by prominent blacks such as Alain Locke.

23. William Wells Brown, *St. Domingo: Its Revolution and Its Patriots* (Boston, 1855), 3, 32.

Southerners who had every reason to fear the ominous events in St. Domingue nevertheless found solace in Toussaint's ability to exercise tight control over the blacks. They were also pleased that he played a role in defeating the French and in discrediting radical French ideas. White abolitionists found in the life of Toussaint a justification for their conviction that blacks were capable of civilization as long as they acted judiciously. By rejecting retaliation against whites for slavery, and by adopting a moral, Christian life, they were reassured that their deepest fears about blacks were unfounded. To black Americans, long starved for real heroes, Toussaint was of primary importance to their struggle for freedom and equality: he showed them that freedom could be won and how it could be done. Toussaint Louverture was the most powerful black symbol of his time, and he affected the history of Napoleonic Europe, the young North American republic, the United States, and the Caribbean. The various meanings and interpretations of Toussaint's symbolic role supported each constituent's position, and thus he exerted a continuing influence on American thought throughout the antebellum period. Further, he personified the whole range of Haiti's impact on America since his time.

Toussaint Louverture, the Black Napoleon

Courtesy the Library of Congress

Bishop Theodore Holly, the first black bishop in the New World
Courtesy the Archives of the Episcopal Church, Austin

Louis Moreau Gottschalk, American pianist and composer, who made great use of Caribbean themes

Courtesy the Library of Congress

James Redpath, abolitionist and agent for Haitian emigration
Courtesy the Library of Congress

Frances Wright, reformer and advocate of black liberty
Courtesy the National Portrait Gallery, Smithsonian Institution, Washington, D.C.

FOUR

THE SOUTHERN RESPONSE TO THE
HAITIAN REVOLUTION

Southerners were keen observers of what was happening in the Caribbean. They were anxious to defend their economic, political, and social system by applying what they saw as the lessons of the French West Indian experience to their own situation. Nor were they reticent about pointing out, for themselves and the rest of the nation, what they felt were threats to their security. Even though the slave insurrection in St. Domingue broke out only a short time after southerners participated in their own rebellion against a European power, they were not prepared to support a violent black struggle for freedom in an area so close to them. The notions of *liberté* and *égalité*, the catchwords for the French Revolution in Europe and in St. Domingue, were anathema to southern planters who lived in fear of a black revolt at home. Whatever revolutionary sentiment there had been in the South during the American Revolution soon lapsed into silence over the ominous events in St. Domingue. Southerners admitted refugees from St. Domingue as a humanitarian act; they cautiously excluded revolutionary ideology as an act of self-preservation.

Heeding the warnings of John Randolph, the Virginia congressman and states' rights advocate, against the "introduction of slaves into this country, or of the maroons, brigands, or cutthroats from St. Domingo," every southern state legislature passed laws designed to curtail the activities of the black population, free and slave, and to prevent the arrival of French West Indian blacks.[1] Since New Orleans was part of Spanish Louisiana during the 1790s, Virginia and South Carolina were the major American ports of entry for refugees fleeing St. Domingue. The French consul estimated that six hundred St. Domingans were living in Charleston by 1796. South Carolina charitably welcomed the unfortunate refugees at first; however, it soon became clear that there were grave risks in admitting blacks—free or slaves—from the island. South Carolinians showed some enthusiasm for the

---

1. *Annals of Congress*, 6th Cong., 3rd Sess., 991, 7th Cong., 2nd Sess., 385.

French Revolution, but after the French abolished slavery in 1793 and the Jacobins in France became increasingly antislavery, South Carolinians and other southerners became alarmed at the implications of what was happening in France and in its colonies. Not only did they fear blacks who had either witnessed or participated in the destruction of the white planter class in the Caribbean, they were quick to see the parallel between their situation and that of the besieged planters in St. Domingue.

Consequently, South Carolina was the first state to take legislative action to abolish the slave trade when, in 1792, it prohibited the importation of all slaves. This ban was in part a reaction to an antislavery document published in London that same year by the Quaker abolitionist Thomas Clarkson, who, in *An Inquiry into the Causes of the Insurrection of Negroes on the Isle of Santo Domingo,* concluded that the major reasons for the insurrection were the large-scale importation of blacks from Africa and the white minority's inability to maintain control over the more numerous blacks. While Clarkson's interest was in curtailing the slave trade, Carolinians were concerned about their safety. Legislators took an additional step toward this end by prohibiting free Negroes from Hispaniola from entering the state, and an article of an 1803 statute specifically barred any Negro or man of color, free or bond, "who heretofore hath been, or now is, or hereafter shall be resident in any of the French West India islands." Two years later, South Carolinians were worried enough about the problem of whites helping blacks to revolt that they passed a law making it punishable by death for "any person in any way to aid in an insurrection." Two witnesses were needed for a conviction. This law was aimed at white Frenchmen, suspected Jacobins, who might be in the state.[2]

The state of Georgia then prohibited the importation of blacks from the West Indies, though the African slave trade remained open for five more years. In a long statute passed in December, 1792, Virginia required that those entering the state had to take

2. John Hurd, *The Law of Freedom and Bondage in the United States* (3 vols.; Boston, 1862), III, 95; *South Carolina Statutes at Large* (10 vols.; Columbia, 1836–41), V, 503; *Acts of the General Assembly of the State of South Carolina* (2 vols.; Columbia, 1808), II, 511; Patrick Brady, "The Slave Trade and Sectionalism in South Carolina, 1787–1808," *Journal of Southern History,* XXXVIII (1972), 609. Brady states that St. Domingue was one of the factors that unified an otherwise split legislature into action.

an oath that they had not imported any slaves from the West Indies or Africa. Virginia legislators tightened their control with a
1793 statute that prescribed the death penalty for any free black
convicted of "exciting slaves to insurrection or murder." In 1795,
North Carolina also prohibited importing slaves from the West
Indies and attempted to promote domestic tranquillity by requiring that a slave could be liberated only if he posted a $200 good-
conduct bond. Maryland, which in 1792 had allowed French subjects to bring their personal slaves into the state, repealed this
dispensation in 1797, thus joining those states that banned West
Indian slaves.³ Louisiana abolished the slave trade but specifically exempted slaves accompanying their masters into the state.
A court case in Louisiana in 1809 illustrates to what lengths
slaveholding communities would go to ensure that the example of
St. Domingue was not repeated in the South. A refugee, Pierre
Dormenon, faced disbarment because he was accused of being
a Jacobin who "assisted the negroes in St. Domingo, in their
horrible massacres, and other outrages against the whites." A
lower court concluded that "no person who has acted in concert
with the negroes and mulattoes of St. Domingo, in destroying the
whites, ought to hold any kind of office here."⁴ Dormenon won
his appeal several years later after he was elected to the Louisiana
State Legislature.

Many Americans, including many responsible southerners,
were convinced that the cause of the St. Domingan slave rebellion
was uncontrolled growth of the slave population. It was natural
that those who advocated closing the slave trade in the United
States would use St. Domingue as a primary example of the necessity of stopping the importation of Africans. While the state laws

3. Hurd, *Law of Freedom and Bondage*, 5–6, 101; Oliver Prince (ed.), *Digest of
the Laws of the State of Georgia* (Milledgeville, Ga., 1822), 442, 455–456; James
Tredell (ed.), *Laws of the State of North Carolina* (Edenton, N.C., 1794), 1; *Laws of
North Carolina* (Raleigh, 1821), 786–87; Samuel Shepard (ed.), *The Laws of Virginia, 1792–1806* (Richmond, 1835), 122–30; *Virginia Argus* (Norfolk), January
27, 1801, reported that a new law that further curtailed free blacks by requiring
that county officials keep accurate, up-to-date records of their whereabouts. For
Maryland, see William Kilty (ed.), *The Laws of Maryland* (2 vols.; Annapolis,
1800), Vol. II, Chap. 75.
4. *Digest of the Laws of Louisiana* (3 vols.; New Orleans, 1828), II, 383–84.
Louisiana passed a law in 1831 similar to the 1803 South Carolina statute that
prohibited any free person of color from traveling between the West Indies and that
state.

prohibiting the slave trade were a direct response to the situation in St. Domingue as Americans saw it, that situation was important in preparing the South to accept the Federal suppression of the slave trade.[5]

These state legislative efforts to keep out dangerous slaves notwithstanding, the demand on the Atlantic seaboard enabled some slaves to get into the country. For instance, a South Carolinian noted that some planters bought Negroes off vessels that came to shore under the pretext of being in distress. These planters, he reported, smuggled the slaves directly to their plantations, bypassing the authorities in Charleston. Still, local communities did what they could to screen incoming slaves. Two shiploads of refugees arriving at Charleston in October, 1793, occasioned a resolution stating that "any vessel . . . from St. Domingo with passengers, negroes or people of color shall remain under the guns of Ft. Johnson till such passengers as the committee may deem improper to admit, and the Negroes and people of color be sent out of the state." Furthermore, Governor William Moultrie ordered "all free negroes and people of color who arrived within twelve months from any other place to depart from this place within ten days." South Carolinians became cautious because they feared, as one official noted, "the lower order of Frenchmen . . . who would fraternize with our Democratic Clubs and introduce the same horrid tragedies among our negroes, which has [sic] been so fatally exhibited in the French islands." St. Domingans and their entourages were now associated with radical ideas that threatened the security of the slaveholding areas of the South. As one Carolinian wrote to a friend: "The account of the intended designs of the French negroes have given us a great deal of concern—we dread the future, and are fearful that our feelings for the unfortunate inhabitants of the wretched island of St. Domingo may be our own destruction."[6]

5. *Annals*, 9th Cong., 2nd Sess.; W. E. B. Du Bois, *The Suppression of the African Slave Trade, 1638–1870* (1896; Baton Rouge, 1965), Chap. 7. Also see *Virginia Argus* (Norfolk), October 3, 1800.
    6. John Bowan to Charles Harris, August 12, 1800, in Keith Read Papers, Ilah Dunlap Little Memorial Library, University of Georgia, Athens; Charleston *City Gazette and Daily Advertiser*, October 9, 1793; Ralph Izard to Mrs. Gabriel Manigault, November 20, 1794, Mary Pinckney to Mrs. Manigault, February 5, 1798, both in Ralph Izard Family Papers, South Caroliniana Library, University of South Carolina, Columbia.

One of the most explicit illustrations of the early influences of the St. Domingan slave insurrection upon the southern psyche was a series of letters published in the Columbia (S.C.) *Herald* during the summer of 1794 under the name "Rusticus." The author was thought to be Alexander Garden, Jr., son of the famous naturalist for whom the gardenia was named. Garden, a revolutionary war soldier and a planter, wrote *Anecdotes of the Revolutionary War in America* (1822). Rusticus was concerned about the news from St. Domingue, particularly southern newspapers' open discussions of those events. Garden called for vigilance against the introduction of dangerous elements into southern society, and he strongly supported the proposition then being discussed in Charleston to "expel from the state all negroes without exception that have within the last three years arrived here from the French West India Islands." He criticized the "excess of humanity" that Carolinians displayed in admitting the St. Domingans and warned that the situation was now more precarious as a result. Black expulsion, he argued, was necessary because "self-preservation [w]as the first law of nature." He also expressed fears that an abolitionist society existed in South Carolina that corresponded to Les Amis des Noirs. Garden was adamant about keeping "French ideas" out of southern society because they would prove "fatal."[7]

South Carolinians heeded his words. In 1803 a St. Domingan refugee, John James Negrin, was arrested and imprisoned for having published in Charleston a pamphlet entitled *A Declaration of Independence of the French Colony of St. Domingo by Dessalines.* The publication, officials said, was intended to "excite domestic insurrection and disturb the peace of the community." Negrin denied any ill intentions, reminding authorities that this material had been previously published with success in Charleston as *The Life of Toussaint."*[8] However, by 1804, attitudes toward St. Domingue had changed. Carolinians were listening to their leaders and trying to keep inflammatory tracts and dangerous persons out of the country. It was St. Domingue, not the attacks of northern abolitionists, that caused the South to turn against freedom of thought.

7. "Rusticus" extracts from Columbia *Herald,* July 14, 1794, in South Caroliniana Library, University of South Carolina.
8. Negrin, memorial of August, 1804, Senate Petitions (MS in South Carolina Archives, Charleston).

Other states were faced with similar controversies. In a congressional debate over taxation of imported slaves, Willis Alston of North Carolina reminded the House that blacks from the West Indies were one hundred times more dangerous than slaves imported directly from Africa. The French reportedly were depositing refractory blacks along the South Atlantic seaboard in spite of efforts to stop the practice. In August, 1802, Colonel William Davies of Norfolk, Virginia, wrote to Governor James Monroe that "a French frigate from Cape François full of negroes [was] off Cape Hatteras . . . and that . . . it was the determination of the French government to transport from St. Domingo such of the blacks as had borne arms against the French." Later, a Virginia newspaper protested that "the infernal French are disgorging the whole of their wretched blacks upon our shores." In the subsequent hysteria, all Alexandria townsmen were apparently as anxious to fight the French as the Negroes. According to one eyewitness, the citizens were prepared to kill all the Negroes who landed, a group estimated at one thousand. Congress received a memorial from the citizens of Wilmington, North Carolina, on the same topic. Several months later the Charleston *Courier* warned that "transports laden with refractory negroes from St. Domingue are to come to America and land their contents on the banks of the River St. Marys." The French did in fact attempt to banish troublemakers from all their West Indian possessions, and some blacks from Guadeloupe did receive permission to land in New England. However, most forcible deportations of blacks from St. Domingue failed.[9]

As we have seen, Governor William C. C. Claiborne expressed concern about some French elements in the population, especially those from St. Domingue, who were intent, he thought, on fomenting divisions between the French Creoles and the Americans. He told Mayor Boré of New Orleans that he thought the municipality's measures to control immigration of "Negroes and free Mulattoes from the Antilles" were expedient. Furthermore, one of Claiborne's first actions as governor was to commission an

9. *Annals*, 9th Cong., 1st Sess., 360; Elizabeth Donnan, *Documents Illustrative of the History of the Slave Trade to America* (4 vols.; Washington, D.C., 1930–35), IV, 171; Alexandria (Va.) *Advertiser and Commercial Intelligencer*, October 23, 1802, February 2, 1803. Also see D. Peeples to Lewis Ayer, December, 1802, in Lewis M. Ayer Papers, South Caroliniana Library, University of South Carolina; and *Annals*, 7th Cong., 2nd Sess., 385, 459–61, 525, 533–34, 1564; Shelby McCloy, *The Negro in France* (Lexington, Ky., 1961), 113–14.

agent, Dr. John Watkins, to report on the military, political, and economic conditions of the territory, including the parishes on the Mississippi River above New Orleans. In his report, Watkins mentioned an incident that illustrated why American authorities were justified in being fearful of blacks from St. Domingue: "Some few weeks ago . . . there passed up the fork from sea a vessel having on board twelve negroes said to have been Brigands from the Island of St. Domingo. These negroes in their passage up were frequently on shore, and in the French language made use of many insulting and menacing expressions to the inhabitants. Among other things they spoke of eating *human* flesh, and in general demonstrated great *Savageness* of character, boasting of what they had seen and done in the horrors of St. Domingo."[10] Throughout this period, Governor Claiborne expressed his suspicions of St. Domingans. In the summer of 1804 a dispute over white–free black relations broke out in New Orleans. Claiborne acted discreetly but quickly to resolve their differences because, as he said, "I remember that the events which have spread blood and desolation in St. Domingo originated in a dispute between the white and mulatto inhabitants, and that too rigid threatment of the former, induced the latter to seek the support and assistance of the Negroes." Claiborne adopted a policy of admitting only African slaves into Louisiana, excluding "those slaves who from late habits are accustomed to blood and devastation, and whose councel [*sic*] a communication with our present Black population may be pregnant with much future Mischief." Nevertheless, fear of "another St. Domingo" continued to haunt Louisiana. Private citizens echoed the governor's concern for their safety and the security of their property. In a letter from Kentucky, the brother of a New Orleans resident marked that he "should tremble for your situation in the event of a war with Spain. But nothing would be so horrid as the idea of the insurrection of your slaves." He, however, felt relatively safe, since his plantation was not as exposed to such a threat as were those in Louisiana. The events in St. Domingue were well known "up the river," as this letter and other docu-

10. W. C. C. Claiborne to James Madison, January 24, April 8, 9, 1804, Claiborne to Mayor of New Orleans, July 25, 1804, all in Dunbar Rowland (ed.), *Official Letter Books of W. C. C. Claiborne* (6 vols.; Jackson, Miss., 1917), I, 344–46, II, 84–85, 88, 366–67; James Robertson, *Louisiana Under the Rule of Spain, France and the United States, 1785–1807* (2 vols.; Cleveland, Ohio, 1911), II, 5–6, 313–14. The Charleston *Courier*, May 17, 1803, January 18, March 13, 1804, has additional examples of "French scares."

ments suggest. Governor Claiborne received a petition from the inhabitants of Pointe Coupée Parish, the scene of an earlier slave revolt said to have been inspired by the example of St. Domingue, warning him of the precarious situation there: "The news of the Revolution of St. Domingo and other Places has become common among our Blacks—and some here who relate the Tragical History of the Revolution of that Island with the General Disposition of the most of our Slaves has become very Serious—A spirit of Revolt and Mutyny has Crept in amongst them—a few Days since we happyly Discovered a Plan for our Destruction."[11] Claiborne's administration took such messages seriously. The governor's vigilance was rewarded: there were no serious outbreaks, though several "plots" were uncovered and several Frenchmen were deported. When the large group of St. Domingan refugees arrived from Cuba in 1809, Claiborne insisted that only blacks accompanied by whites or free blacks who chose to flee the insurrection be allowed to land.

The southern response to the St. Domingan refugees changed from humanitarian acceptance to increased vigilance and constraints. Southerners relied upon exclusion, of émigrés and slaves and of attitudes they deemed hostile to slavery, as a way to protect their social system. Their actions were a portent of their response to domestic militant abolition in the 1830s: it was in the 1790s and the early 1800s that the South began to erect its intellectual blockade against potentially dangerous doctrines. As one concerned South Carolinian said in an address to an agricultural society in Charleston in 1825, with the Denmark Vesey plot no doubt still fresh in everyone's mind, "God will raise up a Toussaint or a Spartacus against us. . . . Our history has verified the melancholy truth, that one educated slave or colored freeman, with an insinuating address, is capable of infusing the poison of insubordination into a whole body of the black population."[12]

11. Rowland (ed.), *Letter Books of Claiborne*, II, 244–45, 254–57; New Orleans Municipal Records, March 7, 1804, in Howard-Tilton Memorial Library, Tulane University, New Orleans; [?] to Brown, December 13, 1805, in James Brown Papers, Library of Congress; Petition, November 9, 1804, in Clarence E. Carter (ed.), *The Territorial Papers of the United States* (26 vols.; New York, 1934–62), IX, 326–27; *Annals*, 11th Cong., 1st Sess., 44.
12. Whitemarsh B. Seabrook, *A Concise View of the Critical Situation and the Future Prospects of the Slave-holding States in Their Relation to Their Colored Population* (Charleston, 1825), 13.

After St. Domingue, the South often felt that it was perpetually under siege and it was increasingly aware of the instability that a slave society provided. One of the many lessons garnered from the events in "hapless" St. Domingue was that supporters of slavery must develop a consensus on the ideological assumptions concerning white and black relations.

There is, however, ample evidence to suggest that the deeds of Toussaint, Dessalines, and Christophe did not go unnoticed by American slaves in the South. Newspaper accounts as well as émigré tales circulated in the South from 1791 until 1809. The slaves' success in establishing an independent republic gave American slaves heart and left some with the desire to emulate their brethren in the Caribbean. Whites had always been aware of slaves as "troublesome property," but only after St. Domingue did they react to the threat as a real one and not just a potential one. As early as 1793, the French minister to the United States, Edmond Genêt, reported to his superiors that American slave owners were "terrified" by the Negro revolt in St. Domingue. Southerners were more concerned, not about the individual acts of black defiance that had always plagued them, but about the possibility of actions that could develop into large-scale insurrection. While there is no way to tell how many individual slaves responded to the events in St. Domingue, we do know that knowledge of those events was widespread among American slaves in Virginia, South Carolina, and Louisiana. Any number of slave plots, real and imagined, were blamed on what happened in St. Domingue. Whether the whites accurately assessed how the Haitians' deeds affected their slaves, St. Domingue gave vivid imagistic life to the South's sense of insecurity.[13]

The first major incident that linked slave unrest in the United States and in St. Domingue was in Virginia in 1793. John Ran-

13. *Annals,* 9th Cong., 2nd Sess., 628–30; F. J. Turner (ed.), "Correspondence of the French Ministers to the United States, 1791–1797," *Annual Report of the American Historical Association* (1907), 245–64. Runaway slave advertisements, such as one published in the *Virginia Gazette and General Advertiser* (Williamsburg), March 14, 1792, often indicated that the subscriber feared that the runaway would "attempt to get to the West Indies." Also see Thomas Dew, "A Review of the Debate in the Virginia Legislature, 1831–32," in *The Slavery Argument as Maintained by the Most Distinguished Writers of the Southern States* (Charleston, 1831), 430–32, 440–42, 483.

dolph discovered two Negroes close to his house, and he overheard their conversation about a plot to kill the whites there just as "the blacks has [sic] killed the whites in the French Islands and took it a little while ago." Another Virginian reported to the governor that the blacks were more insolent than before because of the arrival of "French from C.F. [Cap François]." Because many St. Domingans lived in Norfolk and Portsmouth, Virginia, those cities shared Charleston's apprehensions in the early 1790s. A citizen of York, Virginia, found a letter purportedly by a black itinerant preacher from Norfolk. It was to a fellow conspirator and spoke of an uprising that seemed well planned and well organized. Six thousand slaves from South Carolina were supposedly standing ready to rise up to destroy the white slave owners; the arms and ammunition had been supplied by a source in Charleston. The letter was immediately copied and circulated among officials in Richmond, York, Norfolk, Savannah, and Charleston, with a dire warning to local militias to be on guard. One worried officer in Norfolk pointed out to the governor that about two hundred Negroes had been brought to that port by their masters fleeing Cap François, and he had no doubt that these slaves would be ready to act against the whites in support of the local conspirators. Perhaps because of the advance warnings and increased military activity, this plot, like many others, never actually got started. Yet the rumors of the revolt traveled widely: in New York it was reported that letters from Charleston indicated that the blacks were becoming "very insolent" because "the St. Domingue Negroes have sown these seeds of revolt." At about the same time, South Carolina Senator Pierce Butler, writing to a friend in Savannah about the insurrection reportedly brewing in North Carolina, warned that "our Eastern and French friends will do no good to our Blacks."[14]

These scares easily spread throughout the South at this time, in part because private letters, public speeches, stories, and travelers kept alive the reports on St. Domingue. A disturbance in

14. *Calendar of the State Papers of Virginia* (Richmond, 1886), VI, 453, 471–72, July 21, 1793 (Randolph's report), and VI, 490, 532–33, 570, 650–51; Ira Berlin, *The Free Negro in the Antebellum South* (New York, 1974), 86–87; [?] to Gov. Moultrie, November 30, 1793, in folder 1, Governors' Messages, South Carolina Department of Archives, Columbia; New York *Journal and Patriotic Register*, October 16, 1793; Pierce Butler to [?], October 28, 1793, in Pierce Butler Letterbook, South Caroliniana Library, University of South Carolina, Columbia.

Charleston led to four blacks being tried for conspiracy to burn the town, a plan said to have "originated among the French negroes." Planters in the lower counties of North Carolina feared the effects of General Leclerc's having promulgated Napoleon's emancipation decree in an attempt to placate the insurrectionists in St. Domingue. Also, the residents of Pointe Coupée again petitioned Governor Claiborne to send reinforcements to lessen the threat of revolt in their area.[15]

Several years later, a serious incident involved some five hundred slaves gathering in St. John the Baptist Parish for a march on New Orleans. Only decisive action by federal troops and local militia thwarted the slaves' plan to usurp lower Louisiana. Sixty-six insurrectionists were killed, and others were later executed. The brutality of the executions—decapitation and display of the severed heads—indicates the intensity of the slave owners' intention to prevent such occurrences. Throughout the South they blamed attempts to orchestrate large-scale insurrections on the example of St. Domingue. The fear reached such proportions that almost any extraordinary occurrence concerning blacks ensured a swift white reaction, and often a brutal one. Minor incidents such as one recorded in Charleston in November, 1795, were replicated across the South during this time of stress. A white citizen, alarmed about several Negroes who gathered at the home of a free person of color, quickly reported it to the authorities, who called out the local guard. The city was in a stir when the guard broke into the house, only to find that the blacks were enjoying a night of socializing and dancing. Still, a full investigation ensued, though nothing came of the matter.[16]

Circumstantial evidence only suggests that the first major insurrectionist attempt in the early nineteenth century, Gabriel

15. Petition, in Carter (ed.), *Territorial Papers*, IX, 326–27. Also see *Virginia Gazette and General Advertiser* (Williamsburg), June 2, 1802; H. L. Pinckney letters, November 24, 1797, in South Caroliniana Library, University of South Carolina.

16. Charleston *City Gazette and Daily Advertiser*, November 22, 1797; David Homes to Capt. Thomas Butler, January 18–19, 1811, in Thomas Butler Family Papers, Troy H. Middleton Library, Louisiana State University, Baton Rouge; Harriet to her father, February 16, 1811, in Peters Family Papers, New York Public Library; Lubin Laurent, "A History of St. John the Baptist Parish" (Typescript in Middleton Library, LSU), 68–72; Alcée Fortier, *A History of Louisiana* (4 vols.; New York, 1904), III, 78–79; Governors' Messages to Senate, 1795, in South Carolina Department of Archives.

Prosser's, was inspired by the events of St. Domingue. At the time, Virginia was inundated with St. Domingans and newspapers were full of the happenings in the ongoing saga. During the subsequent trials of Gabriel's would-be insurrectionists, testimony indicated that Frenchmen were to be spared during the carnage. Southern newspapers drew an analogy between Prosser and Toussaint, and one warned that "the insurrection . . . appears to be organized on the true 'French plan.'"[17] Certainly antislavery advocates in the North saw the connection. Taking advantage of this well-publicized plot, the *New England Palladium* contained the following dire warning to southerners:

> Remember ere too late
> The tale of St. Domingo's fate.
> Tho' Gabriel dies, a host remain
> Oppress'd with slavery's galling chain
> And soon or late the hour will come
> Mark'd with Virginia's dreadful doom.

This poem catches exactly what southerners most feared. They often accepted reports of plots no matter how unlikely the prospects: eight thousand slaves were thought to have been potentially involved in Gabriel's conspiracy. In many cases, the French were seen as provocateurs. The sense of insecurity in southeastern Virginia in 1800 soon spilled over into North Carolina. Former governor William R. Davie wrote to his successor, outlining a slave plot brought to his attention by a reliable friend. Davie's information linked the Prosser revolt with some North Carolina slaves and raised the specter of St. Domingue.[18] But nothing came of this particular scare. In Bertie Country, North Carolina, in 1802, however, eleven blacks were executed as the result of an alleged plot. In South Carolina, a northern visitor to Columbia reported "considerable alarm" over a plot to burn the town, and

17. *Calendar of the State Papers of Virginia,* IX, 150–52, 159, 260; Thomas Higginson, *Travellers and Outlaws* (Boston, 1889), 185–214 (which appeared as articles in *Atlantic Monthly* in the antebellum period); *Liberator,* September 17, 1831. The modern black novelist Arna Bontemps, in *Black Thunder* (Boston, 1936), thought that Prosser was inspired by the events in St. Domingue.

18. *New England Palladium* (Boston), January 6, 1801; *Virginia Argus* (Norfolk), October 3, 1800, reprinted from the Philadelphia *Aurora.* Also see Joshua Coffin, *An Account of Some of the Principal Slave Insurrections and Others . . .* (New York, 1860), 25–26, reprinted in *Anti-Slavery Tracts;* George Kirkland to General William MacPherson, September 28, 1800, in W. H. Horner Collection, Pennsylvania Historical Society, Philadelphia; Hooker to parents, January 6, 1806, in Edward Hooker Papers, William R. Perkins Library, Duke University, Durham.

two of the confessed leaders were executed. The observer noted parenthetically that the "consequences of introducing so many [slaves] into the state . . . must sooner or later be serious."[19]

The role of St. Domingue in Denmark Vesey's plans for a black takeover of Charleston in 1822 was more discernible than it was in the Gabriel debacle. Vesey had been in the West Indies in his youth as a servant to his master, Captain Joseph Vesey, a slave trader. Denmark Vesey bought his freedom in 1800, and twenty years later began laying plans to lead a rebellion that was to rally blacks in the Charleston area. The authorities uncovered his extensive, well-coordinated network of recruits prior to the date set for the beginning of the revolt. In the aftermath, authorities found that Vesey apparently wrote to President Boyer of Haiti, seeking aid for his plans. A captured conspirator confessed that Monday Gill, one of the leaders, wrote to Haiti and delivered the letter to a steward on a brig headed for the island. It appears likely from the testimony that Vesey was both inspired by and reliant upon some encouragement and support from the black republic. Another participant testified that Vesey told the conspirators that they would not be safe unless they agreed "not to spare one white skin alive, for this was the plan they pursued in St. Domingo."[20] While not the only impetus to Vesey's desire to overthrow the slavocracy in South Carolina, St. Domingue played a role in his thinking. Whites laid the blame there as well: Henry Desaussure, a prominent Charleston lawyer, wrote to his friend Carolina Congressman Joel Poinsett just after the Vesey plot was suppressed: "We have been much shocked and grieved here, to learn that the suspicions of insurrectionary movements among the blacks were but too true: and that there has been a necessity to resort to measures of severity. I fear this kind of property is fast losing its value . . .

19. John S. Strickland, "The Great Revival and Insurrectionary Fears: North Carolina, 1801–1802" (Paper delivered at the meeting of the Organization of American Historians, Atlanta, April 7, 1977).

20. James Hamilton, *Negro Plot: An Account of the Late Intended Insurrection Among a Portion of the Blacks of the City of Charleston* . . . (Boston, 1822), 42. Also see Achates [Thomas Pinckney], *Reflections Occasioned by the Late Disturbances in Charleston* (Charleston, 1822), 6–9; [?] to Hammet, 1822, in William and Benjamin Hammet papers, Perkins Library, Duke; William Freehling, *Prelude to Civil War: The Nullification Controversy in South Carolina, 1816–1836* (New York, 1965), 58–60, 112, 114; John Lofton, *Insurrection in South Carolina: The Turbulent World of Denmark Vesey* (Kent, Ohio, 1964); Marina Wikramanayake, *World in Shadow: The Free Black in Antebellum South Carolina* (Columbia, S.C., 1973), 140–53; and Robert Starobin (ed.), *Denmark Vesey: The Slave Conspiracy of 1822* (Englewood Cliffs, N.J., 1970).

for the vicinity to the W.[est] I.[ndia] Islands, and the great inter-course with them, must introduce among our people many of those who have engaged in Scenes of blood in the West Indies, who will beguile our Slaves into rebellion with false hopes and idle expectations." In the aftermath, citizens of Charleston asked themselves how and why such a thing could have happened. In *Reflections, Occasioned by the Late Disturbances in Charleston, by Achates*, General Thomas Pinckney unequivocally connected the Vesey plot to "the example of St. Domingo, and [probably] the encouragement received from thence." Pinckney, a prominent Federalist statesman and soldier, also blamed northern abolition-ists whose "indiscreet zeal in favor of universal liberty" endan-gered the South—if they succeeded, "it would be a war of exter-mination to their fellow-citizens, their wives, and children; as was the case in St. Domingo." Pinckney's solution was to strengthen slavery by reducing the slave population in the cities and by hav-ing more control over the hiring out and teaching of slaves.[21] This personal reaction, to tighten the bonds of slavery, was typical of an educated, thoughtful individual such as Pinckney and of the en-tire South, slave owner or not, as well. At this early period in its history, the South presumably had not yet developed a sense of sectionalism, but the region was remarkably in agreement about both the lessons of and the response to the events of St. Domingue.

Shortly after the Vesey plot was aborted, white Carolinians took measures to ensure that free blacks were given even less freedom of movement and more supervision than before, and that black sailors, frequent visitors to Charleston, were not allowed to mix with local blacks on the streets of the port city. In December, 1822, the South Carolina legislature enacted the infamous Free Colored Seamen's Act, requiring that all free Negroes employed on incoming vessels be detained in jail while their ship was in port. Thus the black population would not be contaminated by what-ever radical views they had been exposed to or held.[22]

There is no direct evidence connecting Nat Turner's short-lived but bloody revolt in 1831 with the Haitians. Several St. Domingan families did settle in Southanpton County in the isolated area of

21. Henry Desaussure to Joel Poinsett, July 6, 1822, in Joel Poinsett Family Papers, Pennsylvania Historical Society; Achates [Pinckney], *Reflections*, 6–8, 22.
22. *Acts and Resolutions of the General Assembly of the State of South Caro-lina* (Charleston, 1822), 9–11; *South Carolina Statutes at Large* (10 vols.; Colum-bia, 1836–41), VII, 461–66.

southeastern Virginia where the revolt took place. Predictably, though, contemporaries did recall the carnage in St. Domingue when they discussed Turner's Rebellion. One slavery apologist attempted to downplay the notion that an insurrection such as had occurred in St. Domingue was possible in Virginia. To comfort his readers, he stated that even there the slaves had to have outside aid, that they could not have done it all alone, as Nat Turner attempted to do. No, he said, "it was the march of intellect among the free blacks that influenced the slaves there [St. Domingue] to revolt." Thus he was able to calm the public and at the same time suggest that free blacks should be proscribed. A New Yorker who was not in Virginia at the time of the revolt offered a different interpretation of its causes. Samuel Warner thought that Turner was clearly trying to emulate the St. Domingan slaves by setting up his own government and bringing slaves in neighboring states to insurrection. In advancing this conspiracy thesis, Walker wrote an emotional narrative about the massacres at Cap François. He even tried to draw an analogy between the Dismal Swamp, near the scene of Turner's revolt in Virginia, and the redoubt in the mountains above Le Cap that Toussaint's troops used as a refuge. Warner concluded: "Such were the horrors that attended the insurrection of the Blacks in St. Domingo, and similar scenes of bloodshed and murder might our brethren at the South expect to witness, were the disaffected slaves of that section of the country but once to gain the ascendancy. In a 'General Nat,' they might then find a wretch not less disposed to shed innocent blood, than was the perfidious Dessalines."[23] Whether or not Nat Turner consciously imitated the example of St. Domingue, many whites were reminded of that example and some were convinced that his inspiration came from his black brethren in the Caribbean. It mattered not to them, for many whites saw smoke rising from the volcano.

One of the first prominent southerners to comprehend the impact of St. Domingue on the South was St. George Tucker, a law professor at the College of William and Mary and an eminent jurist.

23. *Constitutional Whig* (Richmond), September 26, 1831; Samuel Warner, *Authentic and Impartial Narrative of the Tragical Scene Which Was Witnessed in Southampton County . . .* (New York, 1831); William Drewry, *The Southampton Insurrection* (Washington, D.C., 1900), 118–23; H. I. Treagle, *The Southampton Slave Revolt of 1831: A Compilation of Source Material* (Amherst, Mass., 1971).

Convinced that a dense slave population would eventually result in a revolt, Tucker pointed out that the number of slaves in the United States would double in thirty years and would be over a million in sixty years. He advocated gradual emancipation and colonization for the freed slaves. The jurist was against the forced removal of freedmen, though he thought that they would voluntarily seek asylum elsewhere if they were prevented from bearing arms, for example, or holding office or exercising the franchise or marrying whites. Tucker called for the emancipation of all female slaves at birth so there would be considerable time between the beginning of the process to rid the country of the "troublesome property" and its accomplishment. Tucker quoted Thomas Jefferson to explain why the blacks must eventually be removed to make America a white man's country: "The recent scenes transacted in the French colonies in the West Indies are enough to make one shudder with the apprehension of realizing similar calamities in this country. Such probably would be the event of an attempt to smother those prejudices which have been cherished for a period of almost two centuries." Jefferson endorsed Tucker's plan to separate the two races, and he added that "if something is not done; and soon done, we shall be the murderers of our children." Jefferson feared what he called the "insurrectionary spirit of the slaves." Convinced that nature had connected the South and St. Domingue by "the strong link of mutual necessity," Jefferson thought that the tropics were for the black man and nothing could stop the rebelling slaves from claiming the region, since it was naturally suited to them. After the Republic of Haiti was created in 1804, Jefferson looked upon that nation as a land of opportunity that would attract America's unwanted blacks to fulfill their destinies. The sense of urgency felt by some slavery advocates was shared by most gradual emancipationists, who were motivated by the fear of black retaliation after years of deprivation and by humanitarian concern: "Let us turn our eyes to the West-Indies, and there learn the melancholy effects of this wretched policy [slavery]. We may there read them written with the blood of thousands. There you may see the sable . . . brave sons of Africa engaged in a noble conflict with their inveterate foes. There you may see thousands fired with a generous resentment of the great injuries, and bravely sacrificing their lives at the altar."[24] This

24. Judge Tucker to Dr. Belknap, n.d., in *Collections of the Massachusetts Historical Society*, III, 5th ser. (Boston, 1877), 405–406; Thomas Jefferson to St.

warning by the Reverend David Rice, a Presbyterian missionary of Danville, Kentucky, was more sympathetic to the cause of the blacks in St. Domingue than were most moderates, yet his preachings do reveal a real concern that St. Domingue would be repeated in the South if preventive steps were not taken.

Most southerners did not agree with this interpretation of the events in St. Domingue or with the remedy suggested by the likes of Tucker, Jefferson, and Rice. A prominent planter-politician, John Taylor of Caroline, was one states' rights advocate who assessed the meaning of St. Domingue in quite different terms. Taylor began writing as early as 1803 of the dangers to the South of a general or a gradual emancipation. Using St. Domingue as his primary example, Taylor argued in his agricultural work, *Arator* (1814), and in his other sociopolitical writings, that emancipation had caused the carnage there. In order to prevent mulattoes and freed slaves from inciting the slaves to rebellion, Taylor urged the removal of all freedmen from their midst. Further, the institution of slavery should be strengthened to ensure that discipline and obedience were paramount. Taylor argued that slavery was a "necessary evil," with emphasis on the *necessary,* since it stood between the white masters and the vengeful hordes. He encouraged southerners to deal directly with the situation: "The fact is that negro slavery is an evil which the United States must look in the face. To whine over it, is cowardly; to aggravate it, criminal; and to forbear to alleviate it because it cannot be wholly cured, is foolish." Taylor's argument, which became popular with successive generations of southerners, was that if something were not done, the South would reap "a harvest of consequences"—as had happened in St. Domingue. He thought that gradual emancipation, as suggested by Jefferson and Tucker, would end in a "war of extermination" between whites and blacks.[25] This theme—that slavery protected the South against a race war and must therefore be preserved—was one of the cornerstones of the proslavery argument. Before St. Domingue it was possible to discuss gradual emancipation as a long-range answer to the problem of slavery in Ameri-

---

George Tucker, August 28, 1797, in Paul L. Ford (ed.), *The Writings of Thomas Jefferson* (10 vols.; New York, 1892), VII, 107–109, VI, 349; Jefferson to William Burwell, January 28, 1805, in Bagby Family Papers, Virginia Historical Society, Richmond. Also see Ford (ed.), *Jefferson,* VI, 80. Rice quoted in Robert McColley, *Slavery and Jeffersonian Virginia* (Urbana, 1964), 197.

25. John Taylor of Caroline, *Arator: Being a Series of Agricultural Essays, Practical and Political* (1814; New York, 1977), 52–53.

can society; after St. Domingue it became increasingly difficult, for southerners had time to develop their sense of events in St. Domingue.

In the same manner, southerners viewed universal equality and liberty as inappropriate and even suicidal in a slave society. Slave owners found the excesses of the French Revolution appalling: St. Domingue was the primary symbol of those excesses, not the Reign of Terror in France. Slaves simply were not ready to enjoy the privilege of liberty, owners observed, and any attempt to force "French ideas" upon them would destroy southern civilization. One slavery advocate railed in a southern journal: "The atheistical philosophy of revolutionary France added fuel to the volcano of hellish passion which raged in its bosom, the horrors of the island [St. Domingue] became a narrative which frightened our childhood, and still curdles the blood to read." Southerners saw themselves as living "on the edge of a precipice," and if they did not guard against radical ideas and radical men, there might come "a crisis which may overwhelm this country as St. Domingo was destroyed—a single false slip may precipitate us—a spark may produce an explosion." Thomas R. Dew, famous for his influential volume of essays *The Pro-Slavery Argument* (1852), excoriated the French for "an intemperate and phrenetic zeal for liberty and equality" that caused the "madness" of St. Domingue—"the bloodiest and most shocking insurrection ever recorded in the annals of history."[26]

Southern politicians were quick to recall the disaster in St. Domingue whenever the issue of emancipation was brought up for discussion in the United States Congress. As early as January, 1795, a debate over a naturalization bill—and a motion to amend, according to which all aliens applying for citizenship should emancipate any slaves they owned—elicited reference to St. Domingue as the primary example of why emancipation was unacceptable to southerners. North Carolina Congressman Joseph McDowell asked the sponsor if he were aware of the consequences of his motion, "when the West Indies are transformed into an im-

26. *De Bow's Commercial Review,* XVI (January, 1854), 35; also see Benjamin Palmer, *A Discourse: The South, Her Peril and Her Duty* (New Orleans, 1860), 10; and Elizabeth Donnan (ed.) "Papers of James A. Bayard, 1796–1815," *Annual Report of the American Historical Association,* (1913), 90; Philip S. Foner, *History of Black Americans: From Africa to the Emergence of the Cotton Kingdom* (New York, 1975), 456; Thomas R. Dew, *An Essay on Slavery* (Richmond, 1849), 4.

mense scene of slaughter." McDowell spoke of the thousands massacred or dispossessed by the former slaves; the sponsor quietly withdrew his antislavery motion. A Quaker antislavery petition placed before the House in November, 1797, met a similar fate. John Rutledge of South Carolina warned against the nihilism that emancipation had wrought in the Caribbean. Several years later, black abolitionist Absalom Jones introduced a petition to Congress to abolish the slave trade as a first step in the eventual emancipation of all blacks in the United States. Rutledge, stating that he for one was thankful that blacks were in slavery, delivered a philippic on the dangers of "new-fangled French philosophy." He later went to great lengths to draw parallels between the early stages of the insurrection in St. Domingue and the attempt by free blacks to petition Congress for their freedom in the United States. These partisan sentiments transcended sectional feelings: a Connecticut Federalist, Samuel Dana, voiced his opposition to any French notions that would likely "produce some dreadful scenes of St. Domingo."[27]

Senate debates over the Breckinridge bill in 1804 occasioned further discussion of the sensitive issue of slave unrest. Senator Jesse Franklin, a North Carolina opponent of slavery, remarked that "negro insurrections have already been frequent—they are alarming. Look in the laws of Virginia and North Carolina made for the purpose of guarding against and suppressing these rebellions, and you will learn our dangers." His fears were echoed by Senator John Breckinridge of Kentucky, sponsor of the bill, who admitted that he heard that "our slaves in the South will produce another St. Domingo." Another senator stated that too many slaves in the Louisiana Territory could well give rise to insurrection—St. Domingue was evoked often in this debate over the danger of large numbers of slaves in the sparsely populated territory. One southern newspaper noted: "When war becomes the topic of discourse, this people [southerners] will turn their eyes to the calamities of St. Domingo."[28] However, there was no need for federal

27. *Annals*, 3rd Cong., 2nd Sess., 1041–44. For a discussion of the influence that the St. Domingue insurrection had on the image of black men as satanic, see Richard Erno, "Dominant Images of the Negro in the Ante-bellum South" (Ph.D. dissertation, University of Minnesota, 1961), 122–25. Also see *Annals*, 5th Cong., 2nd Sess., 667, 6th Cong., 1st Sess., 230, 234, 241–42, 13th Cong., 3rd Sess., 527, 1469; and Diary of Captain Leigh, 1795 (MS in Middleton Library, LSU).

28. "Senate Debate on Breckinridge Bill for the Government of Louisiana, 1804," *American Historical Review*, XXII (1917), 340–64 (March 19, 1803); Diary

officials to remind Louisianians of the danger of slave insurrection. *Digest of the Laws of Louisiana* warned slaveholders of their responsibilities in keeping the threat of a race war to a minimum. The law strove to "impress upon the minds of the inhabitants the necessity of attention to their slaves, and of keeping them in that state of content and subordination which would alienate them from the wish to acquire a freedom which has cost so much blood of those in St. Domingo."

Two decades later, the image of St. Domingue still held sway when these topics were discussed. During the congressional debates over the controversial admission of Missouri as a state in 1819–1820, senators were again reminded of the danger of a race war between masters and slaves. Massachusetts Federalist Harrison G. Otis predicted that extending slavery into the trans-Mississippi territory would give emissaries from St. Domingue (the island had been called Haiti for nearly twenty years) an opportunity to foment revolution there. James Barbour of Virginia countered that the westward expansion of slavery was essential precisely because of the "lessons of St. Domingue." Southern expansionists pointed out that the success of the black insurrection rested primarily on the ten-to-one ratio of blacks to whites in the former French colony. And westward expansion would redistribute the potentially dangerous concentration of slaves in the East. Southerners saw the West as an area that could absorb virtually all potential troublemakers, both red and black, in their region. In this same debate a Delaware Federalist, Louis McLane, reminded his colleagues that eventual emancipation could cause another St. Domingue. Furthermore, he said, "we cannot fail to admire the cautious wisdom of our ancestors in not hazarding the great object of the struggle, by suddenly letting loose the unfortunate, though degraded, slave population."[29] These sentiments were

---

of Leigh; Thomas R. R. Cobb, *An Historical Sketch of Slavery, from the Earliest Periods* (Philadelphia, 1858), 181–87; G. W. Featherstonhugh, *Excursions Through the Slave States . . .* (2 vols.; London, 1844), II, 190–91. During the War of 1812, southerners were particularly concerned about the reliability of blacks, since St. Domingue was still fresh on their minds (see *Annals*, 12th Cong., 2nd Sess., 701; and Col. Alexander Declouet to [?], September 19, 1814, in David Rees Papers, Howard-Tilton Memorial Library, Tulane).

29. Debates reprinted in *Annals*, 8th Cong., 2nd Sess., 1567, 16th Cong., 1st Sess., 225–26, 330–34, 1155. Also see the Richmond *Enquirer*, February 19, 1820, on the speech by North Carolina Senator Nathaniel Macon. For other versions of

echoed loudly by a concerned southerner when he wrote, in the wake of the Vesey plot, that "our negroes are truly the Jacobins of the country; that they are the anarchists and the domestic enemy; the common enemy of civilized society and the barbarians who would, IF THEY COULD, become the DESTROYERS OF OUR RACE." By this time, the conventional wisdom on the "lessons of St. Domingue" was to maintain slavery unequivocally, watch the freedmen carefully, and show a united front against attacks on the institution; otherwise, race war was inevitable. The prospect of a war between masters and slaves was argued again and again throughout the South, right up to the Civil War. A newspaper stated during the nullification crisis of 1828: "An attempt by the General Government to emancipate our slaves . . . would not only threaten to deprive us of a large part of our property; it would also produce immediate danger of the massacre of our families, and of a horrid servile war."[30] Although the South linked its destiny in part to the history of St. Domingue, it was not prepared to secede at this time. One reason for staying in the Union was that the Constitution guaranteed southerners the right to control their slaves, and the government assisted them in doing that. They were thus relatively safe from slave insurrection and did not worry about becoming a minority in any new postsecession nation.

In the winter of 1831–1832 a rare debate took place in the Virginia legislature concerning the possibility of abolishing slavery in the state. As a result of the fears caused by the Nat Turner revolt as well as the changing economic situation, Virginians en-

---

this expansionist view, see *Annals*, 5th Cong., 1st Sess., 305ff., 2nd Sess., 1310, 10th Cong., 1st Sess., 25–26, 1171–1218; Frank Blair, *On the Acquisition of Territory in Central and South America* . . . (Washington, D.C., 1858). The fear of large concentrations of blacks, as in St. Domingue, led some southerners to support colonization (see Mathew Carey, *Reflections on the Causes That Led to the Formation of the Colonization Society* . . . [Philadelphia, 1832], 2; and Robert E. May, *The Southern Dream of a Caribbean Empire 1854–1861* [Baton Rouge, 1973], who covers this topic well).

30. Edwin C. Holland, *A Refutation of the Calumnies Against the . . . Southern States* (Charleston, 1826); *Federal Union* (Washington, D.C.), August 25, 1831). Also see Calvin Cotton (ed.), *The Works of Henry Clay* . . . (2 vols.; New York, 1897), I, 219–20. James Birney was a moderate antislavery publisher who advocated gradual, carefully planned emancipation. He received letters from southerners (many of whom were not slave owners) protesting even this moderate plan because they feared black retaliation and violence (see Dwight Dumond [ed.], *Letters of James G. Birney* [2 vols.; New York, 1938], I, 197–200, 240–41).

gaged in a lively debate that revealed the schism between the slaveholders in the eastern portion of the state and the white yeoman farmers in the west. Some participants in this unique event in antebellum southern history were astonished at the divided opinions on slavery, which were also freely expressed and given wide coverage in newspapers and pamphlets. There was, however, common ground: the issue of whites' security. Having been drawn together by the Turner Rebellion, those who favored immediate abolition, gradual abolition, or no abolition all agreed that whatever the fate of slavery in Virginia, freedmen and free blacks must not be allowed to remain in the state as a threat to whites. For instance, General William H. Broadnax, a Tidewater slave owner and a colonizationist, had commanded the militia in the vicinity of Southampton County. A moderate on the slavery issue, and chairman of one of the legislative committees to investigate the problem, he nonetheless declared that any talk of emancipation would have to follow the removal of all blacks. Otherwise, only the most horrible of servile wars and massacres would result. His more conservative colleagues, represented by James Gholson of the Piedmont region, argued that any sort of emancipation raised the specter of St. Domingue. While disagreeing with these positions, Thomas J. Randolph, grandson of Thomas Jefferson and spokesman for some other views, agreed that blacks and whites could not "exist upon the same soil in an equality of condition; one will govern by force, the other will rebel in bloody massacre." Randolph quoted his grandfather's conviction that "it [emancipation] will come . . . whether brought on by the general energy of our minds, or by the bloody process of St. Domingo." The more moderate apologists turned to colonization as the way to rid the country of a quarrelsome segment of the population. Thus, Jefferson favored colonizing freedmen and free blacks in St. Domingue, Thomas Dew favored sending them to other slave states in the lower South, and many Virginians took up the cause of African colonization.[31] This historic debate ended in compromise, with

31. Theodore M. Whitfield, *Slavery Agitation in Virginia, 1829–1830* (Baltimore, 1930); *Speeches of . . . [various delegates] . . . in the House of Delegates of Virginia on the Abolition of Slavery* (Richmond, 1832), particularly those of T. J. Randolph (13, 17) and John T. Brown (30). See Alison Goodyear Freehling, *Drift Toward Dissolution: The Virginia Slavery Debate of 1831–1832* (Baton Rouge, 1982), 90–93, 103, 111–13, 117, 121, for an excellent summary of the slavery advocates associating emancipation with slave insurrection and retaliation.

nothing done about a plan of general emancipation. One area of consensus was that to remain safe, Virginia was going to be a white man's country no matter what measures would be adopted to keep it that way. The fear of racial disharmony was an important backdrop to the future of slavery in the United States.

During the late 1830s southerners were increasingly defensive about their peculiar institution in the face of direct attacks from northern abolitionists and Britain having abolished slavery in its West Indian colonies in 1833. They soon declared that emancipation there was every bit the failure it had been in St. Domingue, particularly in Jamaica, the largest and most troublesome island. Southerners decried the declining agricultural output, but they were especially sensitive to the presence of so many freed blacks near their shores. Hugh S. Legaré warned that those emancipated in the British West Indies, if "added to St. Domingo, will present. . . , at the mouth of the Mississippi, a black population of some 2,000,000 free from all restraint and ready for any mischief."[32] Southerners saw, in Legaré's words, the dreadful fruition of Jefferson's warning about the Africanization of the tropics.

The Atlantic community seemed to be heading in a direction that caused white southerners increasingly to fear for their lives and property. Following a pattern set by their interpretation of the events of St. Domingue years before, and continued with emancipation in the British West Indies, the South began to close ranks as a region and to exclude "radical" ideology. It is not surprising that slaveholders in the French West Indies had responded in just this way. Southern politicians in Congress argued against emancipation, state laws were passed to better control the movement and lives of freedmen, communities set up local committees to monitor the dissemination of "incendiary publications," and a new generation of southern leaders formulated a more aggressive ideology in the face of outside opposition. Southern literary figures such as William Gilmore Simms also took up the defense of slavery and southern ways. In a rejoinder to Harriet Martineau, who, in her *Society in America* (1837), argued that slave owners were incorrect that outside agitators, abolitionists, were responsible for slave outbreaks in the South (such as the Nat Turner revolt),

32. Joe B. Wilkins, "Window on Freedom: The South's Response to the Emancipation of the Slaves in the British West Indies, 1833–1861" (Ph.D. dissertation, University of South Carolina, 1977), 41–42, 75, 116, 135.

Simms stated that the South was a more secure region because it was aware of the dangers of abolition. Simms saw the tragedy of St. Domingue as the introduction of troublesome ideas and people into a stable slave society.[33] The southern chorus now sang in unison: the need to protect the system against outside or inside agitation was vital to their security.

Throughout the sectional controversies of the late 1840s and the 1850s, De Bow's Review represented the South's consciousness of the danger of race war. Its editor, James D. B. De Bow, was a South Carolinian educated at the College of Charleston when there were St. Domingan refugees on its faculty. Although some fifty years had passed since the age of Toussaint, articles in De Bow's journal often warned that "a war of the races would begin following any emancipation attempt." A respected publication that was available throughout the South, De Bow's Review was interested in the economy of the South, in commercial and trade information, and in the proslavery argument. De Bow reminded his readers that "revolutions, tumults and disorder, have been the ordinary pursuits of the emancipated blacks."[34] In the late antebellum period, then, slavery advocates again and again conjured up the image of St. Domingue to dissuade Americans from allowing notions of freedom and equality to reach such a dangerous portion of the population. No matter what the topic—abolition, free black rights, colonization, attempts to reopen the slave trade, or the future of slavery in the South—the specter of St. Domingue was primary in the mind of southerners:

> These slaves, inured to labor, possessed of great physical strength, ignorant, and of course under the influence of brutal passions, if turned loose as a body of emancipated freemen, with arms in their hands . . .

33. William G. Simms, "Miss Martineau on Slavery," Southern Literary Messenger, III (November, 1837), 65off.; Dickson D. Bruce, Jr., "Racial Fear and the Proslavery Argument: A Rhetorical Approach," Mississippi Quarterly, XXXIV (1981), 461–78.

34. De Bow's Review, XVI (1856), 595. For additional examples, see ibid., XI (1851), and XXVII (1859), 36–38; Ronald Takaki, A Pro-Slavery Crusade: The Agitation to Reopen the African Slave Trade (New York, 1971), 58–59; Louis M. Gottschalk, Notes of a Pianist (1881; rpr. New York, 1964), 13; and William Drayton, The South Vindicated From the Treason and Fanaticism of the Northern Abolitionists (Philadelphia, 1836), 246. De Bow shrewdly used the example of St. Domingue to keep nonslaveholding southerners from advocating emancipation (see his "The Non-Slave-holders of the South," The Interest in Slavery of the Southern Non-Slaveholder [Charleston, 1860], 12).

would occupy a position so full of danger so frightful of collision, that the interval between the act of abolition and the outbreak of war would be as the flash that precedes the thunder. This result is inevitable. The two races cannot mix and mingle in social and political equality. Oil and water could as soon unite. The history of the French and British West Indies is proof of this.[35]

As the debates over slavery heated in the decade before the Civil War northern newspapers with southern sympathies warned of the impending crisis should blacks be set free in large numbers. Drawing on "the bloody history of Hayti," the New York *Herald* (which supported John C. Breckinridge, the states' rights candidate for president in 1860) cautioned that abolition would result in "a perpetual war of races" that "cannot cease until the black race has been exterminated or driven from among us." Another observer claimed that southerners misunderstood the lessons of St. Domingue because they feared black emancipation, though he did acknowledge that this concern was caused by the Haitian Revolution. In a poignant characterization, he said that "the darkened mind of the slaveholders, filled with fears and prejudices, can see nothing but bloodshed and devastation in the path of voluntary emancipation."[36]

Perhaps the most telling statement was by the antebellum South's elder statesman, John C. Calhoun. In his *Disquisition on Government* (published posthumously in 1850), he voiced his concern for liberty, which "when forced on a people unfit for it, would instead of a blessing, be a curse; as it would, in its reaction, lead directly to anarchy—the greatest of all curses." Calhoun implied what most southerners thought, that emancipation would end in race war, and that blacks were capable of civilization only under the guiding hand of their white masters or of a strong-willed military dictator like Toussaint. When Dessalines founded the first black republic, southerners observed the "experiment in black freedom" with devout interest. Unfortunately, Haiti in the

35. H. F. James, *Abolitionism Unveiled! Hyprocisy Unmasked! And Knavery Scourged* . . . (New York, 1850), 8, 9, 27; Nehemiah Adams, *South-Side View of Slavery* . . . (Boston, 1854), 119; Drayton, *The South Vindicated*, 254–75. Also see Thomas H. Benton, *Thirty Years' View in the U.S. Senate* (2 vols.; New York, 1854), I, 577; and Richmond *Enquirer*, November 30, 1819.

36. New York *Herald*, September 19, 1860; New York *Journal of Commerce*, October 26, 1860; G. B. Stebbins, *Facts and Opinions Touching the Real Origins, Character, and Influence of the American Colonization Society* (Boston, 1853), 64–65.

nineteenth century suffered civil wars, massacres, and assassinations. That history only served to reinforce white slave owners' fundamental skepticism of the capabilities of blacks living in freedom. Southerners looked to Haiti more than to the northern states to evaluate what freedom meant to blacks. Given their orientation, slaveholders found further evidence to bolster their tendencies toward racist views.[37]

The example of St. Domingue convinced white southerners that slavery was an institution that not only protected them from the horrors of race war but also protected the slaves from themselves. White observers of Haiti concluded that the unfettered black, left to himself, would regress to a more primitive state such as had presumably existed in Africa. Whites also claimed that slavery gave blacks a civilized alternative to a savage life. Watching closely the events in Haiti, white southerners concluded that black freedmen were incapable of civilization without slavery and that any attempt to free the unprepared slaves would end in race war, and in the destruction of southern culture.[38]

To prove their point, slavery supporters were fond of comparing the lush French colony before the revolution and the faltering, decrepit black republic of Haiti during the nineteenth century. As the only nation known to be controlled by blacks, Haiti was the sole symbol of what former slaves could accomplish if left to themselves. Southerners were unforgiving in their interpretation of the island's history. The destruction of the economy during the struggle for St. Domingue, the bitter rivalries between mulatto and black that caused unending internal instability, and Haiti's

37. R. K. Crallé (ed.), *The Works of John C. Calhoun* (6 vols.; New York, 1854), I, 54. As James Leyburn noted in *The Haitian People* (New Haven, 1941), 89: "Of the 21 heads of state between 1843 and 1915, only one served out his prescribed term of office, 3 died while serving, one was blown up with his palace, one presumably poisoned, and one hacked to pieces by a mob; one resigned. The other 14 were deposed by revolution after incumbencies ranging in length from 3 months to 12 years."

38. For a typical example, see William Harper, *Memoir on Slavery Read Before the Society for the Advancement of Learning of South Carolina . . .* (Charleston, 1838). Some northerners also supported this view (see New York *Daily News*, April 10, 1861). For an interesting comparison of American attitudes toward the Indians as also incapable of civilization, see Brian W. Dippie, *The Vanishing American: White Attitudes and U.S. Indian Policy* (New York, 1981); and Bernard W. Sheehan, *Seeds of Extinction: Jeffersonian Philanthropy and the American Indian* (New York, 1973).

complete isolation by the republics that shared the Caribbean were not part of southerners' evaluation of the black experiment with freedom. One American observer commented on what he saw as the difference between the old colony and the new republic: "The inhabitants are the laziest and most criminal I have ever seen. . . . I can never believe that it is [good] . . . to give a people their freedom who their whole lives have been slaves. On the island of St. Domingo one sees proof of this."[39] This personal assessment was reiterated in southern newspapers throughout the antebellum period. The theme was paradise lost. One editor admonished his readers to support the breaking of the Negroes' iron scepter that "has already crushed all the fair fruits of European culture, and in a few years by a series of cruel wars and revolutions will convert these beautiful plantations into an African wilderness."[40] Even moderates warned against indiscriminate emancipation because of what happened when "heedless enthusiasm took control over reason in St. Domingue." In his widely read works, Professor Thomas Dew illustrated the results of emancipation in St. Domingue and Haiti in a chart that showed exports in 1791, in 1802 under Toussaint when he attempted to reconstruct the plantation system without slavery, and in 1822 under President Boyer. Exported commodities declined in 1802 but had fallen precipitously by 1822.[41] It was true that staple-crop production suffered. But the only lesson proslavery southerners could draw was that blacks would not work unless they were required to do so, presumably by white overseers and masters.

In a speech before educators in Charleston, Chancellor William Harper, whose *Memoir on Slavery* (1837) was regarded in the South as one of the most important of the proslavery arguments,

39. Christian Koch, Diary (1831–36), 62, 69 (MS in Middleton Library, LSU). Also see Benton, *Thirty Years' View*, I, 578; William Gooch to Secretary of State, February 7, 1843, in U.S. State Department, Consular Despatches . . . Aux Cayes. Predictions of blacks' inability to govern themselves came quite early (see Philadelphia *Gazette of the United States*, December 8, 1794; *Virginia Gazette and General Advertiser* [Williamsburg], November 9, 1796).

40. Charleston *Courier*, March 11, 1803. Also see *Virginia Gazette and General Advertiser* (Williamsburg), May 11, 1802; *Louisiana Gazette* (New Orleans), March 17, 1807. The Richmond *Enquirer* of May 28, 1805, predicted that Haiti would be another "barbarous pirate state like Tripoli." The same attitude prevailed half a century later (see *De Bow's Review*, II [1849], 314–31).

41. *Annals*, 16th Cong., 2nd Sess., 1155; Dew, "Review of the Debate," in *The Slavery Argument*, 430–32, 440–42, 483. Also see Matthew Estes, *A Defense of Negro Slavery As It Exists in the United States* (Montgomery, Ala., 1846), viii–ix.

praised slavery for its ameliorating effects on ignorant blacks. Convinced that the peculiar institution was the conservator of stability and order in southern society, Harper pointed out that because slavery had been abolished in the Caribbean, "St. Domingo is struck out of the map of civilized existence, and the British West Indies will shortly be so." Harper developed a geopolitical argument for using slaves in tropical regions: the languid character of such climates caused slavery to flourish in Greece, Spain, Portugal, Italy, and the Caribbean. Further, both the American South and the West Indies needed slave labor to be productive. In the words of another slave apologist: "The negro was made for the South." This polemicist used St. Domingue to warn antislavery supporters: "Destroy our slavery and you put a stop to all progress, all improvement in the South: you throw it back to its primitive state, in which it is only fit for the residence of beasts of prey."[42]

American commercial agents in Haiti were an important source of information, since the United States did not have diplomatic relations with the black republic. Their reports were remarkably negative throughout this period. An agent at Aux Cayes wrote to John C. Calhoun, then secretary of state, that "there are very few blacks capable of conducting the affairs of the island, and . . . they will soon commence fighting each other and separate themselves into clans and become like Africa." Another agent reported to James Buchanan that the country continued in a "pitiable state and that the "licentiousness of the lower classes can hardly be conceived and daily increases." This agent later predicted that without outside help Haiti would "become a disgrace to the civilized world." Still another agent referred to Haiti as "an agricultural wasteland."[43]

A spate of pamphlets and lectures by slavery apologists appeared when the Compromise of 1850, increased abolitionist criticism, the Kansas-Nebraska question, free soil, and the founding of the Republican party reinvigorated the debates over slavery.

42. Chancellor William Harper, *Memoir on Slavery Read Before the Society for the Advancement of Learning of South Carolina at Its Annual Meeting in Columbia* (Charleston, 1837), 43; Estes, *Defense of Negro Slavery*, 161, 183.
43. Gooch to John C. Calhoun, April 29, 1844, and agents to Buchanan, December 31, 1845, August 26, 1847, all in U.S. State Department, Consular Despatches . . . Aux Cayes. Also see "Diary of Secret Mission to San Domingo," in David Dixon Papers, Perkins Library, Duke.

These polemics emphasized the Haitian experiment as a clear example of the effects of emancipation. As one lecturer noted, the black republic was "the exclusive architect of its own institutions and destiny," and so "they have relapsed into pristine barbarism." Many other apologists, viewing the agricultural decline in Haiti as evidence of the failure of black freedom, came to the same conclusion. They saw the tropics as "Africanized," with all the emotional overtones that term held for advocates of the necessity of slavery in the New World. The scenario was described by a slavery sympathizer: "The negroes would perform just labor enough, in addition to what they could rob from the whites, to live a lazy, dancing dissolute savage life till the whites, finding it impossible to live with them, would abandon everything and fly with their families to the free states; then, the negroes would fall upon and butcher one another."[44]

De Bow's Review took particular delight in reminding its readers of the deplorable state of the black republic. Charts were often published as dramatic evidence of economic decline. Summing up his arguments over the years, De Bow pronounced the republic a failure and offered the following observations:

> What the destiny of Hayti may be, we will not attempt to determine further than the revolutions of 1842, 3, 4, 5, and 6—the expulsion of President Boyer—the atrocities committed by the negroes on the colored races—the contests and distractions between the former political men on the island—the insecurity that prevails—the non-payment of the installments of indemnity to France—the neglect of agriculture, the consequent want of products for trade, and the lax morals and indolence of the population, are all subjects, deliberately considered, that do not leave us much good hope for the prospects of Hayti.

This unhappy situation was caused by "the want of means and intellect on the part of the slaves," who are, as another slavery advocate argued, "savages in the midst of society, without peace, security, agriculture, or property—ignorant of the duties of life

44. Ellwood Fisher, *Lecture on the North and the South* (Cincinnati, Ohio, 1849), 42–45; also see, for example, *A Defense of the South Against the Reproaches and Incroachments of the North* (Charleston, 1850); Rev. Iveson Brooks, *A Defense of Slavery Against the Attacks of Henry Clay and Alexander Campbell* (Hamburg, S.C., 1851); *A Lecture . . . Showing African Slavery to be Consistent with the Moral and Physical Progress of a Nation* (1851; New York, 1969); and B. F. Stringfellow, *Negro-Slavery, No Evil; Or, The North and the South* (St. Louis, 1854); "Amor Patrie," *Slavery Con and Pro; Or, A Sermon and Its Answer* (Washington, D.C., 1858).

. . . averse to labor, though frequently perishing of want—sus-picious of each other, and towards the rest of mankind, revengeful, and faithless, remorseless and bloody minded." These devastating opinions found expression in mockery as well. James B. Hope, a Norfolk essayist and newspaperman, wrote to his mother about his meeting with "his nigger *highness*," Soulouque, during a trip to the Caribbean. Hope's contempt for what he thought was the Haitians' presumptuousness was apparent throughout his long letter, which made fun of the "funny costumes and inky faces" of the black "bafoons." He concluded that "more villainous dogs I never saw." Some southerners expressed both interest in and fas-cination with Haiti. Mary Boykin Chesnut noted that the same emperor, Soulouque, was the subject of a biography that was popular in her area during the 1850s.[45]

Such sentiments were not confined to southerners. James K. Paulding, a friend of Washington Irving's and the author of numer-ous books including *Slavery in the United States* (1836), ex-pressed his support for the theory that emancipation would de-stroy southern society. He predicted that abolition would produce a "new Africa" in the South, where society would experience the same "decay" and "ruin" as had St. Domingue. While others in the North had southern sympathies or at least agreed upon some of the same interpretations, they were seldom as vocal. Not sur-rounded by slaves or personally involved with the abolitionist crusade, they were content to watch from the sidelines, no doubt happy to sit this one out. Given the widespread acceptance of white supremacy, the northern public wanted nothing to do with either the Negro or slavery. The lessons of St. Domingue did not preoccupy them, nor did they look to Haiti to learn about Ameri-can blacks' capabilities. The slavery controversy raged for more than fifty years, consuming some, hardly touching others. It seems, though, that one could not help but read about the growing

45. *Commercial Review*, V (May–June, 1848), 498–99. For additional ex-amples, see *De Bow's Review*, XVI (1854), 32–38; Dunbar Rowland (ed.), *Jefferson Davis, Constitutionalist: His Letters, Papers and Speeches* (10 vols.; Jackson, Miss., 1923), I, 289 (February 14, 1850); *Annals*, 12th Cong., 2nd Sess., 701, and 16th Cong., 2nd Sess., 1016; Richmond *Enquirer*, June 19, 1818; *De Bow's Re-view*, XIV (1853), 276; John Jacobus Flournoy, *An Essay on the Origin, Habits . . . of the African Race* (New York, 1835), 56; [James Hope] to his mother, April 14, 1852, in James B. Hope Papers, Earl G. Severn Library, College of William and Mary, Williamsburg; C. Vann Woodward (ed.), *Mary Chesnut's Civil War* (New Haven, 1981), 88.

antagonism between the North and South—no small part of each week's news. But St. Domingue and Haiti were issues of no importance to the general public of the North.[46]

The Haitian experiment, as it evolved in the mind of the South, had an important effect upon the development of formalized racial dogma during the late antebellum years. Whites with visceral feelings about black inferiority began to philosophize, using what they thought was irrefutable evidence that blacks were incapable of attaining equality. Actually, several Frenchmen familiar with the experiences of St. Domingue developed these racial theories about the races' incompatability. No less an observer of American life than Alexis de Tocqueville was convinced that a race war would naturally and inevitably result from freeing blacks and allowing them to stay in the United States in any proximity to whites. He warned Americans that "the most formidable of all the ills that threaten the future of the Union arise from the presence of a black population upon the territory." Tocqueville viewed history from the perspective of one race always controlling the other. Where the whites were in control, degradation of blacks and slavery resulted; whenever blacks were the strongest, "they have destroyed the whites." "This," he said, "has been the only balance that has ever taken place between the two races."[47] The most influential French theoretician of racism in the early nineteenth century was Comte Joseph Arthur de Gobineau, whose *Inequality of Human Races* (1853–1855) was translated and widely read in the United States. Gobineau developed a pseudoscientific explanation of the races, and he used Haiti to prove that blacks were incapable of freedom without white stewardship. Gobineau argued that blacks had had every opportunity to develop a cultured society because of the French legacy in St. Domingue. So the Haitian experiment with black self-government was a failure, and perhaps doubly devastating to the blacks, he reasoned, since the tropical environment was best for them. Gobineau's work gave intellectual expression to what southerners had thought all along; namely, that blacks were innately inferior, and to remove them

46. See Eric Foner, *Free Soil, Free Labor, Free Men: The Ideology of the Republican Party Before the Civil War* (New York, 1970); and Eugene H. Berwanger, *The Frontier Against Slavery: Western Anti-Negro Prejudice and the Slavery Extension Controversy* (Urbana, 1971).

47. Alexis de Tocqueville, *Democracy in America* (1832; 2 vols.; rpr. New York, 1945), I, 373, 390. Also see James, *Abolitionism Unveiled*, 119.

from slavery was against the laws of nature and science.[48] There were others, St. Domingan refugees and French officials among them, who also wrote accounts that influenced southerners. Hugo's *Bar Jargal*, set in revolutionary St. Domingue, was translated and reprinted in the United States.

Southerners elaborated on these theories to bolster the argument, increasingly strident, that slavery must be part of the future of an expanding America. In 1851, southern sympathizer Joseph Campbell drew upon Gobineau's argument in his treatise on racial inequality. He relied heavily upon the Haitian example to support his case. Campbell particularly stressed the savagery of blacks, referring to Dessalines's massacres of whites as an "act of crafty ferocity, which history cannot parallel." In his vitriolic denunciation of the concept of black equality, Campbell characterized the Haitians, and all free blacks, as "idle, improvident, licentious and immoral."[49]

George Fitzhugh, as much a critic of free society as he was a defender of slave society, was a patrician who published regularly in the Richmond *Enquirer* and *De Bow's Review;* his *Sociology for the South* (1854) and *Cannibals All!* (1859) were classics of proslavery thought. Fitzhugh joined the chorus of those who were convinced that blacks were not ready for freedom. In an essay published in *De Bow's Review* entitled "Free Negroes in Hayti," Fitzhugh claimed that "the fruits of freedom in that island, since its independence, in 1804, are *revolutions, massacres, misrule, insecurity, irreligion, ignorance, immorality, indolence,* and *neglect of agriculture."* Since the "Queen of the Antilles" had lapsed into a "New African" barbarism, Fitzhugh concluded that "wherever this race is found in a state of freedom, a blight and curse seem to follow."[50] Other, more vitriolic racists made the same comparisons and the same claims. New Orleans physician, ethnologist, and proslavery crusader Dr. Samuel Cartwright agreed

48. Comte Joseph Arthur de Gobineau, *The Inequality of Human Races,* trans. Adrian Collins (New York, 1915).
49. Joseph Campbell, *Negro-Mania, Being an Examination of the Falsely Assumed Equality of the Various Races of Men* (Philadelphia, 1851), 495–501.
50. George Fitzhugh, "Free Negroes in Hayti," *De Bow's Review,* XXVII (1859), 526–49. Also see "Experiment of the Independence of Negroes in Hayti," *ibid.,* XXV (1858), 31–34; David Christy, *A Lecture on African Civilization* (Columbus, Ohio, 1853), 42–43; Josiah Nott, "Statistics of Southern Slave Population," *Commercial Review,* IV (November, 1847), 289; and *Reply to Dr. Dewey's Address Delivered at the Elm Tree* (Charleston, 1852), 22–23.

with Fitzhugh's argument, as did northerner John H. Van Evrie, who published extensively his proslavery and anti-Negro views. They concluded that in Haiti what kept the black man from extinction was "the banana trees and the half-wild hogs."[51]

These arguments seemed infallible. Haiti was a commercial failure: the former slaves had lapsed into subsistence farming, the plantations were destroyed, the mountains, denuded of trees, were severely eroded, and the country was in constant turmoil caused by the rival mulatto and black factions. Having destroyed white culture when they destroyed slavery, Haitians were left to their own devices by a world bent on keeping them isolated as an anomaly. These factors obviously brought about the conditions that southerners so readily recalled. But they could not see that the institution of slavery as a system of oppression, not the character of blacks, had led to the decline of Haitian society. Slavery's legacy was little literacy, no schools, no commercial traditions, no banks, no political stability—a situation from which Haiti has in fact never recovered. Had southerners been interested in preparing for black emancipation, the history of the region might have been quite different. There were lessons to learn from Haiti, and one of them was that the transition from such a system to freedom is fraught with difficulty. But to see Haiti in that light, whites would have had to admit that the value of slavery in "civilizing" the black was simply nonexistent. It was creditable that the Haitians and their own former slaves did as well as they did.

On the eve of the Civil War, southern leaders once again conjured up the images of St. Domingue and Haiti because they feared that an insurrection and possibly a race war might well occur. John Brown's ill-advised raid on Harpers Ferry in 1859 caused an uproar in the South, where beleaguered slaveholders immediately concluded that Brown's actions represented an abolitionist conspiracy to instigate a slave uprising. One outraged

51. Samuel Cartwright, *Ethnology of the Negro or Prognathous Race* (New Orleans, 1858), 12–13, 15; Samuel Cartwright, "Negro Freedom an Impossibility Under Nature's Law, *De Bow's Review*, XXX (1861), 648–59; "Dr. Cartwright on the Caucasians and the Africans," *ibid.*, XXV (1858), 52. Later Jefferson Davis denied that blacks had created their own government (see Rowland [ed.], *Jefferson Davis*, V, 30; *Free Negroism or Results of Emancipation in the North and the West Indian Islands . . .* [New York, 1862], 10–13; and S. D. Carpenter, *Five Hundred Political Texts: Being . . . Results of Slavery Agitation and Emancipation . . .* [Madison, 1864], 12–14). *De Bow's Review*, XVII (1855), 711.

southerner charged that the raid was "nothing more nor nothing less than an attempt to do on a vast scale what was done in St. Domingo in 1791." Robert Toombs, a prominent lawyer and Whig politician from Georgia, suggested that northern abolitionists intended to "destroy it [slavery] by exciting revolt and insurrection among the slaves." Another southern spokesman concluded from Brown's raid that "there is in the South a wide-spread organization of conspirators whose object is servile insurrection and the conflagration of Southern society." He warned that the South was in danger and that the "law of self-preservation" required the region to resist "Northern Jacobinism." This theme, that abolitionists had a "lust for Southern blood" and that the North's policy was "to make slavery unpopular and unprofitable, by sending emissaries amongst our slaves and exciting them to insurrection and bloodshed, to burn down our towns and buildings of agriculture," pervaded southern writing and oratory in the months after the raid on Harpers Ferry.[52]

The southern response was quite emotional and reflected the assimilation of St. Domingue's haunting lesson that race war would be inevitable should slavery be abolished or outsiders allowed to upset the system. Lurid scenes were dominant rhetorical features—the volcano was beginning to awaken. What makes this aspect of their reaction so telling is that sixty to seventy years had passed since the events of St. Domingue, yet no orator had to explain when that was his primary example of what the worst would be. Southern versions of the lessons of St. Domingue were common assumptions throughout the antebellum period and went beyond visions of marauding slaves. White abolitionists were misguided Jacobins, inappropriately interfering in a volatile situation that could cause enormous destruction. In response to reports that Lydia Maria Child was nursing John Brown's wound while he was in prison awaiting execution, the wife of the governor of Vir-

52. Louis Schade, *Appeal to the Common Sense and Patriotism of People of the United States* . . . (Washington, D.C., 1860), 6–36; R. Toombs to E. B. Pullin and others, in U. B. Phillips (ed.), "Toombs, Stephens, Cobb Correspondence," *Annual Report of the American Historical Association* (1911), 521; entries for November, 1859–May, 1861 Diary of John C. Gutherford (MS in Virginia Historical Society, Richmond), 11–13; C. W. Jacobs, *Speech of Col. Curtis M. Jacobs on the Free Colored Population of Maryland, Delivered in the House of Delegates on 17 February 1860* (Annapolis, 1860), 4–5; John Townshend, *The Doom of Slavery in the Union: Its Safety Out Of It* (Charleston, S.C., 1860), 5, 23.

ginia wrote: "You would soothe with sisterly and motherly care the hoary-headed monster of Harper's Ferry! A man whose aim and intention was to incite the horrors of servile war—to condemn women of your own race, ere death closed their eyes on their sufferings from violence and outrages, to see their husbands and fathers murdered, their children butchered, the ground strewed with the brains of their babies." Such a passage could easily have been written by a St. Domingan refugee in the 1790s. It was as if the lessons they had learned, the stories they had been told, were all coming true. Images of the apocalypse abound: "Fanatics and infidels ruled the hour; crying out that there was no God. . . . They embraced and kissed Negroes . . . set free more than 300,000 savage blacks. . . . There suddenly set loose on 30 or 40 thousand defenseless whites, who were barbarously massacred, their dwellings burned, property destroyed, and the island left desolate, from which it has not recovered to this day." The attitude behind these images was widely held in the South on the eve of the Civil War, particularly in those areas where slaves were concentrated. It was not difficult for southerners to conclude, however reluctantly, that fighting to keep slavery stable and northern Jacobins out of the South was essential. At this point it did not matter whether slavery was profitable or would last forever. What mattered was protecting homes and loved ones against the evils associated with Jacobinism. This feeling was best summed up in a Confederate imprint, *The Relation Between the Races at the South* (1861). The author supported secession as necessary to southern "free self-government," particularly since the North threatened slavery, an institution "universally felt through the Southern States as essential to the well-being of those States." The author appealed to the laws of nature and the lessons of history to prove his point. Using St. Domingue as his analogy, he inveighed against outsiders' influence on southern blacks: "The Negroes in Hayti did not emancipate themselves, but, under the influence of ignorant, foreign fanatics, they murdered their protectors, and relapsed into barbarism. The fanatical French demagogues of that day incited the St. Domingo negroes to their unnatural and brutal outbreak, which has issued only in the degradation and barbarism of the St. Domingo negro." Emphasizing a southern shibboleth, the author stated that "the St. Domingo negro has never taken a place among civilized nations; he has only relapsed into barbarism, by withdrawing himself from the humanizing protection of the white, who is the natural elevator of the negro race."[53] Most slaveholders saw no contradiction between their relations with and their images of blacks. Slaves were happy and docile, though childlike and in need of supervision; only because of outside influences did they regress to a savage state. As the author of *The Relation Between the Races* pointed out: "No attempt at insurrection in the South has ever originated from the domestic negro; but such nefarious designs have always been fomented from other sources—such as Vesey, of St. Domingo, and Northern incendiaries." He concluded with the most characteristic feature of the southern attitude toward slavery in the late antebellum period: "The relations of the white and black races in the Southern States is no mere accidental one, but one which, however brought about, is a fulfillment of a law of nature, whereby the negro shall accomplish an important destiny in the development of the resources of the civilized world, and shall be himself elevated in the scale of humanity." Not only was it a "law of nature" that the black man was subordinate to the white man. An article in the New Orleans *Bee* said: "The black man in his own home is a barbarian and a beast. . . . When emancipated and removed from the crushing competition of a superior race he demonstrates his utter incapacity for self-restraint, grows idle and thriftless, indulges his passions without the slightest check, descends step by step down to the original depths of his ignorant and savage instincts, and at length is debased to nearly the state which he is found in the wilds and jungles of Africa. To this complexion is he approximating in Hayti." The editor concluded this assessment of blacks' capabilities by asserting that the "normal condition of the negro is servitude."[54] To proslavery southerners and slaveholders, God, history, and their own sense of the world convinced them that slavery was essential to their survival. This view made logical their acceptance of a war for southern independence in the face of an outside threat.

While the southern consensus about black freedom and slavery

53. "Correspondence of Lydia Maria Child and Governor Wise and Mrs. Mason of Virginia," in *Anti-Slavery Tracts* (Boston, 1860); *African Servitude: When, Why and By Whom Instituted Shall It Be Maintained* (New York, 1860), 28–30; *The Relation Between the Races at the South* (Charleston, S.C., 1861).
54. *The Relation Between the Races*, 16; New Orleans *Bee*, March 16, 1861.

was overwhelming, there was some opposition to the conclusion that secession was the best course of action. Some Unionist planters thought that it was only within the Union that slavery could be protected from insurrectionists. One argued that the fire-eaters' violent rhetoric served only to stir up the slaves and might easily set a spark that would explode in a bloody uprising, such as "was seen in France [St. Domingue] in 1792."[55]

Despite many southerners' initial enthusiasm when the war began, they did not forget the threat to their security at home. As one student of this period noted: "Fears of Negro insurrection were greatly intensified by the outbreak of hostilities. The degree of anxiety varied with time and place, but letters and diaries of the period indicate that this dread hung like an ominous cloud over the Southern mind throughout the long conflict." These fears were particularly acute in late 1862, when Abraham Lincoln promulgated the Emancipation Proclamation. Across the South this action was seen as an attempt to incite the slaves, and St. Domingue was once again a vivid image in the southern mind. The Confederate Congress passed a joint resolution that condemned Lincoln's attempt at "inciting servile war"; one southern politician later accused Lincoln of trying "to convert the South into a San Domingo by appealing to the cupidity, lusts, ambition, and ferocity of the slaves." And as one southern officer in the field wrote home: "I look upon it as a direct bid for insurrection, as a most infamous attempt to incite flight, murder and rapine on the part of our slave population."[56]

During the war the manpower shortage threatened to cripple the Confederate cause. Battle losses, disease, desertions, and a numerically superior enemy caused some Confederates to seek different sources for recruits. Inevitably the question of using blacks

55. James L. Roark, *Masters Without Slaves: Southern Planters in the Civil War and Reconstruction* (New York, 1977), 4.

56. May S. Ringold, "The Role of the State Legislatures in the Confederacy" (Ph.D. dissertation, Emory University, 1956), 129–30; "Address of Congress to the People of the Confederate States," January 22, 1864, in *The War of the Rebellion: A Compilation of the Official Records of the Union and Confederate Armies* (130 vols.; Washington, D.C., 1880–1901), Ser. IV, Vol. III, pp. 132–33; *Journal of the Congress of the Confederate States of America, 1861–1865* (4 vols.; Washington, D.C., 1904), II, 393; James Matthews (ed.), *The Statutes at Large of the Confederate States of America* (Richmond, 1863), 1st Cong., 3rd Sess., Resolution 5; Robert M. Myers (ed.), *The Children of Pride: A True Story of Georgia and the Civil War* (New Haven, 1972), II, 967.

as troops surfaced. No one had considered such a drastic measure—most southerners thought the war would be short and they
would easily win. Slaves were used throughout the war as personal servants and forced labor on fortifications and capital projects. Aware that there were black troops in the Union army, and
facing a diminishing Confederacy, southerners came to evaluate
such a scheme. In early 1864, President Jefferson Davis proposed
and the Confederate Congress passed a bill "to increase the effi-
ciency of the Army by the employment of free Negroes and slaves
in certain capacities," including work on fortifications, in maté-
riel production, and in military hospitals, but excluding combat.[57]
    The controversy really began, however, with Major General Pat-
rick R. Cleburne, a brilliant young officer serving in the Army of
Tennessee against the steadily increasing army of Union General
William T. Sherman. Cleburne stated in his proposal to Com-
manding General Joseph E. Johnston that "the enemy already op-
poses us at every point with superior numbers . . . and he has already in training an army of 100,000 negroes as good as any
troops." Cleburne wrote that emancipating and enlisting former
slaves would strip the North of sympathy and assistance, dry up
Union recruitment of southern blacks, and deprive the North
of its fanaticism. In the South, increased troops could then take
the offensive, and slavery's inherent weakness and vulnerability
would be dissipated. Cleburne was sure that Negroes would rather
fight for their native South than the alien North if they were given
their freedom. No doubt Cleburne thought that the South was
fighting for more than slavery, for a higher cause. However, his
bold plan was suppressed by the Davis government, since it under-
mined much southern ideology about blacks and the need for
slavery. A year later the Confederate government was desperate
enough to consider unorthodox proposals, but Davis modified
Cleburne's to make it more palatable. Davis wanted the Confederacy to provide some black laborers, expressly not armed, who
would be induced to enlist by the promise of freedom after the
war. Davis explained that "the policy of engaging to liberate the
negro on his discharge after service rendered seemed to me prefer-

57. Robert F. Durden, *The Gray and the Black: The Confederate Debate on
Emancipation* (Baton Rouge, 1972); James M. McPherson (ed.), *The Negro's Civil
War: How American Negroes Felt and Acted* (New York, 1965); Benjamin Quarles,
The Negro in the Civil War (1953; rpr. New York, 1968).

able to that of granting immediate manumission, or that of retaining him in servitude."[58]

Opposition to and resentment of Davis' proposal were predictably bitter. A Confederate congressman asked rhetorically, "Will the African save us?" Many of those who felt betrayed by the mere suggestion of emancipation in exchange for military service used St. Domingue once again as a reminder of the danger of such a policy. One editorial evoked the "horrors of the French revolution" and noted that "the negroes are to be armed, and society is to be not merely upset, but destroyed. Every evil which followed in the wake of French emancipation will afflict us here, if this policy be adopted." Another cried that "when we arm the slaves, we abandon slavery."[59] Not even the support of General Robert E. Lee could nullify most Confederate leaders' hostility to the plan. When finally, in desperation, Congress did pass such a measure, it was a meaningless act. The war had already been lost on the battlefield as the debate continued in late January, 1865. Most southerners were spared this last humiliation and were left only with their cherished notions about black inferiority and northern fanaticism. The South had learned its lessons of history all too well— the specter of St. Domingue was one cause of whites' inability to see blacks as anything but brutes, a myopia that prevented them from using valuable manpower even to save themselves.

Thus, southern slave owners and their sympathizers used St. Domingue and the Haitian Revolution as one of the cornerstones of their argument against all critics of their "peculiar institution." From the earliest reports of the events in St. Domingue in 1791 until the last days of the Confederacy in the spring of 1865, they offered their own self-serving historical interpretation of the Haitian Revolution as bona fide evidence of the dangers of a humanist ideology in a slave society. These attitudes, expressed in every decade of the antebellum period, were found not only in private letters, official correspondence, and newspapers but also among the more influential proslavery spokesmen. It was a lesson they

58. *The War of the Rebellion*, Ser. I, Vol. LII, Pt. 2, pp. 586–92, Vol. III, pp. 797–99.
59. Durden, *Gray and the Black*, 103–105, 109–42; *Policy of Employing Negro Troops, Speech of Hon. H. C. Chambers (of Mississippi)* (N.p., November 10, 1864), pamphlet in Flowers Collection, Perkins Library, Duke; Frank Vandiver (ed.), "Proceedings of the Confederate Congress," *Southern Historical Society Papers*, LI (1958), 295, LII (1959), 226–27.

never forgot. Nor did they ever tire of using it to justify slavery or their abhorrence of antislavery sentiment. Indeed, the mere mention of Haiti became one of the primary shibboleths of the South, for it validated their cherished notion of white supremacy and was a major factor in the development of racism as a doctrine. The southern interpretation of the Haitian Revolution and the way it was used strongly suggest one of the reasons why it took a civil war to emancipate the slaves.

FIVE

BLACKS AND THEIR ALLIES RESPOND

Both black and white abolitionists were intrigued by the events in the French West Indies and the history of Haiti during the antebellum period. The accomplishments of Haitian leaders who struggled against overwhelming odds to establish a government of their own played a major role in the development of pride and dignity among American blacks, who were bombarded with theories of racial inferiority and with discrimination in their own country. Blacks thought Haiti was the instrument by which whites in the New World would be compelled to acknowledge Afro-Americans' basic humanity. Blacks also hoped that Haiti would become a powerful guardian of the rights of black citizens in the Western Hemisphere. But Haiti was too unstable and poor to have any major direct impact on the United States or the Caribbean, as far as actually protecting blacks was concerned. Haiti was also isolated in the Caribbean. France did not recognize its former colony until the 1820s, and the United States waited until midway through the Civil War. Yet, as a symbol of black nationalism (and as a place for some emigrants), Haiti was essential to the black psyche. Ironically, it was primarily because of their loyalty to and belief in the American "Dream" that most free blacks did not see moving to Haiti as the answer to racial problems in the United States.

American blacks paid close attention to the developments in the French West Indies. The St. Domingan example influenced several militant antislavery advocates to suggest early on that perhaps violence was the only method of ameliorating the black man's condition in American society. In *Appeal to the Colored Citizens of the World* (1829), outspoken black militant David Walker called for blacks to rise up to overthrow the invidious system of chattel slavery in the South. As historian Herbert Aptheker has pointed out, Walker liberally used the term *citizen* to suggest the French Revolution to opponents of emancipation, though the *Appeal* was punctuated with biblical allusions as well. Walker did not dwell on St. Domingue specifically, but his admonishing slaves to cast off their chains, by force if necessary, certainly referred to the black insurrectionists there. Walker taunted his slave brothers with the rhetorical question, "'Are we MEN?'" He implored the slaves to "read the history particularly of Hayti, and see how they [blacks] were butchered by the whites, and so you take warning." Like Caliban in *The Tempest*, Walker was telling his kinsmen that they should learn of the white man's nature from the white man himself: it was the white slave owner who taught the black slave about violence. Walker was one of the first protestors against slavery to make the point that became the sine qua non of twentieth-century anticolonial leaders such as Franz Fanon: taking one's own destiny into one's hands was an act of manhood that created self-respect as well as freedom. Walker's *Appeal* may have affected the slaves, but it certainly influenced northern abolitionists, who debated his thesis and mourned his martyrdom (Walker mysteriously disappeared from Boston soon after the publication of his *Appeal*, never to be heard from again). Walker's rhetoric surely struck terror in the hearts of southerners because he forthrightly said violence would help achieve black freedom. Furthermore, Walker's *Appeal* was a call to action. Haiti was the example of how the black man took his destiny upon himself and succeeded in throwing off the shackles of slavery.[1]

   Another startling document that linked the events in the French West Indies with the violent overthrow of slavery in the United States was the letter received in Southampton County, Virginia, shortly after the Nat Turner revolt. It was forwarded to the governor of Virginia, James Floyd, who used it in his annual message to the state legislature to prove that outsiders were bent upon destroying slavery in the South. "Nero" begins the letter pointedly: "Oppression and revenge are the two prominent traits in human character; and as long as the former exists, the latter is justifiable." The author, referring to both St. Domingue and Haiti, stated that "our object is to seek revenge for indignities and abuses received—and to sell our live[s] at as high a price as possible." Nero assured blacks that they were strong enough and well armed enough to begin their retribution, and that "Hayti offers an asy-

   1. Herbert Aptheker, *One Continual Cry: David Walker's Appeal to the Colored Citizens of the World (1829–1830)* (New York, 1965), 60. For reactions in the South to Walker's *Appeal*, see William Pease and Jane Pease, "Walker's Appeal Comes to Charleston: A Note and Documents," *Journal of Negro History*, LIX (1974), 287–92.

lum for those who survive the approaching carnage." This un-usual letter may have been wishful thinking, but in the wake of Turner's revolt, and the southern fear of slave retaliation, its shrill cry must have resonated in the southern mind.[2]

A decade later, a black abolitionist again advocated violence as useful in the fight against slavery. Reflecting Walker's frustration, Henry Highland Garnet gave an inflammatory speech at a National Negro Convention meeting in the North. After cataloging the accomplishments of several black leaders, among them Toussaint Louverture, Garnet cried out: "Brethren, arise, arise! Strike for your lives and liberties. Now is the day and the hour. Let every slave throughout the land do this, and the days of slavery are numbered. You cannot be more oppressed than you have been—you cannot suffer greater cruelties than you have already. Rather die freemen than live to be slaves. Remember that you are FOUR MILLIONS!" This speech was too radical for most delegates; black militancy was not a significant force for the majority of black or white abolitionists. Yet these occasional outbursts reminded many of the possibility of violence and convinced some anti-slavery whites that direct action was necessary to defeat the slavocracy. One such convert was James Redpath, an abolitionist editor who became sure that drastic, outside pressure had to be brought to bear on the southern slave system. Redpath, later an ardent advocate of Haitian emigration, and after the Civil War a promoter for the traveling lecturer-humorist Mark Twain, wrote that "unless we strike a blow for the slaves—as Lafayette and his Frenchmen did . . . —or unless they strike a blow for themselves, as the negroes of Jamaica and Hayti, to their immortal honor, did—American slavery has a long and devastating future before it."[3]

Nor did moderate blacks completely reject insurrection and violence. The editor of the *Weekly Afro-American*, for example, defended such seemingly rash actions as "the uprisings of a people keenly sensible of their oppression, and willing to sacrifice life in

2. Ira Berlin (ed.), "After Nat Turner: A Letter from the North," *Journal of Negro History*, LV (1970), 145–51.
3. Henry Highland Garnet, "An Address to the Slaves of the United States," in Carter G. Woodson (ed.), *Negro Orators and Their Orations* (Washington, D.C., 1925), 157; James Redpath, *The Roving Editor; Or, Talks with Slaves in the Southern States* (New York, 1859), 256–57.

their endeavor to throw it off and substitute liberty."[4] Blacks wanted their freedom peacefully if possible, but they were not prepared to sacrifice it simply for the sake of order. Haiti showed the black community that freedom would be forthcoming, but only if they took an active part in their liberation even as they chose not to incite insurrection.

Except for these notable exceptions, then, the majority of black and white abolitionist allies did not advocate violence as a solution to the problem of slavery in American culture. They shunned violence because they thought it impractical: the federal and state governments were too strong; slaveholders were too well entrenched politically and socially; color prejudice, even in the North, was too widespread; and the ratio of blacks to whites was too small for abolitionists to hope for the sort of cataclysmic occurrences that brought an end to slavery in St. Domingue. Slave culture in the South was quite different from that in the West Indies. Generations of blacks had been born to slavery and the South, and the many hidden passages for upward mobility within the slave ranks did not foster cohesion. In fact, blacks often informed their white masters or others of an impending scheme, usually in order to spare a favorite or kindly white acquaintance. The lack of successful large-scale revolts in the American South did not in any way blunt the potential threat of one, which served to keep whites always on edge. The image of a slumbering volcano indicates slavery's place in the antebellum mind: there did not have to be an eruption for the villagers living nearby to realize that at any time death and destruction could suddenly be their lot. And many free blacks in the North were reluctant to risk those few privileges that they did enjoy; nor did they want to alienate their white abolitionist allies. Many were deeply religious and felt that violence was morally wrong, and those who were politically active were not anxious to promote an insurrection whose results would be unpredictable at best. Political and moral suasion seemed their best strategy—civil "obedience" was their primary weapon against the slave system. Many free blacks of the North were determined to represent citizenship as best they could in spite of their precarious position even in the free states.

Whites who were antislavery approached emancipation and abo-

4. *Weekly Afro-American*, January 21, 1860.

lition much more gingerly than did blacks. In the American revolutionary era, the northern states abolished slavery without much fuss. The ideology of the time militated against holding slaves, and the institution was not significant economically or socially there. Opposition to slavery in the South centered in the late eighteenth century upon the Quaker campaign for gradual emancipation—it was quiet and, while earnest, not particularly engaging. This campaign was thwarted by the news of the "race war" in St. Domingue and by the development of the cotton economy. By 1820, slavery had positive and negative reasons to be the mainstay of southern agricultural production. New lands in the lower South, new markets in England, and the cotton gin spurred would-be planters to migrate from the upper South to the areas opened up by Andrew Jackson and others who drove the Indians westward. The deeds of Toussaint Louverture and the Haitians after him represented the negative reasons, since many Americans assumed that the misguided attempt to emancipate slaves not ready for freedom caused the carnage in St. Domingue. Liberals in the upper South found it difficult to maintain their hope in gradual, peaceful abolition after Dessalines's massacres. Until that time, Virginians led the nation in emancipating slaves: there were some ten thousand manumissions during the 1780s thanks to a policy established in 1782. This law was repealed in the 1790s during the struggle for St. Domingue because Virginia feared wholesale emancipation and having freed blacks among the residents.[5] With this shift in southern thinking about slavery, black abolitionists of the North had increasingly to motivate their white colleagues to get them actively involved in the antislavery movement. And the white abolitionists became more strident, since the South now seemed even less willing to listen. Although more aggressive, white abolitionists were reluctant to use St. Domingue as a model for slaves to follow in casting off the yoke. They did, however, warn white southerners, not the slaves, that the inevitable result of slavery would be a holocaust. White abolitionists were careful not to suggest that they themselves advocated catastrophe. Rather, black, and very often divine, retribution would eventually destroy the South should slavery continue. White abolitionists thought

5. Stephen Weeks, "Anti-slavery Sentiment in the South," *Publications of the Southern Historical Association*, II (1898), 88–89; David Robinson, *The Structure of Slavery in American Politics* (New York, 1971), 49–51.

slaves should not revolt; if blacks did, however, they were within their rights. In an early journal article entitled "Rights of Black Men" (1791), northern readers were reminded that "freedom did not depend upon color," the implication being that even slaves should pursue their freedom by any means at their disposal. If St. Domingue proved anything, white abolitionists said over and over again, it was that time was running out. For instance, Quaker merchant Thomas P. Cope claimed that "so long as seven hundred thousand fellow beings are held in chains in these United States, their cruel and hardened oppressors may look for plots, conspiracies, and insurrections—nature revolts at the idea of bondage." Commenting on the discovery of Gabriel's plot in 1880, Cope noted that he could see in the slaves' discontent "a gathering storm which may one day burst forth and overwhelm the oppressor and the oppressed in one general undistinguished ruin." Cope also mentioned rumors of an insurrection near Charleston said to have been instigated by some "Frenchmen," an allusion to what was happening in St. Domingue.[6]

In 1801, Thomas Branagan wrote about slaves' vengeance and warned unsuspecting Americans that "the fate of St. Domingo is Fresh" in blacks' minds. In solemn warning he observed that the "tragical, the bloody scene, which has recently been acted in that unhappy island, should ever be re-acted among us, God forbid. I do not prophecy; I caution and warn." But Africans were certainly capable of revenge, Branagan said, as the bloody history of St. Domingue illustrated.[7]

According to Theodore Dwight, one of the Connecticut Wits and brother of clergyman Timothy Dwight, the situation in St. Domingue was simple to explain: "A succession of unjust and contradictory measures . . . at length highly exasperated the negroes, and roused their spirits to unanimity and fanaticism. Seized by the phrenzy of oppressed human nature, they suddenly awoke from the lethargy of slavery, attacked their tyrannical masters, spread desolation and blood over the face of the colony." Dwight

6. J. P. Martin, "Rights of Black Men," *American Museum, or Universal Magazine*, XII (1792), 299–300; Thomas P. Cope Diary, I (1800–1801), September 22 (MS in Quaker Collection, James P. Magill Library, Haverford College, Haverford, Pa.).
7. Thomas Branagan, *A Preliminary Essay on the Oppression of the Exiled Sons of Africa* . . . (Philadelphia, 1801), 218–19.

applauded blacks for establishing themselves on the "firm pillars of freedom and independence," and warned southerners that they had "the utmost reason to dread the effects of insurrection."[8] Antislavery spokesmen thus countered southern assertions that St. Domingue proved slavery's necessity. Catastrophe, they said, resulted primarily from the "haughtiness and imprudence of the white planters" and from the "remembrance of the former barbarity of masters." One pamphleteer succinctly captured the argument that slavery would cause the South's violent downfall: the South was "a nursery of vice," he said, that God and the slaves themselves would destroy.[9]

Black editors were even more specific: "The day will come when . . . the horrors of St. Domingo will be enacted before your eyes.[10] In his *Appeal*, David Walker stated that not only was the black man angry, but the white man taught him and still teaches him to be so. Walker played off the southern interpretation of St. Domingue as well: "Color," he said, "will root some . . . [of you] out of the very face of the earth." Walker's stance found expression elsewhere, as in the following poem published in the *Liberator*, the foremost abolitionist newspaper:

> Behold! oh, horror—Hayti's bloody strand!
> Mark! how the lesson erst by white man given,
> Now vainly taught the barbarous sable band,
> To claim the birthright held alone from heaven.

The *Liberator* reflected Walker's influence when William Lloyd Garrison wrote: "The name of Walker alone is a terror in the south, and it is probable there are or will be more men like him.

8. Theodore Dwight, *An Oration Spoken Before the Connecticut Society, for the Promotion of Freedom and the Relief of Persons Unlawfully Holden in Bondage* (Hartford, Conn., 1794), 18–19. Also see Thomas Branagan, *Serious Remonstratives Addressed to the Citizens of the Northern States . . . With a Simplified Plan for Colonizing the Free Negroes* (Philadelphia, 1805); George Ritter, *A Speech . . . Called the Proficuous Judicatory; Concerning the Advantages That Would Be Derived from the Total Abolition of Slavery . . .* (Philadelphia, 1802), 10–11; and "Humanitas," *Reflections on Slavery; With Recent Evidence of Its Inhumanity . . .* (Philadelphia, 1803), 7–17.

9. Jesse Torrey, *A Portraiture of Domestic Slavery in the United States and a Project of a Colonial Asylum for Free Persons of Color* (Philadelphia, 1817), 22–23; Morris Birkbeck, *An Appeal to the People of Illinois on the Question of a Convention* (Shawneetown, Ill., 1823), 12, 18.

10. *Freedom's Journal*, October 17, 1828. The same notion appeared in an antislavery song (see W. W. Brown [ed.], *Anti-Slavery Harp* [Boston, 1849], 6).

Negroes have shown their mental capacity in St. Domingo. . . .
That example of bloodshed and misery is before the eyes of our
slaves; that tragedy . . . will soon be enacted on an American stage
. . . unless something is speedily done to prevent it." He warned
that the retribution predicted in the Bible was at hand. Garrison
in a later editorial asked, "What kindled the fire of Seventy-Six?
Oppression! What created the bloody scenes of St. Domingo? Oppression! . . . What has infuriated the southern slaves? OPPRES-
SION!!" Mentioning Nat Turner, and relying heavily upon the image of the horrors of St. Domingue, Garrison ended his philippic,
saying that "the blood of millions of her sons cries aloud for re-
dress. IMMEDIATE EMANCIPATION can alone save her from the vengeance of Heaven, and cancel the debt of ages."[11]

In one of his fieriest Fourth of July orations, Garrison, who acknowledged that over the years black militants had influenced
him, lectured on "the danger of insurrection" caused by the evil of
slavery. Using commonplaces of antebellum abolitionist rhetoric,
the firebrand predicted that without justice being done quickly, "a
bloody catastrophe" would come that would "blot out the memory of the scenes of St. Domingo." He continued: "They are the
premonitory rumblings of a great earthquake—the lava tokens of
a heaving volcano!" Garrison's message was consistent and clear:
"Unless we abolish slavery in our country . . . we must expect
soon to be involved in the horrors of a servile insurrection." Put
into verse, it was the same:

> Though distant be the hour, yet come it must—
> Oh! hasten it, in mercy, righteous Heaven!
> When Afric's sons, uprising from the dust
> Shall stand erect—their galling fetters riven
> When from his throne Oppression shall be driven
>
> . . . .
>
> Wo if it come with storm, and blood, and fire
> When midnight darkness veils the earth and sky:
> Wo to the innocent babe—the guilty sire!
> Mother and daughter—friends of kindred tie
> Stranger and citizen alike shall die!
> Red handed slaughter his revenge shall feed,

11. Aptheker, *One Continual Cry*, 83; *Liberator*, October 29, May 14, October
15, 1831, April 14, 1832. Also see *Liberator*, September 3, December 3, 1831, January 7, February 18, April 14, 1832, and April 13, 1833; and Walter Merrill (ed.), *I
Will Be Heard: The Letters of William L. Garrison* (2 vols.; Cambridge, Mass.,
1971), I, 135.

And havoc yell his ominous death-cry
And wild Despair in vain for mercy plead
While hell itself shall shrink, and sicken the deed!
Thou who avengest blood! long suffering Lord!
My guilty country from destruction save![12]

Angelina Grimké tried to convince southern women that as protectors of the home they could contribute a great deal toward the security of their society by persuading their menfolk to rid themselves of their troublesome property. A southerner herself, Grimké argued against the popular proslavery notion that emancipation would mean a race war, as it had in St. Domingue: "Perhaps you have feared the consequences of immediate Emancipation, and been frightened by all those dreadful prophecies of rebellion, bloodshed and murder, which have been uttered. . . . Slavery may produce these horrible scenes if it is continued five years longer, but emancipation never will."[13] Thus she argued, as was the abolitionist claim, that slavery, and France's attempt to reinstate it, caused the bloodshed in St. Domingue. This assessment was more accurate than was the proslavery view in which only slaves were on the rampage. The French resisted freeing the slaves, retaliated when they could, and tried to reinstate slavery once it was abolished. They also were engaged in a civil war that precipitously armed and used the blacks against one another.

Black abolitionists and their allies became increasingly aggressive and their warnings more strident during the late 1830s. The Reverend Paul Quinn, an abolitionist traveling throughout the western states, reacted to the rumor that South Carolina had reopened its slave trade: "The Africans are as capable of gratitude and revenge as any other people. . . . The fate of St. Domingo is fresh on their minds, as well as in all our memories and . . . will provide a solemn warning to you."[14] These statements seemed to address directly the proslavery image of slaves as happy children. The southern "plantation myth" had no place for vengeful characters, but it was hardly accurate—as free blacks in the North repeatedly reminded America.

12. William L. Garrison, *An Address Delivered in Marlboro Chapel, Boston, July 4, 1838* (Boston, 1838), 22, 28, 37, 47–48.
13. A. E. Grimké, "An Appeal to the Christian Women of the South," *Anti-Slavery Examiner*, I (September, 1836).
14. Paul Quinn, *The Origins, Horrors, and Results of Slavery, Faithfully and Minutely Described* . . . (Pittsburgh, 1834).

William Wells Brown's lectures began boldly and reflected his growing impatience in the late antebellum period: "Hereditary bondsmen! Know ye not who would be free, themselves must strike the blow?" After a long discussion of the rebellion in St. Domingue, and the role of black leaders, Brown evoked a comparison: "Who knows but that a Toussaint, a Christophe, a Rigaud, a Clervoux, and a Dessalines, may some day appear in the Southern States of this Union? That they are there, no one will doubt. That their souls are thirsting for liberty, all will admit." In closing, Brown warned: "The exasperated genius of Africa would arise from the depths of the ocean, and show its threatening form; and war against the tyrants would be the rallying cry."[15] These oft-repeated charges left no doubt that the slaveholder, not the slave, would be responsible for the carnage that would surely come. The volcano was due to erupt.

The abolitionists sought to reassure the South that race war was not a foregone conclusion of emancipation. Focusing on St. Domingue, one abolitionist said that in the attempt "to reduce the blacks again to slavery, a civil war commenced which ended only with the complete extermination of the whites."[16] Garrison tried to reassure southerners that whites and blacks could live together in harmony: in St. Domingue, he said, half a million slaves "were liberated in a day, without preparation, or even warning and their transition from bondage to freedom was accomplished with safety and ease." Another abolitionist assured southern skeptics that "it was injustice, outrage, cruelty, that excited the passions, and impel men to retaliation—not concession."[17]

15. William Wells Brown, *St. Domingo: Its Revolution and Its Patriots* (Boston, 1855), 3, 32. Also see *Annals of Congress*, 8th Cong., 1st Sess., 1069, for the idea that blacks thirst for liberty. This notion countered the southern argument that blacks did not innately desire to be free and did not have any "natural" rights.

16. *Liberator*, April 14, May 5, 1832. For additional examples, see Lydia M. Child, *The Right Way, the Safe Way* (New York, 1836), 86–88. Child went to great lengths to prove that the French were the butcherous villains in the struggle for St. Domingue (Lydia M. Child, *An Appeal in Favor of That Class of Americans Called Africans* [New York, 1836], 24, 58. Gerda Lerner, *The Grimké Sisters from South Carolina: Rebels Against Slavery* (Boston, 1967), 140–41.

17. *Liberator*, April 14, May 5, 1832; William Jay, "Inquiry into the Character and Tendency of the American Colonization and American Anti-Slavery Societies," in *Miscellaneous Writings of Slavery* (Boston, 1853), 171–85; Theodore Sedgwick, *The Practicability of the Abolition of Slavery: A Lecture* (New York, 1831), 40–41.

Abolitionist appeals were not effective in convincing or reassuring southerners who lived in the midst of what they thought was a threatening population. Both sections of the country were convinced that their interpretation of history was correct. Abolitionist warnings about the impending holocaust only exacerbated southern fears, and they became more intolerant of the opposing viewpoint. The schism over the history and course of slavery in the New World is one reason why southerners began to question their place in the Union.

At the same time that abolitionists were warning the South, free blacks and their allies were clearly proud of the history of the former French colony. Like southerners, the abolitionists tended to use St. Domingue in one sense and the history of Haiti in quite another. If St. Domingue was a portent of events should slavery continue, the Republic of Haiti was a source of racial pride that enabled abolitionists to counter the argument that blacks were inferior and incapable of being citizens. The overthrow of a white slave regime and the self-government of Haiti gave American blacks a much-needed psychological boost in their struggle for recognition. With few heroes to emulate and fewer deeds to extol, they took Haiti as a wellspring of pride. From that source and others, black nationalism and self-help grew and became fully developed in the years after the Civil War.[18]

If anything, Haiti proved to blacks that slavery was doomed and that they would eventually uplift themselves. Shortly after the beginning of the insurrection in St. Domingue, a black Methodist preacher, Prince Hall, reminded his impatient brethren in a Masonic lodge in Massachusetts that the slaves there had only recently heard the "snap of the whip," yet the scene had now changed. Hall admonished them to pray for strength in their troubles, because the day of deliverance from bondage was at hand. He focused on St. Domingue: "Thus does Ethiopia stretch forth her hand from slavery to freedom and equality." James Forten, a wealthy black merchant in Philadelphia, also saw the hope and promise in Haiti, and he predicted that "their people will become a great nation." Forten thought the history of Haiti was an

18. Herbert Aptheker (ed.), *A Documentary History of the Negro People in the United States* (New York, 1968), 87.

indication that the status of blacks would change dramatically in the nineteenth century.[19]

Haiti also provided positive evidence of "negro character." Congratulating Haiti on the anniversary of its independence, one editor noted that "the proceedings of the people of Haiti . . . furnish stronger arguments in favor of the mental ability of the blacks, than ever have been or ever can be adduced by those who profess to believe in the doctrine of their inferiority." The author saw Haiti as an "asylum of oppressed virtue," both real and psychological, that spoke to the future of blacks after emancipation. In 1826, John Browne Russwurm, later a black activist and journalist, was Bowdoin's valedictorian. In the tradition of uplifting talks, Russwurm chose "The Conditions and Prospects of Hayti" as his topic. He described Haiti as the symbol of black regeneration: "Thirty-two years of their Independence so gloriously achieved have effected wonders. No longer are they the same people. They had faculties, yet were these faculties oppressed under the load of servitude and ignorance. With a countenance erect and fixed upon Heaven, they can not contemplate the works of Divine munificence. Restored to the dignity of man to society, they have acquired a new existence—their powers have been developed: a career of glory and happiness unfolds itself before them." Thus from Walker's militant *Appeal*, which showed whites that "there is an unconquerable disposition in the breasts of blacks . . . who would be cut off to a man, before they would yield to the combined forces of the whole world," to the proud college graduate, Haiti was on the minds of blacks in the 1820s and 1830s.[20] Haiti's relative political stability during this period helped initiate the first black emigration movements. The *Colored American*, for example, ran articles about Haiti both to encourage free blacks to emigrate and to praise the blacks' accomplishments. One series of articles that appeared between 1837 and 1841 were typical: they described the political situation, and discussed education, agri-

19. Prince Hall, "Pray God Give Us the Strength to Bear Up Under All Our Troubles," in William Nell, *The Colored Patriots of the American Revolution* (Boston, 1855), 64; William Loren Katz, Introduction to *Thoughts on African Colonization*, by William L. Garrison (1830; rpr. New York, 1968).

20. *Genius of Universal Emancipation*, March, 1822; Philip Foner (ed.), "John Browne Russwurm: A Document," *Journal of Negro History*, LIV (1969), 393–97; Aptheker, *One Continual Cry*, 84, 89.

culture, and cultural life. All these articles, somewhat akin to promotional travel literature, praised blacks for their ability to progress unhindered by slavery.

The same arguments were made in the late antebellum period, particularly by the Reverend J. Theodore Holly, a black clergyman who went to Haiti to live permanently. Holly published a great deal in American abolitionist newspapers about Haiti, especially its role as "the vanguard of the race . . . as the [black] Eden of America." He emphasized blacks' role in the history of the French West Indies; he pointed out that the mulattoes and the black slaves took control when the whites were hopelessly impotent during the struggle. Furthermore, he said, former slaves founded an independent republic despite almost universal white opposition, and they managed to maintain that independence. Holly was not concerned that, by some white standards, Haiti was unstable; to him it was important that the republic had survived. Northern newspapers often reported that free people of color in several United States cities celebrated the independence of Haiti, and that some of these blacks looked to the island as "their hope and future home."[21]

Not all criticism of blacks' role in American society came from southern slaveholders. Responding to the comment of white abolitionists such as Theodore Parker that blacks were too passive, physician and lawyer John S. Rock assured a Boston audience that his black brethren might well strike back against slavery. Dr. Rock, one of the first black men accredited as a lawyer before the Supreme Court, insisted that blacks were not passive or cowardly. In his speech "I Will Sink or Swim with My Race," he proudly pointed to "the history of the bloody struggles for freedom in Haiti, in which the black man whipped the French and the English and gained their independence in spite of the perfidy of that villainous First Consul."[22]

In addition to the various speeches and articles that kept the

21. J. Theodore Holly, *A Vindication of the Capacity of the Negro Race* (New Haven, 1857), 44; *Freedom's Journal*, June 1, 1827. Also see *Frederick Douglass' Paper*, April 15, 1855; James F. Clarke, *Conditions of the Free Colored People of the United States* (New York, 1853), 249; *Niles' Weekly Register*, September 3, 1825, p. 4.

22. John S. Rock, "I Will Sink or Swim with My Race," *Liberator*, March 12, 1858.

history of Haiti before the northern antislavery audiences, several book-length histories were published during the antebellum period. One of the earliest was by Prince Saunders, an American black who served as an agent for the Haitian government in London and later emigrated to Haiti. *Haytian Papers* was intended to bolster Haiti's image for prospective emigrants and for a skeptical white world. Saunders' purpose was to "give people . . . correct information . . . of the enlightened system of policy, the pacific spirit, the altogether domestic views, and liberal principles of the government, and to . . . evince the ameliorated and much improved condition of all classes of society in that new and truly interesting Empire." Saunders chose to publish laws and proclamations, hoping that readers would see how enlightened was the constitutional monarchy of Henri Christophe, the black general and Toussaint's former lieutenant who ruled the northern portion of the island. No doubt the British agreed with Saunders that the "greatest happiness of a nation is that of possessing a wise and valiant King," but the platitude would hardly change Americans' hostility to Haiti and monarchy. Saunders' work unintentionally revealed a major problem, the conflict between the blacks of the north and the mulattoes who controlled the south. Saunders launched an attack on Christophe's enemies, particularly the mulatto president Alexandre Pétion, thereby virtually proving that Haiti was not a stable society. Saunders' work also revealed grand deeds, secret intrigues, and strategic considerations within the ruling class that showed to blacks elsewhere that the Haitians were involved in the same politics of power as whites were. His history was among the first works that did not stress blacks' African background, tribal practices, and some form of pagan savagery. Rather, it was a book about European-style polity as conducted by blacks. In the same decade a similar work appeared in the United States, *An Essay on the Causes of the Revolutions and Civil Wars of Hayti* (London, 1823), written by the Baron de Vastey, a member of King Henri Christophe's court until he fell from royal favor in 1820. Vastey's thesis was like Saunders'. He praised Christophe's rule and castigated Pétion's, and treated the early history of St. Domingue and Haiti with a decidedly anti-French bias. Ironically, both Saunders' and Vastey's works reflected racial animosity in the treatment of the conflict between the blacks and mulattoes.[23] These portrayals undoubtedly sparked little interest among American blacks for emigrating to Haiti, but they familiarized many Americans with the history of Haiti.

Because white and black abolitionists and southerners were continually using the "example of St. Domingo" or the "history of the Republic of Haiti" in their theories about slavery and freedom in the Americas, it is not surprising that numerous articles about the island appeared in antebellum journals and newspapers. To counter the slaveholders' negative views, abolitionists kept the reading public informed about freedom and national success in the black republic. This image was not confined to such partisan organs as the *Liberator* and *Frederick Douglass' Paper*. The most extensive coverage of Haiti throughout the antebellum period was in *Niles' Weekly Register*, a Baltimore magazine that reprinted articles from other sources as well as its own original pieces. An article of this period typically began with a discussion of Toussaint's rise and the events of the revolution, usually laying blame for the bloodshed on Napoleon and the French attempt to reinstate slavery. Then came details of the black nation's stability, probably to encourage both migration and commercial investment. Such an article also contained long descriptions of laws and customs and political anecdotes. After 1820, when the island was finally united under President Jean Pierre Boyer, a mulatto who ruled Haiti for twenty-five years, these articles were even more positive. All this literature stressed the accomplishments of blacks who had only recently been slaves—from the chains of slavery to the halls of government: "When we consider how short a period has elapsed since the Haytians established their independence . . . we cannot behold, without admiration, the rapid advances which they have made." This literature was aimed at both whites and blacks, showing what could be done and what was being done; it also stressed blacks' desire for freedom and the accoutrements of civilization, not bloody revenge. In Haiti, one article proudly announced, "the negro stands erect in all the dignity of man." Given where the Negro had started, the accomplishment was extraordi-

23. Prince Saunders, *Haytian Papers: A Collection of the Very Interesting Proclamations and Other Official Documents* . . . (London, 1816), vii–viii, 192. For an article on Henri Christophe as a despot, see *Niles' Weekly Register*, June 13, 1818.

nary, outdoing "the best efforts of any people in ancient or modern times."[24]

If Haiti as a black nation was the model of what could be attained by blacks free from slavery, a personal account of how one former Haitian slave exemplified the American Dream was even more appealing to American abolitionists. A memoir appeared in 1854, written by a New Englander anxious to prove that former slaves could thrive in a free society. The subject was Pierre Toussaint, a slave from St. Domingue (and apparently no relation to Toussaint Louverture), who faithfully and voluntarily followed his mistress to New York, fleeing the troubles in the colony. Toussaint became a successful hairdresser in New York City and supported his penurious white owner throughout her life. On her deathbed, she gave him his freedom. This black nineteenth-century version of the Horatio Alger story was consoling to a generation of whites who worried over the conduct of freed blacks. Pierre Toussaint was a model of decorum and loyalty, a hardworking man who accepted his lot in life, which in the end led to his being freed. The message was unmistakable: faithfulness, Christian living, hard work, and Christian resignation would eventually be rewarded. In Pierre Toussaint's obituary, his life was compared to that of Uncle Tom in Harriet Beecher Stowe's recently published novel.[25] Salvation by hard work and "knowing one's place" were logical conclusions of abolition's religious overtones and should guide the future behavior of freed blacks. The same message was later stressed by black leaders such as Booker T. Washington, whose philosophy owed a great debt to these early examples of black upward mobility through diligence and hard work. To the abolitionists of this ilk, the path to freedom was opened by good citizenship not by good swordsmanship, and former slaves were quite capable of achieving such high Christian standards, as the blacks in Haiti had demonstrated.

24. *Niles' Weekly Register*, September 3, 1825, p. 4; *Freedom's Journal*, March 16, 1827. Also see *Telescope*, August 27, 1825; *Niles' Weekly Register*, February 11, 1826, p. 384; *Liberator*, June 25, July 2, August 6, 1831; *Anti-Slavery Reporter*, June–November, 1833; *Anti-Slavery Record*, November, 1835, pp. 126–127, and March 1836, pp. 1, 7; *Colored American*, June 9, 1838; and James McCune Smith, *A Lecture on the Haytian Revolution, with a Sketch of the Character of Toussaint Louverture* (New York, 1841).

25. Hannah Farnham Lee, *Memoir of Pierre Toussaint, Born a Slave in St. Domingo* (Boston, 1854).

The inveterate champion of the significance of Haiti and the capabilities of the free black was William Wells Brown. The only subjects in his *Black Man* who did not live in the United States were Haitians, who accounted for more than 10 percent of the black heroes. The list included Toussaint Louverture, Jean Jacques Dessalines, Henri Christophe, André Rigaud, Alexandre Pétion, Jean Pierre Boyer, and Fabre Geffrard. It is possible to construct a composite of these leaders' favorable reputation among abolitionist groups in the United States. Representative is one passage from Brown's seven-page sketch of Henri Christophe: "Christophe's aims were great, and many of them good. He was not only a patron of the arts, but of industry; and it gave him pleasure to see his country recovering the ground lost in the revolution and the civil wars, and advancing in name and wealth. He promised industry . . . [and] was also the patron of education. . . . In one respect he excelled Charlemagne,—he could write his name." Brown proselytized endlessly in behalf of blacks, and he left no doubt about what he believed the history of Haiti portended: blacks would eventually control their own destiny. There were a number of blacks in the United States whose achievements were worthy of note, but only in Haiti could antislavery advocates such as Brown find blacks in key positions making decisions that affected an entire nation. American blacks were proud of the black republic and its leaders: militant Martin R. Delany named his first-born son Toussaint Louverture and another son Faustin Soulouque.[26]

White Americans' attempt in the nineteenth century to remove blacks indicated that they conceived of the New World as a white man's country. Although all whites did not support such institutions as the American Colonization Society, most undoubtedly hoped that the "Negro problem" would somehow disappear. Colonizing free blacks was one specific remedy that caught the imagination of many white Americans and some blacks as well. James G. Birney, a Kentucky antislavery leader, a gradual emancipationist who was later an immediate abolitionist, and the Liberty party candidate for president in the 1840s, reflected the view of many liberal southerners: "If the Colonization Society does not

26. William Wells Brown, *The Black Man, His Antecedents, His Genius and His Achievements* (New York, 1863), 138; W. W. Brown, *St. Domingo*; Victor Ullman, *Martin R. Delany: The Beginnings of Black Nationalism* (Boston, 1971), 50.

dissipate the horror of darkness which overhangs . . . southern society, we are undone."[27] The southerners of the upper South and border states saw the freedmen as a danger to white society, an anomaly that contradicted the southern rationale for slavery and the white rationale for white supremacy.

The idea of removing blacks from the American continent was current before the formal organization of colonization societies between 1817 and 1823. It was Thomas Jefferson who first advocated colonization in his *Notes on the State of Virginia*: he suggested that freedmen be "removed beyond the reach of mixture." Jefferson said what whites felt: get rid of an embarrassing problem by sending it away. Moderate slavery advocates and gradual emancipationists founded the American Colonization Society in 1816 to better organize the removal of free blacks and freedmen from American society. Southerners usually wanted to get rid of the troublesome Negroes, but northern antislavery advocates often supported colonization, realizing that only with the promise of removing the former slave would slave owners manumit their slaves. Jefferson and his followers first thought Haiti was the most likely spot to send blacks, but as southerners came to realize the dangers there, they sought other places. By the mid-1820s, Africa became the most popular site for colonization, though Haiti still encouraged and received some colonists. To most whites, Africa somehow represented a home for the prodigal sons, even though most American blacks had never been there. Haiti, however, was closer, but it was in some respects too close for whites looking to entirely remove the "negro problem." Sending blacks back to Africa meant not only returning them to their ancestral home but also the appealing possibilities of dispatching missionaries to the Dark Continent and of perhaps laying the groundwork for commercial ties with American merchants. The complexities of such a migration, and the response of many free blacks themselves, soon had white "philanthropists" looking for sites in the New World as well.

The earliest plan for colonizing blacks in the West Indies came in 1797. The Pennsylvania Abolitionist Society was in contact with French abolitionists of Les Amis des Noirs in Cap François.

27. Dwight Dumond (ed.), *Letters of James G. Birney* (2 vols.; New York, 1838), I, 27.

The correspondence reflected the sanguine hopes that the colony could become an exemplar for white-black relations in the New World; that is, that former white masters and freed slaves could continue producing sugar, coffee, and cotton after slavery was abolished. The Jacobin correspondent from St. Domingue described a scene of racial bliss as whites and blacks lived and worked in an integrated society run by a black general and white officials. Workers without land could earn a living on government plantations, receiving one quarter of the produce in a system of sharecropping that seems to have been part of most emancipation schemes. The writer also pointed to large tracts of unsettled land in the Spanish part of the island that would be available to black emigrants from the United States.[28] The Pennsylvania Abolitionist Society was interested, but Napoleon's attempt to regain control precluded further consideration of colonization. During the early days of Haitian independence, when Haiti was divided by civil war and France threatened to retake its former colony, American abolitionist groups and free blacks expressed little interest in emigrating to the island. The history of colonization plans was related to the level of oppression in the United States and the stability in foreign sites that could be considered suitable for emigrants.

After Boyer unified the island, Haiti was more stable and was interested in actively recruiting skilled American blacks who could contribute to the development of the country's resources. Haiti lacked a sufficiently large middle class, and the island suffered years of debilitating wars and internecine rivalries. Agricultural production and managerial skill were not sufficient to invigorate the economy. Boyer initiated a campaign to encourage American blacks to emigrate. The Haitian government ran long articles in American journals and newspapers that stressed the freedom and security that blacks would enjoy. One article, for example, stated that "no white man, of whatever nation he may be, shall ever set his foot on this territory under the title of master or planter"—a quotation from the Haitian constitution.[29] There was

28. Benjamin Giroud to [?], January 17, 1797, both in "Committee on Correspondence, 1794–1809," Pennsylvania Abolitionist Society Papers, 42–48, Pennsylvania Historical Society, Philadelphia.
29. *Niles' Weekly Register*, October 17, 1818, pp. 117–18, September 21, 1822, pp. 36–37, July 16, 1825, pp. 310–11, August 27, 1825, pp. 403–404.

a small but not insignificant migration of blacks to Haiti during this period.

Loring D. Dewey, a white agent from the American Coloniza-tion Society (ACS) and later a commercial agent in Haiti, wrote to President Boyer with specific questions about the emigration of blacks to Haiti because the ACS was pleased at the interest in American freedmen. Dewey represented the ACS as a philan-thropic agency motivated by its concern for the welfare and future of the degraded black man in the United States. Boyer promptly replied, assuring him that American blacks would be warmly wel-comed and would all be eligible for Haitian citizenship. Boyer also argued that Haiti offered a better choice for emigration for the "children of Africa" than did Africa itself. He generously offered to defray part of the costs of transporting the migrants if the ACS would pay the rest. Boyer promised that each emigrant family would receive thirty-six acres, fee simple and at no cost, if they agreed to pay future taxes on the improved land. Boyer, serious about the need for skilled migrants, sent an agent to the United States to handle the arrangements and to represent the Haitian government in any future colonization proposals. Boyer autho-rized the agent to seek out as many as six thousand prospective emigrants for the first year, certainly an indication of his vision of Haiti's future. Boyer hoped to have these productive immigrants strategically placed in groups of several hundred in areas where coffee, cotton, and tobacco were grown. He instructed his agent to "travel into the interior of the Northern States wherever you are permitted to go, and where you think your presence will deter-mine those to emigrate who are disposed, and at liberty to do so."[30] Anticipating some of the problems that his agent might en-counter, Boyer provided him with $6,000 to help indigent prospec-tive emigrants cover their costs up to $6 each (repayable in Haiti within six months of arrival). Antislavery colonizationists re-sponded with enthusiasm to Boyer's invitation and initial steps to welcome the emigrants. While some saw an opportunity to induce "masses of coloreds to withdraw from the country," others thought that "there is no place in the world, known to us at present where the colored man can have greater opportunities to acquire riches,

30. The entire correspondence was reprinted in "Correspondence Relative to the Emigration to Hayti, of the Free People of Color, of the United States . . . ," *Niles' Weekly Register*, July 3, August 7, 1824, esp. p. 28.

or will be more completely invested with the rights and privileges of civil and religious freedom, than in the Republic of Haiti."[31]

The state colonization societies were all-white, philanthropic groups usually located in areas not dependent upon slave labor, such as the western Piedmont counties of the Carolinas and Virginia or the eastern parts of Tennessee and Kentucky, or in areas where slavery was declining. These organizations saw removal as the logical extension of emancipation and as the solution to the race problem, since they were convinced that blacks and whites would not and could not live together. They were sufficiently sure of the righteousness and necessity of their cause that they declared it an "act of humanity" to remove blacks from white society in an effort to save them from race war and cultural annihilation, not to mention that removal would also benefit white society. They repeatedly reminded skeptical slave owners that gradual emancipation, removal, and colonization could be achieved without the danger of "another St. Domingo."

One of the most active state organizations was the North Carolina Manumission Society, which was dedicated to the proposition that the "human race however varied in color are Justly entitled to Freedom."[32] The society made several trips to Haiti with emigrants, and their experience characterized most of such projects, both in Haiti and in Africa. Agents invariably underestimated the logistical problems in such a significant relocation of indigent people to an unfamiliar environment. There were always contract disputes. In one case an agent and the captain of the ship engaged to transport the emigrants argued about the terms of the contract and the captain threatened to cancel the trip, even though all the emigrants had arrived. Unscrupulous ship captains often either took too many emigrants on board or carried extra cargo. Any delays in departure, no matter what the cause—arguments, bad weather, late arrivals, or cargo-loading problems—created additional expenses and later resulted in a shortage of food and water for the passengers. On one voyage the ship was so undermanned that inexperienced passengers had to fill in as sailors. Emigrants

31. *New England Farmer*, October 22, 1824; *Genius of Universal Emancipation*, May, 1830, p. 67. Also see *Freedom's Journal*, January 16, 1829.

32. The following account is taken from the North Carolina Manumission Society Papers, 78–79, 94–97, and Minutes of the North Carolina Manumission Society (1816–34), January 11, 1817 (both in Southern Historical Collection, University of North Carolina, Chapel Hill).

often had to spend the entire voyage on the exposed docks, even in bad weather. The emigrants usually arrived in Haiti or elsewhere totally debilitated, often very sick, and all at great expense. The North Carolina Manumission Society was always frustrated in its attempts to improve traveling conditions or to cut its costs. In spite of these hazards, Haitian emigration had support during Boyer's administration.

Because many whites favored African colonization and did not want the Haitian scheme to interfere with their plans, those whites who favored Haitian emigration formed a subsidiary organization, a "Society for Haiti," that cooperated with the ACS. This group established good relations with some northern black societies, led by Samuel Cornish of the Colored Presbyterian Church in New York City. In October, 1824, Benjamin Lundy's abolitionist newspaper the *Genius of Universal Emancipation* carried commercial articles on the merits of providing skilled American blacks for the Haitian economy, a response to the program initiated by President Boyer. Lundy opened an emigration office in Baltimore from which he sent eighty-five former slaves to freedom in Haiti. *Niles' Weekly Register* in its editorials and articles spoke to the advantages of Haitian emigration, which would "accelerate the annihilation of slavery [and] . . . arrest the progress of corruption which now preys upon [Haiti] . . . [and] it will forever establish its happiness, its glory and its independence."[33]

The Maryland State Colonization Society wrote Boyer, reiterating its desire to seek suitable sites, for the "colored race can never, whilst among us, attain that moral and intellectual worth or . . . happiness and importance, for which . . . Divine Providence has equally designed them." Ironically, the history of Haiti had contributed to this conclusion, and Haiti was to solve the problem. Colonization proceeded: the cost of transporting blacks was $15 each to the Caribbean and more than $30 to Africa. Other colonizationists thought the easy life in the tropics was best for lazy individuals, especially on an island with an established government. If there was any doubt about their views, some called African colonization a failure because "Negroes are not good pioneers nor are they well calculated for missionaries."[34]

33. *Niles' Weekly Register*, September 11, 1824, January 8, 1825.
34. Stage Managers Book, April 10, 1832, in Maryland State Colonization Society Papers, Maryland Historical Society Baltimore; Philadelphia *Daily News*, November 22, 1860.

While the exact number of emigrants to Haiti will probably never be known, several thousand did migrate there in the 1820s. Some stayed permanently; but a significant number returned to the United States after a few years. One of the first emigrants to achieve success in Haiti was Prince Saunders, a Vermont free black who represented Haiti in London, wrote several treatises about the island, and died in 1839 as the attorney general of the black republic. At this time, other American blacks went to Haiti to witness firsthand the development of a black nation—George Vashon, for example, as a young man spent a year in Haiti. Some prominent blacks planned to go to Haiti but circumstances changed their plans—Edward J. Roye, the fifth president of Liberia, who studied French at Oberlin College with the intention of emigrating; and John Russwurm, the founder of *Freedom's Journal*. Some American blacks responded to Boyer's initiative and the state colonization societies' efforts. As one journal reported, 270 emigrants located in one area of Haiti "where land had been given to them, on which some are already at work to improve, and are much encouraged to be industrious. The mechanics seem to do excellently well in the towns, and there is every prospect that the condition of those who are sober and discreet will be greatly ameliorated, at an early date."[35] Such good news influenced several hundred others to give Haiti a chance.

One of the most energetic abolitionists to be involved with Haitian colonization was Frances Wright, a reformer, activist, and freethinking feminist. A well-to-do Scot who visited the States between 1818 and 1820, she wrote *Views of Society and Manners in America* (1821), which won her the admiration and affection of the Marquis de Lafayette, with whom she returned to America for his triumphal visit in 1824. Wright met Thomas Jefferson and James Madison, and, after being influenced by Robert D. Owen, decided to stay in America to help Owen with reform movements from his New Harmony community. Sensitive to the slaves' plight, she devised a system whereby slaves could work off their purchase price and free themselves. Wright bought eight slaves and two thousand acres in western Tennessee just north of Memphis. She

---

35. Richard Bardolph, "Social Origins of Distinguished Negroes," *Journal of Negro History*, XL (1955), 236; *Frederick Douglass' Monthly*, October, 1862. Also see Philip May, "Zephaniah Kingsley, Non-conformist, 1765–1843," *Florida Historical Quarterly*, XXIII (1945), 145–59; *Dictionary of American Biography*, XVI, 212; *Niles' Weekly Register*, March 12, 18, 28, April 12, 1825.

called her experimental community Nashoba after the Indian name for the Wolf River that ran by the property. Although ill-equipped for an arduous life of farming, Wright wanted to provide a model by which slave owners could eventually achieve gradual emancipation without sacrificing money or safety. Like many nineteenth-century utopian experiments, Nashoba suffered from exalted expectations, poor planning, lack of funds, crop failures, sickness, and improper management when she was not there to oversee the operation. Nashoba was abandoned in 1829.

Frances Wright did not abandon the blacks who had participated in her hard-pressed community. In October, 1829, this determined white woman accompanied thirty of her former slaves to Haiti to take advantage of Boyer's generous offer to resettle American blacks on farms there. She returned to the United States six months later, having seen her charges living on small agricultural plots. While in Haiti she met, and later married, a French educator who assisted her during the difficult early months there. An abolitionist all her life, Wright was never again involved in specific experiments to uplift slaves, but her commitment to antislavery was genuine, if more abstract, after the failure of Nashoba and the relocation of her freedmen. Other individuals helped their former slaves settle in Haiti as well. One generous Virginia slave owner went to Baltimore to make arrangements to send his eighty-eight slaves to the black republic, and he provided them with $130 worth of farm implements with which to carve out their new lives in the tropics.[36]

By the 1840s, antislavery leaders estimated that from seven thousand to ten thousand American blacks had migrated to Haiti, though it was not known how many survived or stayed there more than a short time.[37] After the initial enthusiasm for Boyer's initiative waned, large numbers of free blacks who had voluntarily gone to Haiti returned to the United States, disillusioned with conditions in the Caribbean. The Haitian government only ceded

36. *Genius of Universal Emancipation*, April, 1830, p. 6; *Liberator*, January 7, 1832; *Niles' Weekly Register*, July 2, 1825; Celia Morris, "Frances Wright," *Ms. Magazine*, III (1974), 15–24; Celia M. Eckhardt, *Fanny Wright: Rebel in America* (Cambridge, Mass., 1984); J. Treadwell Davis, "Nashoba: Frances Wright's Experiment in Self-Emancipation,: *Southern Quarterly*, XI (October, 1972).

37. *Liberator*, September 1, 1843. Some American blacks jumped ship in Haiti (see U.S. Department of State, Consular Despatches . . . Aux Cayes, July 30, 1821, May 29, 1838).

land to an emigrant after improvements were made, and a new-comer was not always prepared to do that right away. Many American emigrants could not deal with the primitive conditions, and the language barrier was a significant drawback. Many apparently suffered culture shock. In addition, the Haitian government found it necessary to suspend subsidized passage to the island, so that those who went initially began to feel isolated and lonely.

One of the problems with the colonization movement was that it required at least the tacit support of both slave owners and northern free blacks. While Haitian colonization had its support-ers, most of those concerned with using colonization to solve the race question were not particularly enthusiastic about Haitian emigration. Slave owners, especially in the lower South, were op-posed because they were not interested in bolstering a black re-public so near their southern shore. During the 1850s the south-ern call for a Caribbean empire blunted any thought of helping Haiti. In response to a call by a free black group in Chicago for emigration, for instance, the New Orleans *Commercial Bulletin* published a disclaimer stating that blacks would be foolish to mi-grate to an island that was so deplorable, where marriage was un-known and "free love . . . reigns supreme." The editor used the occasion of the National Negro Convention meeting in Chicago to ask why free blacks of the North were thinking of emigration if they were so happy there. He concluded that southern blacks were better off than those in the North, and if blacks wanted to leave American society, they should go back to Africa, presumably be-cause it was farther away and would not hinder the South's plan for a Caribbean empire. In another incident, the citizens of Mo-bile, Alabama, were alerted that an emigration agent was trying to recruit blacks for Haiti. They had the sheriff run them off—such solicitations of free blacks were against Alabama statutes.[38]

The American government was no less reluctant than were most slave owners to become involved officially with colonization schemes in Haiti, particularly since many key government figures at this time were either southerners or southern sympathizers. American commercial agent Ralph Higinbothom wrote to Presi-dent Martin Van Buren, complaining that he received no support

38. New Orleans *Commercial Bulletin*, May 6, 1859; "A Fresh Catalogue of Southern Outrages Upon Northern Citizens," *Anti-Slavery Tracts*, no. 14 (New York, 1860), 22.

whatsoever from the secretary of state, a Georgia Democrat named John Forsyth, who had pointedly instructed Higinbothom to quit meddling with the issue of black emigration to the island. Higinbothom's enthusiasm for Haitian emigration and colonization was founded on his belief that there would be great commercial opportunities for American merchants. This interpretation was consistent with that of all the commercial agents in Haiti in the antebellum period. And in such matters, the southern viewpoint prevailed, until the administration of Abraham Lincoln and the official recognition of Haiti.[39]

Enough blacks did express an interest in Haiti or actually migrated there for the Baptist General Convention of the United States to assign a missionary for the dispersed fellowship of American black immigrants in 1835. The Reverend William C. Monroe of Detroit was dispatched, and he preached his first sermon in Port-au-Prince "within the sound of the Marshal Drum" and lectured at night "within the sound of the Congo Drum." Monroe stayed in Haiti three years, long enough to build a small church in the capital city before returning to the United States after the death of his wife. At about the same time, William L. Garrison was consoling an acquaintance who was about to journey to Haiti but was apprehensive about speaking neither French nor the native patois. Garrison assured him that he would be fine—"thousands of American colored residents . . . scattered all over the island" precluded his having to speak a foreign language. An American authority on Haiti, having lived there thirteen years and having advocated Haitian emigration, estimated that of the thirteen thousand American blacks who came to the island by the mid-1830s, only a handful who could learn the language and adapt to Haitian ways stayed permanently. Giving credence to the notion of cultural foundations common to the Caribbean and the American lower South, Benjamin Hunt noted that those blacks who came to Haiti from the Deep South, especially Louisiana, fared better than did those from other areas. Still, Hunt envisioned Haiti as the best chance for the free black man, a "black tropics" that had been humanized if not civilized." Thus the initial stage of significant American black emigration to Haiti ended inconclusively. Haiti was evidently not going to be the long-term

39. U.S. State Department, Consular Despatches . . . Aux Cayes, April 1, 1839.

solution to the race problem in the United States, though it did offer some hardy souls the chance to live in a black nation. Regardless of its suitability or success as a colonization site, abolitionists, white and black, were still interested in Haiti because they assumed that a stable black republic in the New World would aid the cause and "hasten the day when emancipation shall be gloriously realized in the United States." With this in mind, the Massachusetts Anti-Slavery Society sent an official representative to Haiti in 1842 to gather information about the state of affairs and the prospects for further colonization. Many American abolitionists were delighted in the spring of that year when President Boyer, who had become too autocratic and disinterested in American colonization to suit them, was overthrown in a bloodless coup.[40]

Rising emotions between the North and South over slavery during the 1850s, and blacks not achieving their goals within the American system, caused many free blacks of the North to conclude that emancipation and equality would be possible only through their own efforts and away from whites. This emerging black nationalism was a result of their deteriorating position in American society and coincided with the rise of southern nationalism in the slaveholding South. Blacks witnessed events that threatened their lives as well as their status: the Fugitive Slave Law, passed as part of the Compromise of 1850, allowed slave owners to claim suspected runaways in northern states without judicial hearings, and in the Dred Scott decision the Supreme Court ruled that blacks were not citizens and were thus not entitled to traditional constitutional protections. These events, and many lesser and more personal episodes of discrimination, were unsettling and contributed to the rise of a black separatist ideology, particularly among the younger generation of free blacks such as Martin R. Delany, Henry H. Garnet, and J. Theodore Holly. They believed in zealous advocacy of all things black, militant exclusion of whites from any control over their organizations and

40. Monroe quoted in Floyd J. Miller, *The Search for a Black Nationality: Black Colonization and Immigration, 1787–1863* (Urbana, 1975), 147; Louis Ruchames (ed.), *The Letters of William L. Garrison: A House Divided Against Itself* (4 vols.; Boston, 1980), II, 146–47, III, 48–49; *Liberator*, April 28, 1843; Benjamin Hunt, *Remarks on Hayti as a Place of Settlement for Afric-Americans . . .* (Philadelphia, 1860), 11, 14, 20.

their destinies, and the establishment of a black nation that would safeguard the rights of all blacks in the New World. Haiti, one of their guiding lights, was one of the places chosen for black emigration after they founded the Negro Emigration movement. Unlike white attempts at colonization, black emigration was to be black sponsored and dedicated to building black solidarity. These men explored and publicized sites in western Canada, the tropics, and West Africa.

J. Theodore Holly was an avowed advocate of black nationalism who sincerely believed that Haiti as a black republic could help elevate blacks in the New World. As pastor of the Protestant Episcopal church in New Haven, Connecticut, Holly emphasized the religious potential of the neglected black nation. He thought that if Haiti was to be the location for black regeneration, sensible emigration by American blacks to convert the natives could build a strong, respected black Christian nation. To gain firsthand knowledge, Holly made the first of several trips to Haiti in 1855, and reported his findings to the National Emigration Convention in Chatham, Ontario, the following year.

Upon his arrival in Haiti, Holly revealed what he considered his private mission: he was "now about entering on a soil that I hope will be the field of my future labors and usefulness in being instrumental in bringing souls into the truefold of Christ."[41] Black nationalism was fused with black messianism. Holly was enthusiastic about establishing a successful mission in Haiti, as his reports to his church superiors and his emigrationist colleagues indicate. Perhaps a little overenthusiastic, Holly even suggested that the emperor Faustin was secretly in favor of Protestantism and that Protestant clergy enjoyed more privileges than did their Roman Catholic counterparts. As for the natives, Holly declared that "the people here are docile and will go to hear Protestant ministers, and will read the Bible." Holly's 1855 report described the various Protestant sects in Haiti, often revealing his own biases as an American missionary. The Wesleyan Methodists, in Haiti since 1816, had been under the guidance of an American pastor, M. B.

41. J. Theodore Holly to [?], August 1, 1855, in Domestic and Foreign Missionary Society Papers: The Haitian Papers, Archives and Historical Collections of the Episcopal Church, Austin, Texas (hereinafter cited as Holly Papers). Also see David M. Dean, "James Theodore Holly, 1829–1912" (Ph.D. dissertation, University of Texas, 1972); and Dean, *Defender of the Race* (Boston, 1978).

Bird, since 1843. Their complex included a stone chapel, a free high school (where English presumably was taught), a rectory, and several other buildings. They were the most successful non-Catholic group in Haiti, and Reverend Bird was interested in additional Protestant activity, reported Holly. The American Methodists, primarily former immigrants and their families, had come to Haiti under the auspices of Boyer's recruitment program. The membership numbered one hundred; about twice that many worshipers attended Sunday services, which were conducted in English. The Methodists were respected in the community because of their American background, and they too were receptive to Holly's proposals. The American Baptists were a new congregation with only thirty members (predominantly native converts).[42]

Holly's report seemed to be written to convince skeptical clerics at home that Haiti was fertile ground for Episcopal missionary efforts. He predicted that a mission would be successful in part because of the Episcopal liturgy: Haitians, he said, loved a show, and when he wore his clerical robes in the streets of the city he was greeted with respect, whereas other Protestant sects were scorned for their secular dress. Haiti seemed to him anticlerical and dissatisfied with the weak Catholic church. Since Haitians did not understand or like the Protestant notions of adult baptism and of revivals, he surmised that the Episcopal church would exactly fill the void between the two extremes. Haitian men also disliked the confessional and were strongly Masonic, according to Holly. For good measure, Holly enclosed the observations of a native Haitian, Judge Emile de Balletée, that were in agreement with his own.

Holly obviously saw this opportunity as his life's work; he continued his campaign to establish a mission in Haiti after his return to the States. A radical change in the Haitian government at that time aided his cause—the more liberal president Fabre Geffrard replaced Emperor Faustin. Holly reminded his superiors that

42. "Report of 1855," in Holly Papers. Rev. Richard Allen was interested in missions to Haiti in the 1820s and 1830s at the time of the Boyer emigration scheme. See Carol V. R. George, *Segregated Sabbaths: Richard Allen and the Rise of Independent Black Churches* (New York, 1973), 91, 103, 118–21, 152; Benjamin Lundy, *The Life and Opinions of Benjamin Lundy, Including . . . a Notice of the Revolution in Haiti* (Philadelphia, 1847), 194. Additional material on the Baptists in Haiti can be found in letters of November 19, December 23, 1846, Phelps Family Papers, Boston Public Library.

American black emigration to the island had recently increased, and that these newcomers offered the best foundation on which to build a congregation. Holly reported that 200 blacks had sailed from New Orleans in May, 1859, followed by another 176 in June, and 81 more in January of 1860. In addition, blacks in Washington, D.C., Florida, and his own area of New Haven expressed a desire to emigrate to Haiti. Holly said that the Baptists had recently sent a new minister from the black refugee community in Canada to Haiti, and that the Geffrard administration was, after seventy-five years, going to reach an accord with the Vatican. This time Holly's corroboration came from the Haitian consul in Boston, Benjamin C. Clark, who wrote a letter to Holly's superiors on the desirability of an Episcopal mission.

Holly finally obtained permission to establish an Episcopal mission in Haiti, and on the eve of the Civil War in 1861, he moved his family permanently to the island. On Trinity Sunday, 1861, Holly held the first Episcopal service in Haiti, and his Trinity Church was named in memory of that event. The black minister suffered the same adjustment period as did most of the new American immigrants. During his first year, fever caused the death of his wife and two children. Yet the determined pastor never gave up. He continued to advocate his mission there, and he pronounced the political regeneration of the black republic under President Geffrard, in the same way that he proposed the spiritual regeneration of the black republic under J. T. Holly. Holly started modestly, with forty-six communicants and twenty-six confirmations, but he soon had a large congregation and six Haitian parishioners studying at the Mission Home in Philadelphia. Holly was not unmindful of what this work would do for his career. His acquaintance with Haitians and American emigrants in Haiti, his personal dedication to the mission, and his success in founding his Trinity Church finally received recognition when, in 1874, he was ordained bishop of Haiti, the first black bishop in the Protestant Episcopal church.[43]

Holly did not accomplish his lofty goal—Haiti did not become the powerful guardian of blacks' political or spiritual rights in the Americas. His church did become the focal point for Protestan-

43. "Report," and Holly to Rev. S. D. Denison, March 19, 1860, both in Holly Papers; *The Spirit of Missions . . . of the Protestant Episcopal Church* (New York, 1867), 53.

tism in Haiti and for those Americans who came to the island. Trinity Church in Port-au-Prince still plays a vital role and is involved in the preservation of Haitian folk culture. Unlike those black emigrants who participated in the white-influenced colonization schemes, particularly to Liberia, Holly, his descendants, and his parishioners took on native ways and were assimilated into Haitian culture after several generations. Because of education and connections, his family was quite successful: several sons became lawyers, doctors, or statesmen. One son followed his pioneering father into the Episcopal ministry. Other of his descendants have returned to the United States and have maintained filial links between the two countries, and the large family is interchangeably Haitian and American.[44] Holly's life and contributions to Haiti represent what shrewd Haitian leaders saw as the primary advantage of having American blacks move to the island.

Shortly before the American Civil War, the Haitian government made another concerted effort to encourage American blacks to settle in the black republic. President Geffrard asked James Redpath to act as an agent. Redpath attacked his new position with vigor: he established the Haytian Bureau of Emigration in Boston to facilitate recruitment in the Northeast, he published *A Guide to Hayti* to promote life on the island, and he founded a newspaper, the *Pine and Palm*, to publicize his project in the antislavery community. Redpath's efforts during these troubled years in American history illustrate black nationalism as a sanguine and a futile solution to the race problem in the New World. In the first edition of the *Pine and Palm*, he advocated "the building up of Hayti, by an enlightened and organized emigration, into the rank of a great American Power. We hold this measure to be now essential for the dignity of the African race and its descendents wherever they exist. The foundation of respect is power. . . . We must create a great Negro Nation." Redpath named his journal to emphasize his belief that the temperate, colder regions of North America, the "Pines," were inextricably united with the more torrid regions of the Caribbean, the "Palms," in a common destiny. There is no

44. Trinity Church today supports a primary school and a local crafts shop. The communicants number more than fifteen thousand and the clergy is exclusively Haitian. Interview with Raphael Holly (the seventy-nine-year-old grandson of J. Theodore Holly), November 17, 1972, Port-au-Prince. Raphael had served on the city council in the capital.

indication that he realized that Thomas Jefferson, a slaveholder, was the spiritual father of that notion. With characteristic bombast, Redpath wrote that Haiti should represent "a splendid colored nationality in the tropics, destined . . . to be the England of the western continent." At various times, this self-proclaimed "ultra abolitionist" predicted that in five years he could produce a thriving colony of 100,000 American black emigrants. As a white man working for a black nation, Redpath became somewhat obsessed, as he declared to a Haitian official: "Je suis Haitien! I wish it were literally true for I have no affection for this enslaving land. If you repeal your 'ancien blanc law' (forbidding whites from being naturalized citizens of Haiti) I would like the honor of being the first white citizen." Redpath made several trips to the island before writing A Guide to Hayti (1861), the most thorough work on the subject then in print. Redpath emphasized Haiti's role in the development of black nationalism: the island was the "only one country in the Western world where the Black and the man of color are undisputed lords . . . where neither laws, nor prejudices nor historical memories, press cruelly on persons of African descent." Redpath's goal was to stimulate a strong migration that would bolster the economy and would surround the "Southern states with a cordon of free labor within which, like a scorpion girded by fire, slavery must inevitably die." This argument told American blacks that they could fight slavery even if they left the country, a point many black activists disagreed with.[45]

A Guide to Hayti included a section on the history of the "Queen of the Antilles," as well as a map and descriptions of the geography, the climate, the soil, and the flora and fauna. The Haitian constitution was given in full, and Redpath offered an analysis of the political situation. One of the most important parts was an invitation from the Haitian government to American blacks (or Indians). The secretary of state cordially said: "Come and join us; come and bring to us a contingent of power, of light, of labor; come and together with us, advance our own country in prosperity." There were promises of subsidized transportation, full protection of the laws until naturalization (in one year), and land at low rates and with reasonable repayment schedule. Redpath ad-

45. James Redpath, Pine and Palm, May 18, 1861, in Boston Public Library; James Redpath Notebook, April 29, 1861 (MS in Library of Congress), 60; James Redpath, A Guide to Hayti (Boston, 1861), 9.

mitted that knowledge of French would be necessary, but he said that one could easily learn the language in Haiti. Redpath attempted to allay the fears American Protestants might have about settling in a Catholic country: "Religious tolerance . . . [was] a prominent characteristic of the Haytian people." He pointed out that the pope was white and that Haitians felt no particular allegiance to him. To Redpath, Haitians were nominal Catholics and very "democratic" in religious matters. After dismissing many of the problems encountered by immigrants, Redpath ended with an appeal to American blacks. In no uncertain terms, he stated that Haiti offered what the black man could then acquire nowhere else in the Western world, security—in Redpath's words, Haiti offered "a home, a nationality, a future."[46]

To promote his emigration scheme, Redpath had eight agents working in Boston, the port of embarkation; nine traveling agents in Canada and the Midwest; one "special" agent; and five agents in Port-au-Prince to work with the Haitian government. His initial annual budget was $20,000, which included emigrants' passage money, agents' salaries, and supplies and equipment. He received an additional $4,500 for the publication and distribution of ten thousand copies of his *Guide to Hayti*. At one point, Redpath tried unsuccessfully to persuade the Haitian government to buy several ships and outfit them specifically for transporting emigrants.

There were, however, numerous difficulties. As it became increasingly apparent that war might break out in the fall of 1861, traveling from the Midwest and Canada to Boston was more and more chancy. More important, newspapers began to report on disenchanted emigrants returning from Haiti. Tales of mismanagement and government inefficiency circulated within the black communities. There were also reports that Santo Domingo planned to invade the unstable black republic. These rumors plagued Redpath, who wrote to the Haitian minister of the interior, detailing the adverse publicity: "The idea that Hayti is in constant Revolution; the assassination of the President's daughter; numerous Re-

46. Haitian Secretary of State, September 27, 1832, in Dumond (ed.), *Birney Letters*, I, 27; Redpath, *Guide*, 99, 175. David Walker had referred to Catholicism in Haiti as "that scourge of nations," but he was hopeful that Protestantism would soon prevail there (see Aptheker, *One Continual Cry*, 84). It had also been reported that Henri Christophe wanted to change the country from Catholicism to Protestantism (see *Niles' Weekly Register*, January 18, 1817, p. 347).

ports of Conspiracies; a furious opposition to Emigration per se; false reports of discontent among Emigrants; worse than all, a total ignorance respecting her; and a suspicion of her founded on the failure of the emigration of Boyer—and lastly, the threatening attitude of Spain, supposed to be prompted by France—all these colossal obstacles I have overthrown by zeal." The beleaguered Redpath was sure that a war with Spain would end it all. Redpath's convictions got the better of him: he suggested a "John Brown" raid from Haiti to Cuba to cause the slaves to revolt, thus diverting Spain's attention from the republic. He also told the Haitians that the Boston *Journal* was reporting that there was a plot to overthrow the government, and that caste feelings between blacks and mulattoes were creating race problems. Redpath was not discouraged, however, and he outlined the four issues on which the future of Haitian emigration from America rested: preserving peace in Haiti, keeping the emigrants together (to ease the acculturation process), immediately purchasing two emigrant vessels, and reorganizing the emigration bureau at St. Marc, the port of entry for Americans, which was reportedly graft-ridden.[47] Redpath's comments reveal some of the reasons why the various colonization schemes attempted in the nineteenth century never succeeded in transferring large numbers of American emigrants in an orderly fashion, particularly to alien regions such as Haiti and West Africa. Furthermore, this outline implies why most American blacks had no desire to leave America, even in the face of white supremacy and oppression.

War between the North and the South did not deter Redpath from continuing his emigration efforts. He argued that free workers in a strong Haiti could help defeat the "villainous Confederates" by breaking their monopoly on cotton. As he wrote to a cotton merchant in Manchester, Redpath envisioned Haiti as the supplier for English textile mills. He reminded the merchant that theirs was a common cause: "You want cotton, I want cotton growers."[48] At the same time, Redpath was trying to convince United States officials that America should recognize the Republic of Haiti. He sponsored a petition signed by Boston merchants trading with Haiti that asked the Massachusetts legislature to so advise Congress. The tireless Redpath traveled to Washington to speak with Secretary of State William Seward and

47. Redpath Notebook, July 20, 1861, p. 144.
48. *Ibid.*, April 10, 1861, pp. 16–18.

Senator Charles Sumner on the matter. Redpath was delighted to be appointed one of two "Commissioners Plenipotentiary to the United States Government for the purpose of procuring . . . formal recognition of the Independence of Hayti." He resigned from this post a month later, however, because he could not work with the other commissioner in Boston, Benjamin Clark.

In these two years, James Redpath was a diligent and loyal advocate of Haitian emigration, and perhaps seven hundred American blacks did settle in Haiti as a result of his efforts. However, events were working against him. Most blacks were not willing to undertake a major relocation to an alien environment, even in a black republic. Redpath himself became convinced that Haitian emigration was not realistic, and he resigned as agent in October, 1862. For the second time in the antebellum period Haiti demonstrated that it could capture only the imagination of American blacks who were striving for freedom and equality. They were content to see the black republic as an important symbol, not as their power base or future home. In fact, they had too much invested in America to leave willingly.

John Brown's raid on Harpers Ferry intensified the acrimony between antislavery forces and the slavery advocates. That Brown's strategy was reminiscent of St. Domingue was not lost on spokesmen for either side. In fact, Brown admitted during his trial that he read widely about militant blacks such as Toussaint Louverture and Nat Turner. To take advantage of Brown's martyrdom, James Redpath wrote and published two books in 1860 that emphasized Brown's plan to free the slaves: *The Public Life of John Brown* was a martyr's biography written by a passionate abolitionist; *Echoes of Harper's Ferry*, dedicated to President Geffrard, was replete with references and encouragements to insurrection by southern slaves with St. Domingue and Haiti as the backdrop. An inflammatory work, *Echoes* quoted Theodore Parker's declaration that slaves had the right to kill their masters to gain freedom, as well as Wendell Phillips' statement that "the lesson of the hour is insurrection."[49] The volcano seemed ready to erupt—northern

49. *Echoes of Harper's Ferry* (Boston, 1860), 45, 74–75, 81. Haitians were particularly interested in John Brown and sent financial aid to Brown's widow (see Benjamin Quarles, *Allies for Freedom: Blacks and John Brown* [New York, 1974], 146–48). One of the boulevards near the President's Palace in Port-au-Prince is named after Brown.

newspapers predicted a slave insurrection, especially after the Civil War began. The Philadelphia *Inquirer* said: "No Christian wishes for servile insurrection, but when the Federal power and the certain sympathy of Northern strength is taken away, they will certainly occur." Another newspaper foresaw "widespread negro insurrections and their attendant atrocities" because the South would be isolated from its suppliers and shortages of food would cause slaves to revolt. As late as 1862, General Benjamin Butler, the controversial Union commander of occupied New Orleans, wrote both officially and privately that it was impossible to free the Negroes "without a San Domingo." He continued: "A single whistle from me would cause every white man's throat to be cut in this city. . . . There is no doubt that an insurrection is only prevented by our bayonets."[50] Whether Butler's comments were accurate or simply self-serving, they indicate the pervasiveness of St. Domingue as the "slumbering volcano" even some fifty years after the events that gave rise to the image.

These sentiments were challenged by many moderates and non-abolitionists in the North, particularly by the Republican candidate for president, Abraham Lincoln, who tried to reassure people that Harpers Ferry and the possibility of another St. Domingue were not inspired by Free-Soilers. In an important pre-nomination speech in New York, Lincoln acknowledged that southerners associated "insurrection, blood and thunder among the slaves" with what they called "Black Republicanism." Not anxious to polarize middle-of-the-roaders, Lincoln pointed out that slave uprisings were no more common now than they had been before the Republican party was organized, and he cited Turner's Rebellion as his example. Furthermore, Lincoln declared, slave insurrections in the South were impossible because of poor communications and because secrecy simply could not be maintained by large numbers of slaves, many of whom were personally close to their masters. Lincoln dismissed Haiti as an exception, a case occurring under "peculiar circumstances." He also reminded his prestigious audience that John Brown's efforts were not successful because southern slaves refused to participate in such violent action. A shrewd politician, Lincoln knew that raising the specter of race war would

50. Philadelphia *Inquirer*, February 1, 1861; New York *World*, April 30, 1861; Butler quoted in William F. Messner, "Black Violence and White Response: Louisiana, 1862," *Journal of Southern History*, XLI (1975), 24.

cost him the support of those northerners who were neutral or who were prosouthern because of their commercial ties or latent racism.[51]

After the election of 1860 and the secession of the southern states, northern Democrats were a minority party vis-à-vis the Republicans, who were waging war against their former colleagues. As the opposition to Lincoln's wartime administration, these Democrats were vocal critics. Catering to the public's commitment to white supremacy, they accused the Republicans of putting blacks' interests before whites'. Throughout the war they charged that Lincoln and the Republicans hoped to destroy southern society and, with it, American society by turning loose blacks who would "Africanize" the country. Some Democratic leaders, among them Stephen Douglas, were publicly neutral on the slavery issue, but those in the Midwest were particularly pointed about how the war would elevate blacks. Indeed, in the Midwest, Republicans and abolitionists were equally strong in their condemnation of blacks. These groups did not often use Haiti as their primary example of what was in store for America if blacks were allowed to migrate to their areas. Nevertheless they steadfastly denounced the black race, drawing the same conclusions southerners had—blacks were inferior, they would degrade white society, they would not work without white supervision, and America would soon become a wasteland. One especially ardent Democrat, Congressman Samuel Cox of Ohio, often used Haiti to illustrate the futility of black freedom. In a lengthy speech in Congress during April, 1862, on the likely results of emancipation, he reminded his colleagues of the history and lessons of Haiti, where, he said, "her freedom is the freedom of fiends." Cox lectured on the decline of commerce, the family, and church and schools. In conclusion, he warned about "what our fate shall be if we are launched on the same stormful sea."[52]

No issue in the North during the Civil War caused more heated debate between Democrats and Republicans than did the arming of blacks to fight in the war. The Democrats were adamantly op-

51. John George Nicolay and John Hay (eds.), *The Collected Works of Abraham Lincoln* (New York, 1890), VI, 316–17.

52. Joel Silbey, *A Respectable Minority: The Democratic Party in the Civil War Era, 1860–1868* (New York, 1977), 27–36; Cox quoted in *Congressional Globe*, 37th Cong., 2nd Sess., Appendix, 243–46.

posed, since the proposal confirmed their suspicions that Lincoln wanted to destroy the South by encouraging slave insurrections there and at the same time inflict blacks on white society in the North. They thought the conflict was a "white man's war," and the Republicans were close to adopting those "Jacobin" measures that led to the destruction of St. Domingue. Republicans who were for the war and most abolitionists were in favor of such a measure because it gave blacks a chance to prove their abilities and aided the war effort as well. Blacks were themselves enthusiastic about the opportunity: black enlistments in the Union army rose dramatically, and colonization schemes and emigration efforts virtually came to an end. Those who supported black military participation in the Civil War rushed into print histories of Haitian generals and accounts of blacks in earlier wars to bolster their claims that blacks were worthy warriors. A lecture that captured the spirit of these arguments was delivered by the Reverend Jonathan C. Gibbs on the occasion of the Emancipation Proclamation. Pastor of the Colored Presbyterian Church of Philadelphia, Gibbs rejoiced that "the long night of sorrow and gloom is past . . . the black people of this country are thoroughly loyal . . . all our hopes and interests lie in the success of our government." He rejected colonization, saying that blacks were too patriotic to leave their native land, America, for Africa or the Torrid Zone. He called for the nation to "enfranchise and arm the black man," and he asked rhetorically, "Will the black man fight?" His answer was emphatic: "What has made the name of Haiti a terror to tyrants and slaveholders throughout the world, but the terrible fourteen years' fight of black men against some of the best troops of Napoleon— and the black men wiped them out. There are some fights that the world will never forget, and among them is the fight of black men for liberty on the Island of Haiti."[53]

The Emancipation Proclamation and the opportunity to fight for their freedom in the Civil War were events that greatly heartened blacks. They also took an interest in the issue of official United States recognition of both Haiti and Liberia. Although the Republic of Haiti had been an independent nation since 1804, the

53. V. Jacque Voegeli, *Free But Not Equal: The Midwest and the Negro during the Civil War* (Chicago, 1967), 97–100; Gibbs quoted in *Christian Recorder*, January 17, 1863.

southern viewpoint held sway in Congress. Some southerners, such as Federalist Thomas Pinckney of Charleston, were willing to maintain trade relations for the commercial advantages and for weakening France's hold on its former colony, but they were not anxious to give Haiti official sanction. Senator Robert Hayne of South Carolina suggested: "We never can acknowledge her independence . . . the peace and safety of a large portion of our Union forbids us to even discuss [it]." This attitude influenced American foreign policy during the 1820s when the new independent nations of Latin America wanted to hold a New World conference to decide upon joint strategies for facing any threat from the former colonial powers of Europe. Such a meeting was held, but the United States, not wanting to align itself with these new nations or encourage any new independence or revolutionary movements in the Americas, did not attend. In addition, American statesmen would have had to meet with Haitian diplomats, a prospect that, as Hayne suggested, was unthinkable. Later Thomas Hart Benton of Missouri remarked that recognition would be misunderstood as "a reward for the murder of masters and mistresses by black slaves."[54]

Abolitionists regarded nonrecognition of Haiti as not only a slight to the black community and black humanity but an insult to the United States as well. A New England antislavery audience was told in the 1840s: "Have we not a country, and is she not dishonored before all the nations, by her inconsistency and shameless violation of faith, in refusing for 30 years to acknowledge the independence of Hayti, with its 900,000 of inhabitants, and its extensive commercial relations, while she sends a vile and refuse population of only 30,000 to take . . . Texas." During the 1850s when blacks renewed their interest in emigration to Haiti and Americans followed affairs in the Caribbean, recognition again became an issue. The Reverend James W. C. Pennington called upon the government to recognize Haiti, "whose trade [with the United States] is only surpassed in value by two other nations."[55]

54. *Annals*, 5th Cong., 3rd Sess., 2766, and 19th Cong., 1st Sess., 161, 166; Thomas H. Benton, *Thirty Years' View in the U.S. Senate* (2 vols.; New York, 1854), I, 69. Also see Hans Schmidt, *The United States Occupation of Haiti, 1915–1933* (New York, 1969), 25.

55. "Address of the Boston Female Anti-Slavery Society to the Women of New England," Letter Book IV, no. 50, in Weston Papers, Boston Public Library; *Proceed-*

A group of merchants in Haiti in favor of recognition sent a petition to Congress through Benjamin Hunt, head of a commercial house. In 1853, entering Haiti were 247 vessels carrying 33,262 tons of cargo, and 233 vessels with 31,369 tons (mostly coffee) departed. At this time, Benjamin Clark wrote *A Plea for Hayti*, in which he said that Haiti was the only nation with extensive commercial ties to the United States that was not recognized officially. Clark described the particular advantages of importing Haitian coffee and mahogany. After a brief history of the island, Clark reminded his readers that Haiti was the first independent nation in the New World after the United States and that Haiti had befriended and supported Simón Bolívar.[56]

Such appeals notwithstanding, only after southern congressmen resigned from Congress did the government decide to initiate diplomatic relations with Haiti and Liberia. In his first Annual Message to Congress, in December, 1861, President Lincoln advocated American "recognition of the independence and sovereignty of Hayti and Liberia."[57] An important consideration for Lincoln was that regularized relations would be most helpful if the colonization schemes he supported should become a reality. Republican congressmen even hoped that Haiti and Liberia would help stop the illicit slave trade from Africa and the West Indies to the South. Loyal Democrats such as Garrett Davis, a Kentucky Unionist in the Senate, were opposed because the American government would have to treat black Haitian diplomats with the same courtesies extended to white statesmen, thus implying equality. Dip-

---

ings of the Colored National Convention Held in Rochester, July 6–8, 1853 (Rochester, 1853). See Howard Bell, "Negro Nationalism in the 1850's," *Journal of Negro Education*, XXXV (1966), 100–104.

56. Petition, June 13, 1854, in Benjamin Hunt Papers, Boston Public Library; B. C. Clark, *A Plea for Hayti: With a Glance at Her Relations with France, England and the United States for the Last Sixty Years* (Boston, 1853), 4–25.

57. Nicolay and Hay (eds.), *Collected Works of Lincoln*, VII, 33, VIII, 97–98. Elizur Wright published in the New York *Tribune* (May 27, 1861) a long article, "The Lesson of St. Domingo: How to Make the War Short and the Peace Righteous," in which he summarized the traditional abolitionist view of that history, namely, that blacks were going to win their freedom. The article is full of references to "black men as raw material to military power"; it states that "His [God's] law for all races is, to baptize their infant greatness in insurrection." The newspaper article also was published as a pamphlet in Boston in 1861. Lincoln and other whites were influenced by such pressure to free blacks, let them fight for their freedom, and recognize black republics as nations (see Benjamin Quarles, *Lincoln and the Negro* [New York, 1962]).

lomatic relations required a reciprocity that many Unionists were not prepared to accept. In spite of these concerns, Senator Charles Sumner of Massachusetts, a consistent worker for the rights of black Americans, guided a bill for recognition through Congress. The United States signed the treaty in November, 1864, thus ending Haiti's anomalous position in the Americas.[58]

Abraham Lincoln had made clear his solution to the race problem in the United States several years before he became president. In his debates with Stephen Douglas, he stated that "the separation of the races is the only perfect colonization." Like Jefferson and many other Americans who struggled with this issue, Lincoln was convinced that the two races could not live in harmony or equality and he supported the idea of removing blacks to Haiti. The abolition of slavery in the District of Columbia in the spring of 1861 was an occasion for Lincoln to advocate colonization and to undermine his Democratic critics who accused him of trying to mix the races. He had large sums appropriated to finance the removal of individual freedmen at $100 each to Haiti or Liberia. He also encouraged several schemes to colonize blacks in Haiti or Panama. The federal government contracted with several dubious entrepreneurs in a pilot project to take five hundred blacks to Ile-à-Vache, off the southern coast of Haiti, in hopes of developing a steady migration. This scheme suffered from poor planning, short supplies, outbreaks of disease, and white cupidity. The white overseers, as it turned out, were hoping to establish a thriving agricultural community based on sharecropping that would make them a great deal of money. More than one hundred black colonists died before Lincoln admitted failure and ordered the United States Navy to evacuate the remaining blacks from the island. American blacks needed no such demonstration that colonization was not the answer to the problem of race relations in America. Their faith in the United States and their hostility to colonization helped cause the demise of such schemes. In the words of Frederick Douglass, "We are Americans, speaking the same language, adopting the same customs, holding the same general opinions . . . and shall rise and fall with Americans. . . . I hold that all schemes of wholesale emigration tend to awaken and keep alive and confirm the popular prejudices of the whites against us. They serve to kindle hopes of getting us out of the country. . . . The hope of the world is in

58. *Congressional Globe,* 37th Cong., 2nd Sess., 1806–1807.

Human Brotherhood; in the union of mankind, not in exclusive nationalities."[59] Lincoln came to realize what black leaders had told him all along—that blacks were in America to stay.

59. Nicolay and Hay (eds.), *Collected Works of Lincoln*, II, 206–207; Frederick Bancroft, "The Ile à Vache Experiment in Colonization," reprinted in Jacob E. Cooke (ed.), *Frederick Bancroft, Historian* (Norman, 1957), 228–58; Warren Beck, "Lincoln and Negro Colonization in Central America," *Abraham Lincoln Quarterly*, VI (1950–51), 162–83; Charles H. Wesley, "Lincoln's Plan for Colonizing the Emancipated Negroes," *Journey of Negro History*, IV (1919), 7–21; Rayford Logan, *The Diplomatic Relations of the United States with Haiti, 1776–1891* (Chapel Hill, 1941), 293–314; Quarles, *Lincoln and the Negro*, 191–94; Walter L. Fleming, "Deportation and Colonization: An Attempted Solution to the Race Problem," *Studies in Southern History and Politics* (New York, 1914), 3–29; Philip Foner (ed.), *The Papers of Frederick Douglass* (5 vols.; New York, 1979), II.

EPILOGUE

Although the Caribbean has played an important role in the cultural development of the United States, it does not resonate in the American mind as an area worthy of much attention. Some historians and anthropologists have studied the region, but Americans are generally not aware that the southern United States shared its history and many institutions with the Creole societies in the colonies of Great Britain, France, Spain, and Holland in the seventeenth and eighteenth centuries. Cultural attitudes, agricultural systems, labor sources, laws, architecture, and vernacular ways of life all developed in a shared diffusion of culture in the Caribbean basin, of which the southern United States was the northernmost extremity. The events in eighteenth-century St. Domingue and the subsequent history of Haiti were only one example of the interaction between the United States and the Caribbean. Yet contemporary observers of antebellum America were far more aware of the Caribbean influences in the American South than are present-day observers of American society. They naturally linked the destinies of the Americas in ways that we have forgotten because history seemed to them a matter of give-and-take, not simply a one-way phenomenon. The inability to perceive this cultural exchange is probably the result of the ethnocentrism and racism that developed in the the United States during the nineteenth century. The rediscovery of the Caribbean as a place for leisure pursuits, exotic foods, and cheap labor in the mid-twentieth century has only exacerbated the problem and widened the gap between American perception and historical reality. The Caribbean has continued to influence the United States, in areas quite different from those that were significant in the nineteenth century, though American attitudes were formed in the period this study covers. The southern view of the Haitian experiment has been incorporated into the national psyche, just as Americans accepted southern and national attempts to exert control over blacks. Eric Foner has shown that control over labor was a major concern in all slave societies in the Caribbean and in Africa.[1] It is, significantly, one extension of the "lessons of St. Domingue and Haiti" that blacks must not be allowed free will. The notions of black vengeance and black laziness came from different sources; however, St. Domingue and Haiti gave whites their most unforgettable and most often evoked image—that of Melville's "slumbering volcano." Like those Italians who live in the shadow of Vesuvius (there have been two major eruptions in two thousand years), southerners became vulcanized about the issue of slavery because of one major eruption. It is possible to write about antebellum culture without mentioning St. Domingue, and many have. In fact, we accept the importance of the cotton gin to southern society without requiring evidence that southerners themselves talked about it very often. Yet one of the most striking aspects of southern history was the frequency with which southerners—and their critics—evoked the history of St. Domingue and Haiti. No issue having to do with slavery and the role of blacks in American society was discussed at so many different times, in so many different ways, for so many different reasons as the lessons of the Haitian Revolution. A few speeches here, several letters and diary entries there, a pamphlet in another place, or from another time—these fragments indicate that the events in St. Domingue made an indelible impression upon those concerned with black history in antebellum America. Furthermore, everyone who used those lessons knew that audiences were also aware of these events. Rarely can one find any events being evoked in heated debate some sixty years—three generations—later. The actual history of the Haitian Revolution did not have to be mentioned by name, though it often was. The conclusions that whites and blacks drew were widespread in antebellum America and carried into the twentieth century; after abolition, however, there was little need to refer to the specific history of slavery in St. Domingue.

1. Eric Foner, *Nothing But Freedom: Emancipation and Its Legacy* (Baton Rouge, 1983). Other sources that put St. Domingue and Haiti into context are: Winthrop Jordan, *White Over Black: American Attitudes Towards the Negro, 1550–1812* (Chapel Hill, 1968), 375–403; Eugene D. Genovese, *From Rebellion to Revolution: Afro-American Slave Revolts in the Making of the Modern World* (Baton Rouge, 1979), esp. 82–99; John Bauer, "International Repercussions of the Haitian Revolution," *Americas*, XXVI (April, 1970), 394–418; and George M. Fredrickson, *The Black Image in the White Mind: The Debate on Afro-American Character and Destiny, 1817–1914* (New York, 1971), 43–70.

The tragedy was that none of the constituencies that spoke of the revolution's lessons took the black republic on its own terms. Always Haiti proved their point—that slavery was good or that slavery was evil. Few concerned themselves with a struggling nation, born in blood, isolated, and subject to debilitating internal struggles. If Haiti became the most poverty-stricken country in the Western Hemisphere, it is in part because it gave much and received little.

The exchange of people and ideas between Haiti and the United States has never stopped. After the Civil War, Frederick Douglass was the American ambassador to the republic. Years later, concern about Haiti's stability during World War I caused the United States government to send an expeditionary force that occupied the island for several decades. The American occupation ended with the administration of Franklin D. Roosevelt. There was renewed interest in the black republic: *Citizen Toussaint*, a biography, was a Book-of-the-Month Club selection, as was *Black Majesty*, about Henri Christophe's life; scholarly articles on voodoo and public health in Haiti appeared in American journals. Melville Herskovits did seminal anthropological work in his *Life in a Haitian Valley*, a glimpse at a distinctive folk culture in the New World.

No longer seen as an island that played a significant role in American history, Haiti calls to mind exotic dances, drumbeats, and the darker side of life—a land reminiscent of Poe's *Adventures of Arthur Gordon Pym*. Works such as Graham Greene's novel *The Comedians* and Robert Rotberg's *Haiti: The Politics of Squalor* accurately depict the ongoing problem of repressive political leadership. The discovery that incorrectly associated a deadly disease, Acquired Immune Deficiency Syndrome (AIDS), with Haitians is but the public-health counterpart to the white Americans' view of Haiti since 1804—it is untouchable.

With political oppression and personal deprivation facts of everyday life in Haiti, the so-called boat people of the 1980s were yet another movement in the history of migrations both to and from the island. There is a long-standing relationship between Haiti and the United States: American doctors, missionaries, social workers, businessmen, and tourists go to the black republic in every-increasing numbers, and there are literally hundreds of thousands of Haitian refugees—doctors, engineers, students, housekeepers, and taxi drivers—in the United States, especially in New

York City and its environs, and in southern Florida. These immigrants diversify American society as have groups from Europe, Asia, and the Far East. Together with the Cubans, Puerto Ricans, Jamaicans, Barbadians, and other West Indians, Haitians contribute to the continuing Caribbean influences in American culture. Unfortunately, because they are dark-skinned, predominantly poor, speak patois, and come from a southern culture without a strong European tradition, their presence and influence have been invisible to white Americans.

INDEX